Betty Melville Smith.

REMINISCENCES OF AFFECTION

By the same writer:

My Dear Timothy
More for Timothy
Shall Our Children Live or Die?
In Darkest Germany
The Case of Adolf Eichmann
The Devil's Repertoire
A Year of Grace
The New Year of Grace
From Darkness to Light
God of a Hundred Names (with Barbara Greene)
Journey Towards Music
The Ring at Bayreuth

BITS AND PIECES

VICTOR GOLLANCZ

REMINISCENCES OF AFFECTION

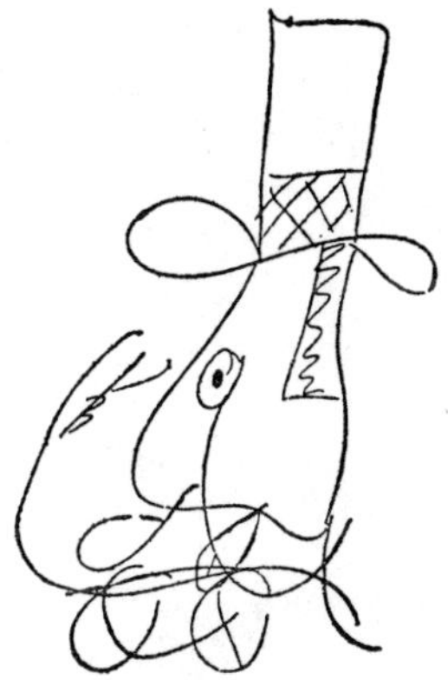

LONDON
14 HENRIETTA STREET COVENT GARDEN
1968

Published by Victor Gollancz Limited
and printed in Great Britain by
The Camelot Press Limited of London
and Southampton

575000007

בָּרוּךְ אַתָּה יְיָ אֱלֹהֵינוּ מֶלֶךְ
הָעוֹלָם׃ שֶׁהֶחֱיָנוּ וְקִיְּמָנוּ
וְהִגִּיעָנוּ לַזְּמַן הַזֶּה׃

For R.G.

Do you remember the Italian hours
When in the greenness of the silent close
We sat encalmed, and knew its nature ours,
And robbed it of its Botticelli rose?

And do you remember—on the Elysian way
"Our spirits grew as we went side by side",
And in the sunshine of that Christmas May
"The hour became your lover and my bride"?

Forgive me, dear, if my mortality
Could seem to rob us of immortal things
  And doom us to the common human fate;
Yet all remains, its essence unimpaired:
The loyalty, the rapture and the grace,
  The union of mate with perfect mate.

In the train to Birmingham, July 22nd, 1948.

CONTENTS

LIST OF ILLUSTRATIONS

FOREWORD

During the four or five years preceding his death on February 8th, 1967, my father had been gathering material for a religious book to be called 'The Sanity of Christ'; but every time he began seriously to think of writing it, another book materialised. Thus we had *Journey Towards Music* and *The Ring at Bayreuth*; and thus, when he returned from his 'sabbatical' towards the end of June 1966, he began writing a book of reminiscences with the working title, 'Bits and Pieces'. As he wrote chapter after chapter—the first chapter first, then the 'Last Chapter', followed by nine others, and one or two shorter pieces, in no particular order—he realised that the book was becoming an important one from the autobiographical point of view, and that it should have a more dignified title: hence, REMINISCENCES OF AFFECTION.

For affection is its keynote: affection for the friends, some famous, some humble, who played so large a part in the shaping of his life; affection for the places that, whether in the reality of experience or in memory, gave him such pleasure; affection for the small mementos—the bits and pieces of his original title—that he and my mother had randomly collected, and which were a constant reminder, during week-ends at the country cottage (where they were used to decorate the sitting-room bookshelves), of so much happiness. For he was a man to find joy in so many things. The chapters also reflect his great love of music; and perhaps above all his affection for erring humanity. And through it all run references to his own life at the time of writing (as in the *Timothy* books), and digressions (as in *Journey Towards Music*) on many events, and aspects of life, and on the particular causes for which he never ceased to fight.

These eleven chapters, some 80,000 words, were written between late June 1966 and October 7th, 1966, when V.G. suffered his first stroke—an affliction that rendered him incapable even of reading over the parts of the manuscript which had not been typed before that date, or of deciding in what order the chapters should appear. For this reason, it has not always been possible to relate chapter to chapter, although throughout them all the descriptions of the memorabilia—the bits and pieces kept on the cottage shelves—provide a linking theme. The book is therefore unfinished in that he himself was not able to make it into a book; and individual chapters may have been unfinished. For instance, I know that there was to have been a long chapter on Naples, culminating in a piece on the caves of Cumæ—I found the following words scribbled on a folder of photographs: "Keep for a final showpiece what should be everyone's goal in this part of the world, namely Cumæ"—and I have included the existing fragment on Naples with the pieces on Assisi and Perugia, although it was the last of all to be written.

And now as to the scheme of the book itself: shortly before my father died, I asked him what he wanted done with the manuscript. He replied, "Publish it as it stands"; but some editing of the unrevised manuscript was inevitable. In addition, among the papers found after his death were the opening chapters for 'Last Words for Timothy' (or *Tim III*, as it has been more familiarly referred to), and the first of these describes, very charmingly, how V.G. courted and married my mother. It seems appropriate, therefore, to print this chapter as a Prelude to what is, after all, an account of the best parts of a very full and rich married life. And again, a few weeks before he died, when he was paralysed in his right side, he learned to write with his left hand, and it seems equally appropriate, even if almost unbearably sad, to show the end of his life in his own words, by printing, as an Epilogue, extracts from the diary he kept in order to mitigate, a little, the inactivity imposed by his condition.

The diary was started as a means of learning to write. It so happened that in January 1967 I (the "Poo" of the diary) was to make the firm's annual trip to New York, and I had expressed a wish that he and I could correspond while I was there. About a month before I left, soon after V.G. returned home from hospital, I suggested that he should try to write a note for me to read each time I visited him (roughly every other day). The first notes were merely short statements, but the speed with which he wrote increased so quickly that he was soon writing a page each day.

A consequence of his stroke was a severe limitation of his mental faculties, and of this he was as aware as of his physical condition; but while his literary style was reduced to a tithe of its former quality (and the comparison is in itself interesting), his ideas were, so to say, stripped down to their bare essentials: to a simplicity that speaks directly, and with no semblance of intellectual inhibition.

My mother and I decided for three reasons that the diary should be printed. For those who have known my father, either personally or through his writing, it shows how he spent the last month of his life: confined to a wheel-chair which he never learned to manipulate himself, being taken for a morning "walk" (the business of dressing into outdoor winter clothes was agonisingly protracted), writing in the diary when he returned; then lunch and his "rest", when he sat dozing in an armchair or read for a while (but he could not concentrate easily on the printed page). It was the return to consciousness in the early morning and particularly after his "rest" that caused him so much distress; my mother also rested after lunch, sleeping upstairs on her bed, not returning to him until a prearranged time; and he made it a point of honour never to disturb her by calling out, no matter how miserable he felt. Somehow, the morning awakening, with nurses busy around him, and the imminent prospect of breakfast, never terrified him in the same way as coming back to life from the afternoon sleep, when he was alone and unable to move.

There were often visitors for tea, or later in the evening; it was talking with people that gave him the greatest pleasure, and he could more easily be persuaded to attempt to stand and take a few steps (supported by two people) if a visitor were there to help, or even watch. But to a man used to living a very full eighteen-hour day the boredom and inability to think clearly were the greatest trials of his invalid existence, and it is not surprising that from time to time he gave way to self-pity. It was his complete dependence on other people that caused him the most acute worry. He hated the idea of having a nurse constantly in attendance; and he was continually aware of the indignity of being able to do almost nothing for himself.

Our second reason for printing the diary is to show how the remnants of a brilliant mind approached and understood such a situation. And our third reason is that, if he could have known that these words, taking as they did so much concentration and self-control to write, would be set up in type and printed, it would have given him indescribable pleasure.

Sitting, as I am now, at his work-table at Bottom House, the cottage that figures so largely in 'Bits and Pieces', and looking from the window to the ripening cornfields, golden in the evening sun, I can remember so well his reaction when I had read the first full page of consecutive writing that he had done with his left hand. I remarked something to the effect that it was practically publishable; immediately the left half of his face lit up with its funny paralysed smile, and his eyes spoke the words he did not dare to say.

So there it is: if sophisticated readers find the diary dull, I would advise them not to persevere with it; but from amongst the self-pity, and the speculation as to the course of his illness, a few of his basic and simple ideas emerge, and, if these are found to be of help or interest, we shall have felt justified in using the diary to show how his life ended.

* * *

A few explanations are necessary. The favourite of all my father's favourite stories concerns Queen Mary, whom he greatly loved. It appears in the first chapter of *Tim III*: and it appears in 'Bits and Pieces'. I have not had the heart to remove it from either.

Some people may be puzzled by my parents' familiar, Moses. His image, many times enlarged, appears on the title-page of this book (drawn by V.G.) and also facing page 121 (modelled by Edmund Dulac). My parents first met Lieut.-Colonel Moses, V.C. (nearly), retired (quite), when he was scootering about on the beam that ran across the ceiling of their bedroom in Campden Hill Square, where they lived immediately after getting married.

He is billions of years old, and only failed to be awarded the V.C. after the Zulu War, when it was found that he had been fighting on the other side. In shape he resembles my father's nose. He came originally on his little scooter, but later acquired an aeroplane, and is rarely seen without his top-hat. His greatest friends are commas. As my father took much delight in drawing his picture, Moses tended to proliferate on such places as the office walls, restaurant bills, and in country-house guest books.

There is a passage on page 165 that is now, I am happy to say, out of date. As this book goes to press I hear that the Home Secretary, Mr Jenkins, has caused to be destroyed those instruments of torture described on that page. Had my father been alive, he would have been the first with his thanks.

* * *

It has not been possible to illustrate 'Bits and Pieces' in quite the lavish manner my father had envisaged—he did not consider illustration from the practical point of view of time and expense when he was writing his manuscript. I assume that he would have modified his ideas had he been able to put the book into production himself; but I have not altered passages that refer to an illustration of a particular picture or object, even if that illustration does not appear. And I have put as many as possible of the objects mentioned (though not the pictures) into the colour-photograph that is reproduced as a frontispiece.

In this connection I wish to thank Mr Edward Schwarz, for giving up valuable week-end time to take this photograph and the one of Edmund Dulac's Moses; Stefan Lorant, Quo Tai-chi and Mme Agnes Maisky for the photographs they took while staying at Brimpton and which they later sent to my mother; and many other people whose snapshots cannot now be identified. I also thank Joanna Goodwin, my father's secretary, who helped him with his research, typed the manuscript and, since his death, has assisted with the work in innumerable ways; Sheila Bush, who corrected the proofs with the loving care to which he has so often referred; and above all my mother. My father's debt to her cannot be stated—indeed, she would consider it no debt—but for myself, to have been able to come here, weekend after weekend, to have been freed by her from household chores, and to have had her wise advice and companionship whenever I have needed them, has made the preparation of this book not only possible, but the greatest imaginable pleasure.

BOTTOM HOUSE
SEPTEMBER 1967

LIVIA GOLLANCZ

PRELUDE

LAST WORDS FOR TIMOTHY

Brimpton, April 19th, 1953

SERENE, BECAUSE WE had one another: children, going hand in hand: content with our bits and pieces—that was Ruth and I, in the days of our young marriage.

*   *   *

For this letter to be of full value, I ought to attempt here an utterly uninhibited record of our married relationship: I ought to expose—with as much honesty as anyone can manage in his own case and as much insight as he can achieve in someone else's—every aspect of that relationship from the May of 1919, when we met again for the first time after the war, to this April of 1953. For genuine marriage, present or absent, is one of the three central factors in human existence—together with an inescapable residue of loneliness (in any case), and one's relation, involving one's work and one's creativeness, with the universe or God or the whole: and as all marriages resemble one another, just as all are unique, the record of a particular example, if reasonably honest, is something everyone can learn from. But I see any number of difficulties. First of all there is the question of sex; and by this I mean its physical aspect (amatory technique, coital positions, elements of fantasy, and so on) quite as much as those other aspects of it which may anyhow be involved—and for the most part *are* involved and involved crucially—with the physical one. Here precision is everything: the detail is the point. Now my qualms about this are unrelated to X (you may remember him from *Tim II*) and his talk about strip-tease: I don't care a tuppenny fig for his censorious stupidities. They are equally unrelated to Ruth—to the fact that I should be uncovering her nakedness as well as my own: she would anyhow read everything before I published it, and if she wanted a detail out, it would go. No, my doubts spring from something quite different. The quiddity of sex is the living of it; and by describing its particulars you reveal, not the mystery that gives it its rightness, but the gaiety, the comicality, the grotesquerie, the enchantment, the rapture, the beauty, the spiritual exaltation and the repulsive animality that jostle one another in its utterly satisfying and utterly frustrating ensemble. So by taking it to pieces, or even talking about it at all, you not only dishonour its nature (which resides in its mystery) but you commit a kind of murder in eternity. Yet if the particulars go awry the mystery vanishes—only particulars remain; and though everyone must learn for himself, the more experienced, maybe, can help a bit. There is a genuine problem here, and I haven't the smallest notion, at this stage, whether or not I shall manage to solve it. I shall have to wait and see. I may be driven back, though heaven forbid, on whispers and hints.

Another problem occurs to me: people invariably misunderstand you when you're frank—frank, so to say, against yourself. I had a beautiful experience of this in the case of *Tim I*. I was frank against myself when discussing my father—omitted nothing I could say in his favour: with the result that people called him a saint, which he wasn't in the least. (I am happy, however, to think that the old man is pleased—as he must be, if he is the same old man.) Similarly reviewers love to mock at a publisher for extravagant blurbs on his dust-jackets: but if once in a blue moon he happens to say what he privately thinks, such as "this is a goodish novel, but nothing out of the way", they are off within five minutes to the man in the Waterloo Bridge Road (or he used to be there in my day) who will take it off their hands at half-price. Now Ruth and I have had our difficulties; and while to suppress them would make nonsense of this letter I should simply hate people to start saying "What a flop they have made of their marriage!" So let me repeat, to forestall them, what I said in *Tim I*: "We know consciously on our honeymoons, what we have known less consciously every minute of our lives since a month before our wedding, that our marriage has been essentially—it is a large claim, and you must note the word 'essentially' —perfect: and that a marriage which is perfect, even if only essentially, would be sufficient justification, in the absence of all other justifications, for the sum of things. 'Blessed art thou, O Lord, who makest the bridegroom to rejoice with the bride.'"

* * *

It was Ruth, after the war (the 1914–1918 war, of course), who pursued me, not I who pursued Ruth. I had felt romantic about her, to be sure, during my first term at Oxford, when I had met her at a single-tax dinner in London and had gazed into her eyes the whole evening. I imagined myself in love with her beauty and goodness—with the combination of them, I mean: and let me add, for the benefit of psychoanalysts, that however lovely a woman may be, however radiant with every glory extolled in the Song that is Solomon's, I can feel no atom of desire for her person unless her goodness is to match, and the other way about. The more owlish of sexual investigators may discover in this oddity an obscure form of sadism—a kind of spiritual tress-lopping: and for all I know they may be right. But don't imagine me a Don Giovanni: I am speaking of desire, not of manœuvres to fulfil it.

At the moment, however, it is a question of Ruth. I wasn't in love with her, it turned out—at that juncture, I mean—after all. This became apparent during the summer term of 1914. Nerves atingle I got her down to Oxford, and arranged a gorgeous lunch. The company was excellent, the meal superb. Ewan Agnew was there, and Harold Rubinstein, and Gilbert Murray's daughter Agnes (whom I was also a bit in love with) and Leah Kay (whom I was also a bit in love with—she was to marry L'Estrange Malone: her father, a friend of my family and born Klingenstein, was an important cigar merchant, and had been kind enough to blood me. I was at his house after dinner one evening—I must have been a bit over fifteen—when "Fictor," he said, "it is time you learnt to shmoke a cigar." We were in his cigar-library: rows and rows of cigar-boxes lined its walls, and there was a rickety little step-ladder to get at them. He wheeled this about, brought it to rest, climbed to the top of it, reached to his right, and selected, not only a box, but a particular cigar in it, with almost worried exactitude. Descending, "Here is vun," he remarked, as he made me the gift of it. "It is a little bit shmashed. I fould not offer it to anypody except you") . . . yes, Leah was there, and a few others I don't remember: we ate salmon mayonnaise and strawberries and cream and drank moselle cup. Afterwards we went on the river. But Ruth dropped a terrible brick: she wore sand-shoes, apt for Margate. I immediately fell out of love with her: I thought she didn't know how to dress. Little could I have imagined what she would look like some twenty years later, when she presided at our first Claridge party in a Primavera *robe de style*.

You can always know for certain whether you are really in love with a woman by the sand-shoe criterion. A friend of mine was ambivalent about a girl with a prominent gold tooth: it suddenly ceased to offend him, and he married her.

I saw nothing of my girl for five years, nor apparently thought of her: but a Ruth without sand-shoes must have remained in my unconscious: and it can be said still more definitely that a Victor, with or without any of the flaws she may have found in him, remained high up in hers. As is clear from the following. She was at the Slade when addicted to sand-shoes (along with Nevinson, Stanley Spencer, the Nashes, Gwen Raverat, and many others now famous): left in August, and took up war-work: and three years later blew her feminist trumpet before the walls of the A.A.—the Architectural, not the Automobile, Association, though part of her war-work, as a matter of fact, had been teaching officers to drive. The walls fell: she was admitted as its first woman student (and I may as well say here, as of course it pleases me to celebrate her, that when she decided she'd like to marry me—in her third year—and told her boss, Robert Atkinson, she'd be leaving, he summoned me to his office and caned me severely for depriving the world of a genius). Now the year in which she joined the A.A., the year 1917, was the year in which Fisher expelled me from Paradise, namely Repton: and I was living at Dryden Chambers, and she was living at Holland Park: and Dryden Chambers is on the road from Holland Park to Bedford Square, where the A.A. had its seat. And it happened, whether by accident or intent, that she always found herself passing my courtyard just at the moment I was emerging from it, and it happened further that she liked the look of me (I was thin then). That I liked the look of her I cannot pretend, for her proximity escaped me.

So off I went to Singapore, our togetherness aslumber within me but already stirring in her.

I was back in England, as you know from *Tim II*, by the February of 1919; and Gertie, Ruth's sister, who was to marry the eminent potatoist, Redcliffe Salaman (they were devoted to London, the Salamans, irrespective of period, but with a bias towards Victorianism: there was Redcliffe (Square), Euston (Station), and Clement ('s Inn)). . . . Gertie saw me one day in the neighbourhood of Oxford Street and reported the occurrence. Ruth acted immediately: I got a card for a dinner party, early in April, at the Lowy mansion on Ladbroke Terrace. (If my language is becoming American the reason is, I am on my way there. The voyage, which promises to be delightful anyhow, will remain in my memory for the following reason: I am eating anchovies, and *sole meunière*, and cold roast beef, and hot roast turkey, and cold roast lamb and mint sauce, and smoked salmon for, human uncertainties apart, the last time. I began being a vegetarian again a few weeks ago, and shall be completely one after returning from America. This is my ultimate fling: my Augustinian "not too soon".) I accepted the invitation, but got the wind up as time slipped away: not at the prospect of being captured, but because I was socially shy. I waited till a minute to midnight—the morning of the event—in an agony of indecision; then telegraphed "Very greatly regret have to go at moment's notice to China" and felt marvellously free. But Ruth must have thought I was exaggerating (she often thinks this), for I got a note the next morning to enquire if a week-end at Hurley, where the Lowys had a cottage, might be feasible in May; and I could hardly have done it in the time, except by flying, which was not yet in vogue. I accepted, and sent no subsequent telegram. So I found myself at Hurley a month later, and within an hour of my arrival was in love, for good and all, with your grandmother and my Ruth.

I was lodging, at the time, in the Colvilles: one of those derelict London quarters, full of cats, broken bells and decaying stucco, where, a hundred years earlier, revelry and popping champagne corks had sounded by night. I shared a flat in a great high house with Douglas Jerrold, and with a friend of his, named Young: everything about it was deep, dark and dusty, and if you hooded your eyes you could still see its splendour. Occasionally, as I sat there playing bridge, I half imagined myself Lord Steyne. But the point about it was this: the Colvilles adjoined the Ladbrokes, so I was living, by some starry conjuncture, almost next door to Ruth. We were also working not too far from one another, she in Bedford Square, I in Parliament Street. The same bus-line, therefore, served us; and during the two or three weeks that elapsed between the first and the second of my visits to Hurley I would execute a manœuvre dictated, in equal portions, by passion and pride. I would arrive at the bus-stop a good ten minutes before she'd be due, barring exceptional precipitancy—and the idea of the ten minutes was to look after that: would do a run towards each bus as it started: would slacken and miss it: would walk slowly away: would do my run again—and *da capo* till she appeared. So we met, more or less accidentally, every morning; and what did I care if the bystanders thought me *meshuggah*, or a policeman looked suspicious? For the rest, we went a lot to the ballet, particularly when Karsavina was dancing; and one night, just as the wedding-march had started in *L'Oiseau de Feu*, silently —the words are beautiful, and endless custom has not staled them —we plighted our troth.

I was back at Hurley on Friday June the fourth. Father Lowy was there, some Lowy sisters, and a couple of friends. We waited, Ruth and I, till the Saturday night: our pledge was between us, but it needed the sacrament of words. We had supper, and the old man—I call him that, though he was but sixty at the time—began a series of stories that turned on stammering. B' b' b', c' c' c', d' d' d'—he threatened to traverse the whole alphabet of consonants. Ruth, fearful perhaps (oh, but faithless!) of the result for our pledge, nodded a signal, and I nodded back. We slipped out. Labouring, we walked in silence till we came to a wicket, nearly opposite Medmenham Abbey: then, all but simultaneously, we asked and replied, "Ruth, will you marry me?" and "Yes, Victor". And so began thirty-four years, and pray God it may be a hundred and thirty-four, of married friendship and love.

Everyone was glad, but I felt ill. I had gone sick at Singapore with a stomach trouble, diagnosed as enteroptosis (or the dropping of the internal organs) but really nervous dyspepsia: a sensation of sinking had been the mark of it. Now it returned. From the beginning Ruth and I were as one: no shyness inhibited us, and as I lay on the bed with my stomach bare she gently massaged it. Next morning we went on the river: I behaved with indiscretion, and a man on the bank shouted bawdily "Your bloomin' luck!". She got another proposal that same morning, by special messenger: she was always getting proposals, and her friends used to tease her about her regiment of forty-seven thousand—the number of perverts (alleged) under blackmail (alleged) from the enemy in Pemberton-Billing's Black Book. The trouble was, we met her latest proposer just as we were punting into Maidenhead, and she had to tell him the news: he looked me up and down with a mixture of surprise and contempt, perhaps because, while a fellow of charm and exceptional parts anyhow, he was also bisexual.

We went off to a field when we got back, and made physical love to one another in the blaze of a low sun. My manhood was bursting its bounds, and we all but became as one flesh. The "all but" is attributable to the atmosphere of our homes and to the power of our traditions. A beauty was murdered by our reluctance. I shall return to this presently.

The next morning we motored to London, and I rang up my parents.

My father was delighted. A whole arsenal of reasons combined to make him so. First of all, I wasn't marrying a *shicksa*—a *shicksa*, my dear Timothy, is a housemaid, but as housemaids in Jewish establishments are normally *goyim* a *shicksa* (pregnantly understood) has come to signify any feminine *goy* a Jew takes up with. Secondly, the Lowys were solid. This was a good old Anglo-Jewish family: Ruth's grandfather, who had arrived in England—from Vienna or thereabouts—in I think 1818, had been one of the two founding Rabbis at Upper Berkeley Street. This, it is true, was a Reform bethel, and my father didn't hold with reform—men and women sitting together, and an organ!: its roster, on the other hand, was choc-a-bloc with fine names—Spanish ones, like Henriques (and even Quixano Henriques), or Italian ones, like Montefiore, or vaguely distinguished ones, like Sebag—and a man, if he asked for the Law and the Prophets, couldn't ask for the Cabbala to boot. A Lowy, bosom friend of a Henriques—good enough, if anyone could be, for a Gollancz! Maternally, too, everything was in order: Toddy Solomon was an R.A. Finally (and I am sure this came third) Lowy was rich. All in all, very nice.

Lowy, unfortunately, wasn't rich at the moment. He was always making fortunes on the stock exchange, and always losing them; and he had lost one quite recently. So we got very little: five hundred for household equipment, with an understanding we wouldn't touch it for anything else, and another five hundred hidden away in a marriage settlement. I, with my modest ideas, thought this marvellous.

Financially, indeed, we were in a position that we might have thought parlous, if the matter had occurred to us at all. I had no capital: not a penn'orth of savings: a debt to Blackwell of Oxford for something in the neighbourhood of a hundred pounds: and a job that was coming to an end in the middle of July. Ruth had nothing—or practically nothing: a pound a week, she reminds me, of her own. Moreover, I was totally untrained for any specific occupation except schoolmastering, and that was obviously closed to me. Yet the idea that all this might be relevant to the date of our marriage couldn't possibly have occurred to us. And I mean this literally: I don't mean we thought little of it, I mean we didn't think of it at all. The eternal existence of our togetherness knew no frontier with material considerations.

We fixed July 22nd for our wedding-day; but as we were

married (for the most part) already there was little to distinguish the month of waiting from the months that followed. I remember three small episodes from this time. We were walking one day, hand in hand, from the flowers at Lancaster Gate towards Kensington Road. We looked, I daresay, very happy. An open carriage passed by: we hardly noticed it: but something must have made us glance back—and we saw a lady, upright and bonneted, vigorously waving to us. It was her late and very gracious Majesty Queen Mary. I couldn't take my hat off, not having one on; so I bowed extra low, in ceremonious gratitude. I am nothing of a royalist, as you will have gathered; but from then to the day of her death I have always loved Queen Mary. I have run into her, if I may put it so—she would like the familiarity, I think—on quite a number of occasions. We used to frequent an antique man in Kingston who had been valet to King Edward the Seventh. A lovely little Sheraton table caught our fancy one day, and we wanted to buy it; but we couldn't—it was reserved for Queen Mary. We bought it, however, eventually, and have it at Brimpton: everyone calls it "Queen Mary's table". And I wonder if I may now tell a story that I was asked not to tell at the time. You will learn, probably from *Tim IV*, of the battle I had with the government, lasting more than a year, over food-parcels for Germany. She was starving at the end of the war, and a lot of people wanted to help her—out of personal rations, not from general supplies: but the government would have none of it, until public insistence forced their hands. They collapsed on a Friday, and next morning announced the arrangements: anybody who wanted to send a parcel must fill in a form, and these would be ready at our office from ten o'clock on the Monday. The first applicant arrived at 10.1 precisely. It was a smart page-boy. I asked who had sent him. "Her Majesty Queen Mary," he replied. Requiescat.

The second of the three episodes I remember from this period was as follows. One morning, just after our engagement, we were walking along Oxford Street in search of a ring, and passing Phillips', the silversmith's, noticed something in his window that attracted us. I thought it might run me into a fiver, and I could manage a fiver, as I still had my job. We went in, and old Phillips, who attended us in person, got it out of the window. It was an affair of Brazilian diamonds, English, eighteenth-century. I thought it would look beautiful on Ruth: she gave me her finger, and we tried: it looked beautiful on her. I asked the price. "Thirty-seven pounds," said old Phillips. I grinned in the way sheep are said to, and slipped it off again. "Don't you want it?" asked Phillips. "It suits the beautiful young lady." "Yes," I said, "but I can't afford it; I haven't got any thirty-seven pounds." He slipped it on again. "Take it," he said, "you'll pay me one day." "But," I asked, "don't you want to know my name?" "No," he replied, "you've both got honest faces." So off we walked, and I paid a year later. It was stolen last week: if the man who took it happens to read this, perhaps he will be good enough to return it to me.

My third little story throws light on Ruth's character. Emmy Destinn was singing Aïda on some night late in June: I hadn't heard her since 1914, and the possibility of hearing her again, and in that part... well, if you're an amateur of *bel canto* and a Verdian you will understand what I mean, and not if you're not. Ruth couldn't go in any case: I could, but—the price! They had nothing but a balcony stall at thirty-five shillings or two pounds, I don't remember which; and this seemed outrageous in view of my financial position and our imminent wedding, and, apart altogether from that, I didn't see myself sitting down there among the diamonds and tiaras, instead of up in the gallery. The whole idea seemed impossibly spendthrift, even a bit pagan: the streak of puritanism in me rebelled. But Ruth spent an hour—on a walk through the Park to my office in Parliament Street—persuading me to go; and off I rushed, got my seat, and sat in a heaven of "measureless content" from *Si quel guerriero io fossi!*, through the fragrance of that midsummer eve on the banks of the Nile, to the lovers' duet—disembodied, one might call it—in the fastness of their tomb. Do you understand what I mean about her character? Enjoy the moment, she was saying: let the future look after itself.

But if the future could look after itself a little assistance would be welcome; and we fell to speculating, as our wedding grew nearer and the ebony bowls began arriving, about the possibility of cheques. X might be good for a fiver; Y, possibly, for twenty quid. Was a hundred conceivable? Yes, it was: and not only conceivable, almost certain. Hadn't I a millionaire uncle, or at least an excessively rich one? This was my Uncle Max, surnamed Michaelson: a son of my maternal grandfather by an earlier marriage, and the success of the family. He had cornered the Baltic sponge trade when still in his twenties, with a couple of partners, and had retired a few years later to a palace at Sydenham, which abutted on the better-known Crystal one. (I thought originally, indeed, that they were parts of one whole, for you could pass between the two by a special wicket-gate: but this was an error.) He had a butler and all that; and occasionally I went down with my mother for a lunch that alarmed me, for I didn't know how to behave. (Mother did, beautifully.) He had married an Andrade: so I am kin to the eminent scientist, and the hardly less eminent antique dealer. At the outbreak of war Uncle Max changed his name: not his surname but his Christian one—from Max to Mac (or both of them, in a sense—he was known as Macmichaelson): and Aunt Hannah became Nanon. At the end of the war he left Sydenham for the Riviera, where he drank champagne as you and I drink water till his death at getting on for ninety or even perhaps a hundred. He flourished, in fact, like the bay-tree.

Remembering all this splendour, or as much of it as I knew of at the time, I felt certain he wouldn't let us down: a hundred was safe, but why not, then, two hundred and fifty? . . . We were unpacking a lot of vases one day, and a further supply of flower bowls, when a vanman staggered in with an enormous packing-case, buttressed about by strips of metal. We got to work with a crowbar in mounting excitement: flung out layers of paper—corrugated . . . brown . . . news . . . tissue: and uncovered a vast silver dish, chased all over with mythology. A little card was attached: "With best wishes for a very happy marriage from Uncle Mac and Aunt Nanon." I rallied at once: I always rally, as you know, when the blow has once fallen. And mightn't the thing, after all, be enormously valuable? It didn't look very old, to be sure, but I was no expert in such matters; and even as silver, to forget the workmanship, its value must be considerable. Yes: perhaps here, in spite of everything, was our hundred pounds—or more.

We turned it about, and discovered the name 'Elkington' impressed on it. Why not take it back there, we thought: why not see what they'd give us for it? So that's what we did. The man immediately asked, where had we got it from? I told him. Is your family masonic?, he enquired. My grandfather, I told him, was a mason—a very high one, I believed. Ah, he said, that explains it: we have here a freemason's dish, about fifty years old. What'll you give me for it?, I asked. Well really, he replied, it isn't worth anything. But surely, I said, simply as silver . . . it isn't silver, he interrupted, it's white metal. What'll you give me for it, I insisted, a precipice of numbers at work in my brain—fifty, forty, thirty, twenty, ten . . . Oh! but certainly *ten*. Really, you know, he began, and then looked at us and broke off. After a moment's hesitation, I'll tell you what, he went on with a beautiful smile: I'll give you a pound. So we added his pound to the little store we were accumulating against our honeymoon.

* * *

Our honeymoon—I've got to it now. And this is the place for an essay on marriage.

* * *

I feel it a graver impertinence to write about marriage than about anything else in this letter, including even God and Christ: and I have hesitated longer before plunging. Sense of responsibility is the explanation. No great harm can accrue if I have been wrong, as of course I must have been on innumerable points, about God or Christ—they, or He, can look after themselves; but the case with marriage is different. I mean: nobody's life, I suspect, has been damaged, at any rate in the long run, by other people's falsehoods about God, who reveals himself, sooner or later, if and as he wills; but lots of lives must have been damaged, in the long as well as in the short run, by other people's counsel

MARRIAGE · 1919

AT BRIMPTON
1935

SILVER WEDDING
1944

about marriage, which can set a man, maybe irrevocably, on the road to unhappiness. And though my views, I imagine, will not carry vast weight with you, Timothy, they may carry a little: indeed, I want them to.

My reluctance is increased by the following consideration. About many of the questions I shall be dealing with in the course of this chapter it is only just on balance that, after thirty-four years of married life, I have made up my mind—I see so vividly both sides of them; and about others I have not even got that far. What sort of guide, then, I ask myself, can such as I be? Yet to say nothing would make nonsense of my letter.

And if indeed I must take off for that perilous country could I choose a better moment? This is June 27th, the first real day of breathless weather: the sort of day on which Demeter, as she sits beside her corn-shoots, veils her eyes with quivering lids against the glare. Beyond me is the great peony-bed, and just above it, fuzzy and olive-hued, a long, low line of trees atop the downs; a briar down the lane tricks off the hedgerow, to my left, under the summer-house eaves, a little mess of last year's hay still lies about. This is Brimpton as we know her at her closest, pledge and token of our later married love: and we shall soon be leaving her—for our days grow disunited, with Ruth so much here and me so much in London: the place is too large, our possessions have involved us too straitly: so we are looking for a cottage nearer town. How could I celebrate the place better, then, or say "bless you, and good-bye" to it more happily, than by talking about marriage?

*   *   *

July 4th

What a pity I have to write about matters so serious! We are spending a delightful week-end with the Harry Walstons; and at the moment a couple of girls—Ruth and another—are picking strawberries in slacks, and giving a heavenly display of their callipygic charms. Catherine Walston—what a joy to bring her into this letter, to do, by the way of celebrating her adorability, even as little as that!—Catherine asked me this morning whether I felt better, now that I was a vegetarian—meaning,

I think, morally better. "*No,*" *I replied,* "*not better, but cleaner.*" *She also asked me why I had taken it up again after so many years—getting on for half a century. If I had brought along a proof of* '*Tim II*' *with me I should have given it her and made her read my remarks about* "*Waiting on God*". *It is a question of desire not to eat my fellow-creatures having grown stronger than desire to please my palate. For I cannot pretend I really like vegetarian food—watery, inflationary, pasty, regurgitatory, sawdusty stuff!: but if a pleasure has gone out of my life, a new joy has come into it.*

By a slightly different token I am "*drinking*" *practically nothing these days—nothing at all, in fact, except when courtesy requires. The reason is: mere existence so directly enthralls me—I am so drunk with it, if you like, and with its author—that . . . well, could anything be sillier than to light candles in the sun? But the image is a poor one: for candles don't diminish the sun, but* "*stimulants*" *do get in the way of a meeting—a meeting utter, face to face, with nothing fuzzy, induced, or semi-imitative about it—between oneself and reality.*

* * *

The argument must turn on monogamy.
Do I "believe in" it?
Yes, after my own fashion.

BITS AND PIECES

I

BOTTOM HOUSE

OUR SITTING-ROOM at Bottom House is unique. Not that it is singular in this respect, for every sitting-room is unique. But ours is unique in a peculiar way.

Bottom House is our cottage—the smallest cottage in England. (My wife, who is in the habit of accusing me, particularly at other people's dinner-tables, of exaggeration—a practice I should long since have divorced her for unless I had found her, and still find her, by and large to my taste—denies this; but even she, for all her devotion to accuracy, would concede that the place is unusually small.) Green expanses of wheat and corn, or brown ones, at another season, of flint-laden earth, slope up from us on all sides: and it would be natural to assume that the Bottom of our title is a mere rural bottom, a piece of inanimate geography. But rumour has it that this is not so, and that an eponymous lady of exceptional attractiveness provides the true explanation. I like to think so, for ever since early childhood I have worshipped at the shrine of Venus Callipygus. I confess indeed that when my wife told me about the place (having seen it announced in *The Times* and taken the next train down, with good and beautiful Dorothy Watson as her companion) it was its name above all that induced me to buy.

Bottom House, built of brick and whitewashed flints, was formerly a gamekeeper's cottage.

I must write a few paragraphs about our garden. There are three levels to it, or, to put it in another way, a ground floor and two terraces: with six courses of brick for the lower retaining wall, and three for the higher. That sounds, I suppose, rather grand: but an outsize pocket-handkerchief, say a Fafner's or a Fasolt's, could easily in fact cover the lot. Only, however, if you think capitalistically. To a larger consciousness, the Garden of Eden, or of

Ninfa, could hardly be more extensive: for our "property" can be seen, from wherever you may stand or sit in it, to merge without a break into another of identical or similar substance, namely England's. To be plainer and less theological, our inconsiderable bottom and the slopes that surround us are one.

The navel of our garden, its botanical tholos, is the greenhouse we built for ourselves when we took the place, eight years ago. We sited it, Picassoishly for a navel, right up against our dining-room window, which forms, to confound the metaphor, most of its backside: so that my wife, coming down in the morning for her coffee and fragment of toast, can already see from the turn of the staircase her floral scarlet and rose. A second later she is inside, holding a potted seedling aloft and quizzing its rate of growth, through strong glasses, with a scientist's curiosity, a scholar's intensity and a mother's solicitude.

Our greenhouse is a modest affair, measuring eight feet by ten: but it has a lot to be immodest about; for you might call it a botanical colony, plonked down there in Buckinghamshire, of Italy and Greece. Its special glory for some time now has been its collection of oleanders from Olympia and Venice, grown from seeds my wife has gathered in those places: the father of the Venetian ones, which are paler in their flowers than the rest, being the tree that confronts you just a little to the left of the *Scala dei Giganti* in the courtyard of the Doge's Palace. Below them, in a large tin trough of transatlantic origin (some New York friends are in the habit of sending us a whole white garden every Christmas in this type of receptacle), various seeds are pushing up as I write, mostly South Americana by way of Ischia: jacaranda mimosaefolia, eucalyptus ficifolia and cercis siliquastrum, or judas tree: but in one case, from the hills above Rome, a group of wild blue columbines. (By "the hills above Rome" I mean the Palatine: but "Palatine" and "columbines" jingle distressingly, so the circumlocution was necessary.) We were furious, or I was, when we, or my wife, gathered the seeds: for the taximan, to get a few more lire, had driven us to the farthest entrance, and I had not yet recovered.

On the ledge opposite the oleanders and trough are five seedlings that excite us more, at the moment, than anything else in the greenhouse or garden. They are Roman acacias, from about two inches high to about six: the two smaller ones still have their nurse-leaves, and the two larger ones have already got themselves diminutive thorns. They excite us for the following reason. We had grown a Roman acacia at Brimpton, the country-house we had to abandon seven years ago: and, ever since, we have been ransacking Rome for a seed from which to replace it. We ransacked with particular vigour this late-May and early-June: with such a lack of success that we all but gave up the search. Our last whole day came; and in weather so tropical, suddenly, that our anglicised bodies could hardly stand it (after all, we are both genetically oriental), we crept up to the Trinità dei Monti, crossed over to the parapet above the Steps, and began strolling along the Via Pinciana. After a moment we looked down—by guidance, some might say: and there in front of us, but just in the front of us, lay a gigantic seed-pod, black, ugly and almost bursting. Absurd to imagine that it was there by accident: equally absurd to imagine that it wasn't. All that mattered, anyhow, was that it was there: and our five seedlings are the result.

Will one or more of them, we ask ourselves, rival the Brimpton one? This was a marvel: it stood in a corner of the walled garden, and within a very few years had topped the house. It looked quite different, somehow, from its stay-at-home relatives: its leaves, for one thing, were much slenderer—you expected, when you touched them, to find them sensitive. Its thorns were a glory—such bundles of them darting about everywhere. But what impressed us most was something athletic about it—an immediately arresting combination of leanness and height. We called it Raji.

(Explanation:

Raji is the *petit nom d'amitié* of Rajani Palme Dutt, Grand Theoretician of the Communist Party of Great Britain, and, even more impressively perhaps, one of the greatest living doctors of Marxist–Leninist rabbinics (or so I am told by those who know). He had been as brilliant a classicist at Oxford as H. H. Asquith or Leonard Stein: first in his year of the six Balliol Scholars, he won all, I think, the legendary prizes. But it was not only in Greek and Latin that he excelled: people said of him that whatever profession he might happen to choose, he was certain to come out top of it. (Not that this means as much as it sounds: the same was said of Gerald Gould, who ended, however, merely as reader to my firm and fiction critic of the *Observer*—and, not so merely, as a man specially loved by an unusual number of friends.) They thought him, among other things, a genius at finance: and legend has it that, while still an undergraduate, he was offered an important post by a leading firm of merchant bankers, which he declined, being already a communist. He was sent down in 1917 for preaching Marxism.

At the time I really knew Raji—for a year or two during the thirties—he was leading a life of austere dedication. He got, I suppose, four pounds a week (leaders of the Communist Party, at any rate in those days, received no more than the most insignificant of the rank and file): his diet, John Strachey once told me, was tea, bread and margarine and a few sardines: and, although I never actually saw him at it, I am certain he sold his daily or weekly quota of *Workers*, whichever of the two is required, outside underground stations—probably, as often as not, in the pouring rain. He has also written sixteen books; has edited the *Labour Monthly* from 1921 to the present moment; and has twice stood for Parliament. In point of character, he was a man (and still is, I am sure) of meticulous loyalty in the communist sense: so that King Street could hardly credit its ears when he was heard to remark, during the Stalin regime, "Some comrades say that Comrade Stalin is a great theoretician.... *This* is an exaggeration." I am not, God forbid, jeering. Extreme antinomian though I have always been—even, I suspect, in the womb—I understand loyalty to the "line" as fully as I understand why, seven or eight years ago, a Catholic told me at dinner that he didn't believe in the Bodily Assumption of Our Lady, and next day, at the same time and place, told me he did. He was a man of the highest intelligence: and when he explained just why the Pope's *ex cathedra* compelled, and honestly compelled, a change of opinion, I appreciated, without agreeing with, his manner of thinking.

I admired Raji Palme Dutt for his austerity and dedication, qualities I am weak in: I loved him (he will be astonished) for the undemonstrative kindness you habitually felt in him: and I reverenced him—for I suppose a peculiar reason. He had won the first Balliol scholarship: I had failed to win even the sixth, or indeed so much as *proxime accessit*. He had won the Hereford and Ireland (or so I have always believed: *Who's Who* is silent on the point); I had won merely a Chancellor's Prize, and that only, I have since heard it hinted, in the absence of an alternative. They say, and it may be true, that there were no other entrants.

But what has all this, it may be asked, to do with our Brimpton acacia? This. The acacia was conspicuously tall and lean: Raji was conspicuously tall and lean: so we called the acacia Raji. Harry Pollitt called him "that long bŏoger".

Harry Pollitt disliked Raji Palme Dutt. He also disliked Hewlett Johnston, whom he was in the habit of dismissing as "that blŏody red arse of a dean". This was unfair, for Hewlett Johnston was a man of parts, at any rate in the Thespian sense and probably in another: his skill as an actor was considerable, and only a trifle impaired by the impression he sometimes conveyed that his spontaneities had been overrehearsed. There was nothing personal at all in Harry's attitude to Palme Dutt and the Dean: they were intellectuals (both, Harry thought), and he distrusted, despised, disliked and occasionally even hated intellectuals as such. Not that Harry himself should be underestimated: he epitomised, I sometimes think, the grandeurs and miseries of communism. For example:

On a morning in the late thirties John Strachey looked in at my office on Left Book Club business, and happened to mention the Willi Munzenberg affair. I had never heard of Munzenberg: he was a rich German Jew, it appeared, who, sitting in Paris, directed the Young Communist International, if that is what it was called. He had been summoned to Moscow: but, fearing that he was suspect (the terror was then at its peak), had fled to some hide-out in the South of France, where he was afterwards found dead—whether naturally or murdered by communists or by fascists was, I think, never discovered.

Later the same day I went to Swindon, where a Left Book Club rally was being staged: a rather large-scale affair, if I remember rightly, with people like Harry and Stafford Cripps, Wilfred Roberts and Nye Bevan on the platform. I wanted to confer with the speakers, so as to avoid overlapping; and arranged to meet Harry in a café, for high tea at six. I shall never forget the look of the place: marble table-tops, assorted sauce-bottles, semicircular coffee-stains. We sat down and ordered: then Harry burst out, in a voice savage with hatred and contempt, "What do you think of Willi Munzenberg? The bŏoger! If I'd been sŏomoned to Moscow, and knew for certain that I'd be shot in the back of the neck the moment I landed, I shouldn't have hesitated for a second." Imagine the background: lower-middle-class England in excelsis, with its pubs and its Saturday nights! I knew that Harry meant what he said, and I thought "How grand in its utter dedication! And how appalling in its unutterable subservience!")

It will be clear from what has preceded that my wife is especially addicted to growing things, especially trees, from seeds, roots, rhizomes, etcetera, she has gathered herself, especially abroad. At Brimpton, besides the Roman acacia, we had a dogwood from Connecticut, which we successfully transplanted to B.H.; blue irises from a Venetian garden; and white ones from the volcanic slag of Las Palmas.

These last went back to the summer of 1945. We had been cooped up in England from before the war: and almost the moment it was over we decided to get away, and took a banana boat to the Canaries.

It was not a conveyance we should have chosen in ordinary circumstances. There was nothing to sit on outside except blazing bits of deck, which seemed made not of wood but of iron: a yard or two from our cabin (where Ribbentrop, so they said, had been captured—the line was an ex-German one) the diesel panted and throbbed day and night, as well as smelling: and dinner was served at five-thirty, and consisted, as often as not, of rather fierce fish and chips. I was a bit nervous, too: I had been conspicuously, even ostentatiously, anti-Franco, and feared that, on arrival at Tenerife, I should be grilled and perhaps tortured, and end up in some villainous jail. I saw the captain, and begged him to get our consul on board as soon as we berthed: he said he would do his best, and when the sub-consul's secretary eventually turned up (the rest were busy), he assured me that I had nothing to fear. No one in these islands had ever heard of me, he felt quite certain: he had never heard of me himself.

We had a scare in Tenerife. We had driven across from Santa Cruz in search of the Botanical Gardens (which are well worth visiting), and were drinking our coffee in the pleasant courtyard of a quiet hotel there when suddenly, from a wing to the right, a terrible voice, more stridently hideous than anything even Nono could have invented, began raging through the air. Only a single collection of words, reiterated at intervals, got through to us from that colossal reverberation: "General Bumf von Bumf, Feldmarschall! General Rear zu Rear, Feldmarschall!" Hitler! So those heroics in the bunker were a myth: he had got away to a Spanish hide-out, prepared months in advance, no doubt. We didn't know what to do: what *could* we do, till we got back to England? . . . But might it not be, my wife wondered, that some Spanish fascists were playing a record? This, I thought at the time, was too tame to be true.

Apart from the greenhouse stuff already mentioned, we have a number of my wife's specialities, here at B.H., out in the open. We have cactuses, quite a little group of them, which we acquired on our way from Domodossola to an uncomfortable holiday at Ascona (I had broken my ankle, and the hotel, it turned out, was on top of a mountain or at any rate a hill). We have a Provençal thyme, and still another acacia—this time from the garden of a house near the Matisse chapel where, till quite lately, Robert and Dorothy Mayer spent their summers; and, best of all, we have a few clumps of wild cyclamen from the woods above Menaggio. Wild cyclamen flowers more sweetly even than basil or lily of the valley: the old b'rōcha might have been specially composed for it

—"Blessed art thou, O Lord our God, King of the Universe, who givest a goodly scent to fruits and flowers."

The latest of our acquisitions is quite out of the ordinary. We were staying with the Walstons last year, and drove over on Sunday morning to the Botanic Garden at Cambridge. A few iris roots were lying about under a tree, and Ruth of course picked them up and subsequently planted them. They came up magnificently this June and July, but were clearly not irises: or rather the leaves were the leaves of an iris, but the flowers were the flowers of something like a common yellow mullein, growing in clusters up a two-foot stalk, six-petalled, with three stamens. And now we have identified it, via a neighbour who consulted an old man at Waterer's. It *is* an iris, but one no longer in regular commerce, being thought of as "very old-fashioned": its name is sisyrinchium striatum.

But I must not give the impression that my wife cares only for plants and trees grown from elements she has gathered herself. These are closest to her, that is all, but she can do, if need be, with any ordinary seed-packet. Indeed it is probably her gerbera, in the greenhouse, that she treasures more than anything else at the moment: and it was grown from a packet given her, three summers ago, by a friend in Maine. Ever since she has had a greenhouse of any kind, a matter of well over thirty years now, she has wanted to grow gerberas: wherever we may have happened to be, at home, in Europe or in America, she has been constantly in search of gerbera seed-packets: but something has always gone wrong—either nothing has ever come up or the seedlings have sickened and died. Failures of the kind have been rare with her.

Now she has succeeded: and her gerbera—she has several, but one in particular—is a glory of vigour and light. Close by it is a fine geranium, and the flowers of both are flame-coloured. But the contrast is extraordinary. In the case of the geranium the colour is matt, on the surface, almost as if applied: in the case of the gerbera it glows outwards, as if from the flower's inner being, and lights up everything. The proud stalk, though pulled a little out of its straightness by the sun (there is a large ripple in it, like the deckle on the edge of hand-made paper), is nevertheless already three feet and two inches high, and next week will be considerably higher; and the topmost flower measures a full four inches across.

I may have given the impression that my wife is a genius at horticulture and aboriculture, and I daresay I have half intended to. This is probably nonsense, as she herself would certainly insist: she is a good gardener and no more, like a million others. If I overestimate her green fingers, it is because mine are green in the other sense: I have no instinct for planting and tending. My function is to snip off dead flowers and generally clean up the borders, but even this she does better than I do. I meticulously tackle everything but leave a lot of unsightlinesses: she goes for the essentials like an artist, and five minutes later the job is done. She gardens impressionistically.

More generally, she is a marvel with her hands, which seem to make her an immediate whole with everything she touches, while I am a nincompoop with mine. You might call her universally chiropragmatical, or all but universally, for she is no good at musical instruments. She paints, and at one time or another has done most of the things, like etching and sculpting, that painters normally do as side-lines. She has driven a car for nearly sixty years without an accident. She makes a great deal of what she wears, as well as dressing-gowns for me, trousers for our housekeeper, and any sort of garment that Livia or one of the other children may ask her for. If a friend takes a cottage and wants curtains for it, it is she who supplies them. When our bird-in-the-box incontinently stopped singing, she took it apart—there were literally hundreds of tiny pieces—and put it together again. For some years she made jewellery, from her own designs. She cuts my hair whenever I let her: the last time I went near a barber's was in 1919.

It is not only in the matter of hands that we differ. I can write, she cannot (but can say: see page 55, line 24). She listens to music with pleasure, I with ecstasy: on the other hand she can sing or hum in tune, and I cannot. She is calm, I am nervous. She is moderate, I am extravagant. Each of us seems to have what the other lacks: thinking of life as a game of bridge, you might say that, whenever either of us could call anything, the other could reply with two no trumps.

After close on fifty years, our pleasure in lunching together, and walking together on hot summer days, is undiminished, my broken thigh, in the latter case, notwithstanding. A passage from one of Meredith's poems often comes into my mind after these and similar occasions: "Our spirits grew as we went side by side. The hour became her lover and my bride."

She is still beautiful: as beautiful at seventy-four, some would have it, as she was in her heyday. But this, as Raji might have said, is an exaggeration.

§ 2

I said, a few thousand words ago, that our sitting-room at B.H. is unique. I must now explain why, for what constitutes its uniqueness is the pith and marrow of this book, and the sole reason for my writing it.

For all its lack of size (though it gives the impression of an intimate spaciousness), our sitting-room is a living museum of our common past, which it shows as having been repeatedly crystallised in some particularly memorable present. Apart from a few pieces of furniture and three or four dozen books, there is nothing "mere" or isolated in it: nothing that fails to recall, as part of a whole, some experience or some friend. Three of the walls, with their wash of pale green, are exclusively given over to an aggregation of coloured "views": the idea having been suggested, the very day we bought the place, by a memory of those corridors in the hotel (formerly a palace) at Fontainebleau through which you delightedly made your way before climbing into bed up a ladder. Our views are mostly gouaches, of the kind that originated in the middle of the eighteenth century and were more or less extinct a hundred years later, with 1820 or 1830 as the date of their maximum proliferation. They were produced all over Europe, probably wholesale, as cheap souvenirs for the visiting foreigner: but their real home must have been Naples (at the turn of the century), for it is the Neapolitan ones alone that have survived in any number. Such a provenance is natural: for if you are thinking in terms of pure imitation gouache, with its transparent luminosity, is peculiarly fitted to reproduce, with an easy exactitude, the glow of those waters and the flush (not to mention the gleaming white clouds) of that sky. We have ten of these Neapolitan ones, ranging in size from two foot four by a foot and a half to three and a half inches by two and a half: and in quality from the attractive to the exquisite. We picked most of them up on the quay-side in Paris when I had an office there in the middle nineteen-twenties, for the equivalent of fifteen shillings or so apiece; and my joy when I came on one—after hours of search at a dozen bouquinistes on either side of the river, through portfolios devoted entirely, it turned out, to flowers, birds, fruits, reptiles, baboons, insects, lepidoptera, costumes, gardens, buildings, paintings, statues (occasionally callipygic), as well as to ordinary "views" in black and white, or the wrong sort of colouring, torn out from old books—my joy was extreme. But the three largest—panoramas of the Bay clearly done as a set, with the central one framed as for a middle-class drawing-room of about 1850, with an edging of respectable gilt—I bought for a pound the lot at a junk-shop in the Charing Cross Road a few doors away, or what used to be a few doors away, from the venerated Beaumont. (I really did venerate Cyril Beaumont in my schooldays, when I was not only an enthusiast for opera but something of a balletomane as well; and it was from him that I bought the wooden cut-outs of Karsavina, Böhm and the rest that used to decorate, several years later, the flat I shared in New Oxford Street with Ralph Rooper and Adrian Boult.)

The best of Neapolitan gouaches are the smaller ones, with the smallest best of all. One of ours might almost be classed as a miniature. The long row of houses along the Via Partenope are drawn with exquisite precision, and so are the couple of dozen men and women who are taking a stroll by the Bay: with, in the midst of them, one of those languorous clippety-clops that are still among the town's greatest pleasures (but you must agree the fare first, useless though this may be: for if, when you descend an hour later, you pay what you bargained for you will feel, by the time the cabby has done with you, either a cad or a criminal). There are boats, one large and six small, on the open water, and pink streaks in the sky.

Little figures are a *sine qua non* of these gouaches, whether from Naples or elsewhere: men and women (looking diminutive, but in fact true to scale, my wife tells me) are invariable, and you sometimes get animals too. Particularly dogs, if the subject is Italian: chasing dogs, fawning dogs, leaping dogs and inquisitive dogs. Italians adore dogs, there can be no doubt of it: I have been certain of this ever since I first saw, some forty years ago, the Carpaccio frescoes in the Scuola di San Giorgio. But the allegation that, *en revanche*, they don't really care for children is a scandalous libel, and you only have to go for a short sbrindolar in the Piazza to know it for such.

We have three Florentine gouaches, all exceptionally fine: and if I prefer the Santa Maria Novella one to either of the other two that is for a reason wholly extraneous. The view is from the colonnade opposite, and in the square between foreground and background people are at those varied activities that are common to the leisured in high summer: strolling, talking, walking their horses, galloping their horses: with, close to the foreground, two priests in a narrow barouche, being driven with considerable vigour by a man with a whip. There are five dogs, characterized in the four ways I have already indicated. In the foreground itself, by one of the columns, two large figures are standing, and I cannot make out what they are doing. One of them, with a bastard top-hat rather like my father's and a purple frock-coat, is gazing intently and a bit frowningly into space, or perhaps at the priests: there are two large besoms by his side. The other, with a similar top-hat but no coat, is probing the column with an enormously long bundle of sticks that reach almost to the capital: either bird-nesting or lamp-lighting, you might have said, if there had been a trace of either bird-nest or lamp. Besides, so far as the latter is concerned, it is clearly high noon.

The reason I prefer this Santa Maria Novella gouache to the other Florentine ones is, some may think, singular. The fact is, it reminds me of a dentist. I woke up one morning in Florence with a considerable toothache, and asked the proprietor of our hotel, whom by that time I knew intimately, for the name of a man who might deal with it. "So and so," he replied, "just alongside Santa Maria Novella. All the Americans go to him." He didn't mention the English, because there was hardly an Englishman at that time in the city: we were getting, if I remember rightly, fifty pounds a person a year (just as at present) in valuta, as it used to be called. "Please tell him," I said, "that I am not an American." "I will," he replied, "I will tell him that you are extremely poor." He had not treated me as such, but I felt greatly obliged to him.

The dentist (whose name, I am ashamed to confess, I have long since forgotten) turned out to be exceedingly eminent—President of the World Federation of Dental Surgeons, or something of the kind. But this I learned only at the end of our session: which started by his asking me, with an air of eager curiosity, "How well do you know Berenson?" "Not at all," I replied. "I have never met him." "A pity," he said—though not in those exact words, for his English was imperfect. "You would find him well worth a visit." He then launched on a rapid survey of his favourite English authors, from Shakespeare, through Dickens, to Ivy Compton-Burnett: ventured on a prophecy or two about literary trends (he foresaw, I now realise, not only Kingsley Amis, but William Burroughs and the whole Calder and Girodias school): and wondered whether I thought, like him, that the real future lay with paper-backs. We then briefly discussed music and the cinema.

He had meantime been doing his job, keeping so tight a hold on my mouth that my own part in our dialogue was not as lucid as I would have wished. At last he began undoing my bib: "Directly you get home," he said, "see your own dentist." "What do I owe you?" I asked: he shrugged and smiled with an air of humble deprecation that in the circumstances meant "Nothing". I insisted, and he substituted something purely nominal: no doubt I ought to have insisted again, but the truth is that I felt immensely relieved, and made off. He took me downstairs and out with typical Italian graciousness: told me how much he had enjoyed my company: and murmured something about Jackson Pollock that I failed, being rather tired now, to catch. I have never seen him since: I have unfortunately never had toothache again when staying in Florence.

I have recounted this episode for the following reason: it played a significant if minor role in my life, for it revolutionised my idea about dentists. With what I now see as a piece of stupid as well as discreditable snobbism I had previously ranked dentists as very low, as nonexistent even, in the cultural and intellectual scale: I had put them on a level with barbers, and had often wished that my wife would add dentistry to her other accomplishments. The basis, if any, for such an aberration is unclear to me, but many undoubtedly share it: when Graham Greene, for instance, wants to show a man for tedious and uninteresting he makes him a dentist. A mouth is as serious as an ear, nose or throat: so why automatically assume that a dentist so far unknown to you must be, ipso facto, less knowledgeable and brilliant, his craft apart, than a Fred Alexander?

What my Italian began, Tischler completed. This sweetest and gentlest of men, who had been famous in Vienna and later dealt with the mouths of the British intelligentsia, would not have ranked letters as among his major preoccupations, though he read widely and always knew what was going on in the literary world as well as or even better than I did: he was above all a musician, and I remember how envious I felt when he told me one morning, as he was drilling a molar (almost to my pleasure, for his craftsmanship was superb), that he would be playing quartets that week-end with Otto Klemperer. He was also an excellent gossip: he had known many people now famous when he was living in Vienna. His method differed from the Italian's: we would talk undistractedly for a good half hour, and only then, towards the end of our session, would he get down to business. His fees, though high, were quite moderate by contemporary standards: I think he must have charged me, in his kindness, only for the odd quarter of an hour. His death was as grievous to his circle as Vicky's was to his.

I was explaining why I prefer our gouache of Santa Maria Novella to the other two Florentine ones. These are of the

Cascine and the Piazza del Duomo: the former with a typical selection of walkers and riders, a lady with parasol included, the latter with the Cathedral façade still rough and bare—it was decorated in about 1850.

More "important" are our two Venetian examples. Over the brick fireplace, and just above a funeral gondola with a stalk of lavender for one of its oars, hangs what, I have just been assured, is or at any rate may be a Guardi: not a Francesco Guardi nor even an Antonio Guardi, but a Guardi none the less. A grandly exuberant composition in gold and blue, this is quite a sizeable affair, measuring, with its mount, two feet two inches by twenty-one inches. A gorgeous bucentaur, showing twenty-four oars, occupies the whole left half of the foreground, against a panorama of the Doge's Palace, the Salute and San Giorgio: and right in front, almost out of the picture, a man is running full tilt with what looks like a wooden rapier at a barking dog. The legend, in a pleasurable eighteenth-century script, runs as follows: "Solennità del giorno dell' Ascenzione durante la Republica di Venezia" [*sic*].

We bought this picture, during fascist times, in the Piazza: from a man called Ongania, who ran a fascinating print-and-bookshop in the far colonnade, I mean the one opposite St Mark's. I remember him with reverence. We were chatting to him one evening—his English was perfect—when a group of Balilla boys came shouting past us: "Miserable little dupes," he cried, pointing a finger, at the top of his voice. On our first visit to Venice after the war we sought him out again, but he had vanished.

At the Guardi exhibition a year or two ago we did our work as thoroughly as my father was in the habit of doing his at the Royal Academy. We were a bit bored, to say the truth, but were recompensed: for after trudging about for what seemed like hours we suddenly came upon a picture by Francesco, identical, except for the medium, with our gouache. I mentioned this to an expert the other day, and he told me that ours was probably by Francesco's son Giacomo, who worked only in gouache and only by way of reproducing Francesco's oils.

Opposite what I shall henceforth call our Guardi is a very

different affair, our Canaletto: a meticulously detailed representation of the Grand Canal, looking upwards (away from the Piazza, towards the station), with the Palazzo Pesaro in the left foreground. This is an engraving, lightly washed over by gouache and water-colour. It is not really a Canaletto, I fear: perhaps it is by his son.

To complete the tally of our gouaches, with one exception, we have a Pisa (with camels); a Hamburg (by the Alster); a Bonn (autographed by Carlo Schmid and other Bundestag officials); the temples at Paestum (with the tiniest of figures in the foreground, exhibiting these marvels with upraised finger to anyone who may care to take notice); and finally Pompei—quite a series, including the forum and the street of tombs.

There seems to have been a craze in the eighteenth century, spilling over into the nineteenth, for looking at topographical pictures through a viewing-machine, or optique, as the French called it; and prints specially made for this purpose had survived in considerable number till at least the nineteen-twenties, when we used to pick them up for a trifle on the Paris quayside. Engraved on metal, they came out, when printed, in reverse, or rather the wrong way round: but the optique reversed them back again, besides throwing them to a distance and greatly enlarging them. They were illumined by candlelight. Thomas Gainsborough had a machine of the kind (but not of course a reversing one) specially made to exhibit his transparencies and generally to aid him in the construction of his works: "Gainsborough," writes the *Somerset House Gazette*, "was in the habit of sketching designs for the show-box exhibition . . . whilst his intimate friends . . . sat and sipped their tea." The same writer refers to the play of light in a particular transparency: "The artist has given considerable interest to this subject by introducing the cottager opening the door: the contrast between the light of the cottage and that of the moon excites the most pleasing associations in the mind, and never fails to produce an instantaneous effect of pleasure and approbation." Similarly, a writer in the *Gentleman's*

Magazine of 1753 enthuses about "men, trees, etc., the sun shining bright, represented with such exquisite exactness as far surpasses the utmost skill of any painter to express."

Some *vues d'optiques* were probably coloured at the time, some certainly later: either with a light wash of water-colour, uniformly applied, or with particular features, roofs and so on, picked out in a solider pigment. They were made in a number of places, France, England and Germany among them: we have an English one (of Florence) with the legend "Published according to Act of Parliament August 1760". Portfolios of them must have proliferated: two prints in our possession are both marked '95', but as the subjects are different the numbering must apply to the portfolio.

We have had a number of these prints at various times, but there is only one in the Bottom House sitting-room, where it agreeably diversifies the gouaches: a fine, stark, flaunting representation of the Imperial Castle at Nuremberg ('*Cum Gratia et Privilegio Sac. Caes. Majestatis*'), with much of the detail—sloping roofs, horses' reins, billowing coats—in obstreperous red. It is of German provenance (though there is a dog in it), but the legend is printed in four languages, Latin, French, Italian and German: an example of the international publishing that has been institutionalised, these last few years, by certain London Houses, who however omit Latin from their repertoire of languages.

Add three straightforward, crudely coloured, early sixteenth-century line engravings—of Salzburg, Munich and Rotenburg—and a panoramic one of Florence, similar in type but almost beautiful in its crowded delicacy (it was given us by John Holroyd Reece, one of the outstanding geniuses of our time), and the tale of those three walls in our Bottom House sitting-room is told.

The fourth wall is taken up by white wooden shelves, which our predecessors used for their books. But we have put them to a different purpose: they now house the bits and pieces of a married lifetime. It is an odd collection, I suppose, though collection isn't the word, for nothing deliberate has gone into its making:

it consists merely of small objects we happen to have picked up (often literally) sometimes in England but mostly abroad, or that friends or in a few cases our children or grandchildren have given us. There are an odd couple of hundred of them, all financially and some aesthetically worthless: several very ordinary ashtrays from Florence; a dozen of those miniature liqueur bottles you get on a flight; three razor shells (I think that is what they are called) from the beach at Bournemouth; bits of mica-schist I casually put in my pocket when we got out of the car for a moment or two on a drive near Avignon; a long fir cone from Duse's tomb at Asolo (we picnicked beside it one blazing day in 1962, with the plain stretching on endlessly below); four fragments of pottery, one with a beautiful lip, from the plateau at Tiryns (my wife searched and searched after we had toiled up the Cyclopean causeway, and I searched and lay in the sun); and many others, some of which I shall deal with in their place. Financially and often aesthetically worthless, certainly: but intensely evocative for us.

Now when I came into our sitting-room on a recent week-end (our first at B.H. since our sabbatical), I suddenly found myself wanting to celebrate it, to get the memories it evoked, of friends and experiences, on to paper before I lamentably died. I made an effort to dismiss the idea: a very different sort of project, namely for a book to be called 'The Sanity of Christ', had been dogging me for years; I had done a great deal of reading for it, on occasion tedious or even repulsive—I refer in particular to several German theologians; and to put off starting it again, as I had done dozens of times already, seemed like shirking. But pleasure won, and that is the explanation of this book.

B.H., Saturday, July 23rd, 1966
7 a.m.

When, about fifteen years ago, I started writing 'My Dear Timothy' —a sort of discursive autobiography, as, in an altogether different way, I suppose this is—suddenly, after the first few pages, I found myself breaking into the narrative and switching from a proper past to an irrelevant present; for I felt obliged to record and talk about an immediate experience, namely walking over Westminster Bridge at seven o'clock on a beautiful morning to see a girl-friend off to America from Waterloo Station. I marked this bit to be printed in italics: and a similar compulsion became so frequent that towards the end of the second volume, 'More for Timothy', as much was marked for italic as was unmarked for Roman. The two time-strands of my life were drawing together, and showing themselves a unity.

It looks as if the same thing may happen in the present instance: for I want at this moment, not to pursue the theme I have outlined, but to get on to paper, while the memory of them is still vivid, a couple of events, one of them tiny and intimate, and the other public and colossal, that occurred two days ago. But first let me say, getting even closer to immediacy (one can never actually arrive there in this life), that the look of our garden on this best of summer mornings, and particularly of the gently swaying border (narrow but how poikilos!) that foots the lower of our terraces—let me say that the look of it, as I sit at work here in the liberating sunshine, suddenly recalls a remark my wife made to me on just such a morning at Brimpton. I had asked her to paint a corner of the garden as an illustration for 'Timothy', and she answered: "What? Try to imitate with dull paints the Light of the World?"

Leaving my office late on Thursday evening, I called in at the Maiden Lane tobacconist to replenish my stock of cigars: to buy my daily ration, that is, of the Willems or Dutchmen which, in these slightly more difficult times—justly, for people like me—I am now reduced to. Now Eileen, the charming chef du cabinet, *always calls me Sir Victor with a certain insinuating emphasis, as if to convey, in the courtesy of her heart, how glad she is about it all: and on the occasion in question I saw a man on the far side—he was clearly waiting to be served—give a little start and look almost eagerly at me, and in a fashion so friendly that I almost smiled back. I got my cigars and hobbled down Bedford Street: and half-way towards the Strand the man caught me up, put his hand on my shoulder and said "Sir Victor Gollancz? I have a signed photograph of Emmy Destinn in 'Andrea Chénier'. May I send it to you? Your 'Journey Towards Music' has given me such pleasure." To compare very small things with very great, I had an inkling, as I shook hands with him, of what Oscar Wilde must have felt when, as he left the Old Bailey and the prostitutes were yelping and kicking up their heels and showing their drawers, Bernard Shaw raised his hat. An absurd comparison? No. All goodnesses, my unknown friend's, who felt moved to express his gratitude for the pleasure I had given him, no less than Bernard Shaw's, when it was a question of showing respect to a human being in torment, are fundamentally one goodness: a goodness that makes nonsense of the cruder type of materialism, and shows it for what it is, namely a pathological aberration, 'existential' nausea and despair. How grotesque too, in the light of what we commonly notice in others and experience in ourselves, is Simone Weil's ferocious dictum that our life in its essence is the life of a farmyard: that human nature, as such, has the permanent itch to peck at, kill or drive from their homestead the sick and suffering: and that it is only by supernatural intervention, by a divine miracle, that a man can feel honest compassion for the socially, morally, spiritually or physically afflicted, or plain fellow-feeling for anyone. She may of course mean that nature and supernature are so closely involved that supernature is always there, however deeply overlaid, as the basis of nature: but this would be a forced interpretation: her doctrine, as I at any rate read it, leaves no room for the 'divine spark', everywhere and in everything, that the mystics have always insisted on. Her (and my) ancestors were wiser. "Blessed art thou, O Lord our God, King of the Universe, who varieth the forms of thy creatures." This is what they told us to say whenever we chanced on gross physical deformity: for they believed that by doing so we should strengthen and activise an emotion by no means unnatural to average men and women, namely a sense of brotherhood with all God's creatures. And as to Simone herself: whatever her theological formulations, and whether or not by extraordinary grace, she felt and acted, from early girlhood to death, like Saint Francis.*

I was on my way to Saint Paul's that evening for a performance of Berlioz' Requiem: part of the Festival of the City of London. This was one of the dozen or so greatest experiences of a musical lifetime.

I have been trying to analyse, as a layman, in what the supremely moving quality of a typical Berlioz melody consists: and conclude that at the heart of it is what the Greeks called πόθος, or, rather, a variety of πόθος—namely a longing for the ultimate beauty, coincident with a regret that it has never yet been experienced, and, the probability is, never will be. Some degree of πόθος, no doubt, is to be found in most good melodies. But Berlioz expresses it more intensely than any other composer, those far greater than himself not excluded: and this is why there is such a heartbreaking pang in the loveliness peculiar to him. Or to put it in another way, the tragic sense of life is his climate. Finally: you realise as self-evident, when you hear him, what you may formerly have only suspected: namely that sensuality, if intense enough, is a mode of the spiritual, and spirituality, if intense enough, is a mode of the sensual. In other words, Berlioz was a peculiarly religious composer (all serious composers are of course to some degree religious): as religious, in his own way, as Beethoven.

There was nothing new for me, to be sure, in all this: nor was the performance itself, in spite of its general excellence and Colin Davis's superb conducting, as fine as several I have heard. What gave it its supremacy was its setting in Saint Paul's.

We were sitting in the third row under the Dome, that is to say almost immediately in front of the vast orchestra and equally vast chorus, with two of the brass bands to our left and right (I really do not know where the other two were). I had expected to be deafened. But nothing of the kind happened: we were just caught up in, became an inner, indistinguishable part of, the great echoing sound. ("The noise swings about you," Colin Davis explained afterwards—with just a touch, I rather felt, of endearing annoyance—when I asked him why, against all probability, I had never been so much as conscious the whole evening, no, not even in the 'Tuba Mirum', of anything particularly loud.) But I should put it rather differently. The vast echoings that coursed through the Cathedral made it impossible to listen, consciously and discretely, to what was coming from the platform: the sounds of chorus and orchestra, and the continuously linking reverberations, merged into a 'sound of the universe' that front and back, left and right, below and above, everywhere surrounded us: and we the audience were just unselfconsciously in it, or, rather, one with it. Of course details were lost: of course clarity had sometimes to suffer. But imperfections such as these went for little in the infinitely moving context of all earth and all heaven at worship.

Acoustics, however, were only part of the story, and the smaller part: to hear such music in a building at once so beautiful in itself and so evocative of England and divinity, this was what contributed most to my awe and joy. I will make a confession: when I enter Saint Paul's, as on very few other occasions, I regret for a passing moment that I was born a Jew. I wish that, infinitesimally, Saint Paul's were mine: I wish that, infinitesimally, I had inherited it. Especially the High Altar. I could see part of it from my place on Thursday evening: and it seemed appropriate, as the performance ended and we were on the point of turning away, that I should slightly incline my head. And I am not only a Jew, but a very Jewish Jew at that.

A week or so before, we had heard Verdi's Requiem—greater than, and not as great as, the Berlioz one—from a very different position in Saint Paul's. The Dean had offered me a couple of places in his Closet, which holds half-a-dozen; and although I had already booked seats in one of the naves I gratefully accepted, mainly because I saw myself, round about 1990, boasting to my youngest great-grandson "Verdi's Requiem? Yes. I once heard it from the Dean's Closet."

The Closet in question is situated back in the Choir, half-way between the Dome and the High Altar: not on the ground floor, but up on what, if the Cathedral were an Opera House, would be called the Grand Tier. There is a singular disadvantage in sitting there, or so at first one would think: you face the backs of the chorus (whose music is as often as not marked fortissimo), and on the other side of the chorus is the orchestra (the same applies), and on the other side of the orchestra are the soloists and the conductor. There is, however, a counter-balancing advantage, spiritually if not musically: you are nearer the Altar.

I was moved, in this situation, every bit as much by the Verdi as by the Berlioz, but, so to put it, oppositely: we were not involved in a singing and worshipping world, we were private, we were withdrawn. You couldn't, naturally, hear very much: even the chorus sounded a bit like an economic 'stop-go', not to mention the orchestra and soloists. But this, as it turned out, mattered little, and in a sense even improved things. For you knew every note, and supplied for yourself what was missing: so that, as often as not, you were listening to ideal music, Platonic music, music 'laid up in heaven'.

And then, being virtually alone, you could do what you could never do at the Berlioz: every now and again—at the 'Inter oves', and the 'Recordare', and the 'Agnus Dei', for instance—you could bend the knee.

One thing, however, I shall always regret: I shall never know how great Gwyneth Jones was.

Henrietta Street, July 28th

At a House of Lords crush (with champagne) yesterday evening, a more-or-less-Labour-Party Bishop enquired of me, apropos of the sterling 'crisis', whether I saw 'any way out'. The face that peered at me from above that triangle of official purple looked more than grave, it looked haggard: the tone of voice suggested a conflict between resignation and despair. What was worrying him to death, it turned out (literally, to judge from his appearance), was the possibility, or even the probability, that we—we, the British, not we, mankind—should soon have our standard of living cut to ribbons, or smashed to smithereens, or suffering whatever fate it may be that standards of living do metaphorically suffer. It was this, to the exclusion of his normal preoccupations, that seemed to be obsessing him.

Four or five hours earlier I had contracted to publish a grim manuscript called 'The Starved and the Silent'. The author, a missionary priest, Father Aloysius Schwartz, has been serving for many years now at Pusan, in South Korea: and he enlightens us as to what things are like there. A vast number of Koreans live in one-room shacks or tents, a dozen to a room, with no sanitation or heating (and the climate is intensely cold in the winter) and no jobs: kept alive, after a fashion, by a meal a day from American relief—for those strong enough to wait for it in the queues.

I have been beastly to the Bishop, who is not only a rather exceptionally good Christian but, what amounts to the same thing or ought to, internationally minded, universal in his feeling and thinking, to an unusual degree. And I have been grossly unfair to him too, for he had merely caught the infection: he was reacting to the 'crisis' precisely as, in the bulk, politicians and statesmen of all parties were reacting to it. But being what he is, and on the assumption that I have interpreted him correctly, he illustrates, with peculiar vividness, an almost routine phenomenon: namely that when their own country appears to be 'threatened', in whatever respect, people automatically begin thinking in strictly national terms—which, the larger-minded automatically persuade themselves, are essentially international too. What is at the moment good for England, they suddenly assume, despite all previous convictions, must in the long run be good for the whole universe of nations.

In the context of values, anyhow, the 'crisis' is a comparatively trivial affair.

Bottom House, 10 o'clock, July 29th

There was a coincidence of two similar (but ultimately identical) beauties earlier this evening. The hush of the 'Emperor'—second movement, the opening bars—came through on the air; and the landscape was gently lit up by an unemphatic sunset. Were they right, I fleetingly wondered, who told their disciples that the sole duty of man is to praise? But no, they were wrong: the major duty of man is to co-operate in the work of creation. Our doctors, with their passion for reading sermons in the minutiae of scripture, expressed it like this:

> *"And Isaac asked the Eternal: 'King of the World, when Thou didst make the light, Thou didst say in Thy Torah that the light was good; when Thou didst make the extent of the firmament and the extent of the earth, Thou didst say in Thy Torah that they were good; and every herb Thou hast made, and every beast, Thou hast said that they were good; but when Thou hadst made man in Thine image, Thou*

didst not say in Thy Torah that man was good. Wherefore, Lord?' And God answered him: 'Because man I have not yet perfected, and because through the Torah man is to perfect himself, and to perfect the world.''

The poet-theologian, Nicholas Berdyaev, put it even better, if a shade melodramatically:

"God himself . . . awaits man's help and contribution towards Creation. But we, instead of turning towards him his own image in ourselves and offering him freely the fruits of our creative strength, have wasted and squandered that strength in superficial self-affirmation."

(I am sorry that Berdyaev has passed out of fashion: he writes of the God-man with a more communicative sense of involvement than do any of such regular theologians as I happen to have read. Even his most famous fellow-countrymen—Bulgakov, Soloviev—cannot rival him in this particular.)

It is the need for human-divine co-operation that the most inspiring and suggestive writer of our time in this sort, Father Teilhard de Chardin, perhaps a little understresses. He sees us tending to the Omega-point at which mankind becomes not only at one, but almost actually one—almost a single Great Man, within whom innumerable personalities co-operate. (A doctrine analogous to that of the Trinity.) I like this opinion, but cannot follow him when he finds, I think perversely, that current history supports the hope of this ultimate consummation. On one condition only can we gain an eschatological City of God: that we ceaselessly work for it. Even the man who, in a single particular, stands witness against ungodliness: even the boy, to give one of a hundred examples, who steadfastly refuses military service, can help on the happy outcome. I am occasionally consulted by young people who abominate the whole idea of violent defence: what, in the nuclear age, should they do when called up to prepare for it? "Say no, say it humbly but loudly," is my invariable reply: a piece of advice, I well know, that comes easy from a septuagenarian. "Utterly pointless," they usually retort. "How could my miserable little protest make the slightest impression on an inexorable machine?" Ah, but men too, however insignificant, and however vain in the immediate context their efforts, can be minute grains of mustard seed; or this at least, against all rationality, is my faith. Anyhow, there is and ought to be only one hope for our race: namely that all who feel an impulse, however transitory and dim, to work for some aspect of righteousness should do so.

But I want to get on now with the proper business of 'Bits and Pieces'.

II

ROSE MACAULAY: AND OTHERS

I SHALL BEGIN with Rose Macaulay: but first, by way of sketching in a background that will figure largely in this narrative, I must write a few paragraphs about Brimpton, which is what we always called our house there.

We bought it early in 1931, when it was already apparent that war was inevitable, if not within a decade, then at least 'in our time'; and with five daughters, the youngest only two, we thought we ought to have somewhere ready for them to escape to when the catastrophe came. A little smaller than medium-sized, it was about eight miles from Newbury and a mile and a half from the not yet notorious Aldermaston; and you might have called it, in its modest way, a microcosm of British architecture, for it was Jacobean at the back, Queen Anne in the middle, and Victorian in front, with, still further in front, a late-Victorian conservatory (people used to stand outside and stare in at my wife's cinerarias). We had a largish garden commanding the downs, only half cultivated when we took over: but we had put it in order by 1933, and, with the further improvements we made, it became so beautiful that, a week before the outbreak of war, one of the magazines devoted to houses and gardens was going to photograph it. Apart from the ordinary borders we had a special one alongside the tennis-court and in front of the ha-ha: triune, with peonies on the hither side, delphiniums in the middle, and rudbeckia and other late-flowering stuff behind. The delphiniums were so tall when at their peak that to touch their diminishing tops I had to stand on my toes.

Then there was a sunk garden for roses, extravagantly constructed by a firm of landscape-gardeners who said they had put fifty thousand bricks into it or something like that, which I did not believe: an orchard, which year after year did nothing until our neighbour, Mrs Bornett, gave us a heap of Steiner compost from Wales to nurse it with: two cottage gardens, as we used to call them, by which we meant beds with nothing but 'old-fashioned' flowers in them: and a pond for goldfish and water-fowl, fronted by an ancient willow with a riven trunk. In the shadow of it stood a stone seat, made for us by Eric Gill: which however failed to please me, for the following reason. The main inscription was in Latin, and ran thus: "R. & V.G. HUNC HORTULUM FECERUNT PIGNUS AMORIS 1933"; but at the bottom was the Hebrew word שלום, which means 'peace'. Gill was ignorant of Hebrew and even of how the letters were shaped: so I got a Yiddish paper from an East End Jew on my staff, ringed the word round in blue, and suggested that he should copy it. Now the Hebrew letter is far stronger than the Roman, and a page of Hebrew looks more like a woodcut than a page of print: but Gill got his values the wrong way round, and produced Hebrew letters so spidery that you could hardly see them, even before they had become more or less obliterated by moss. The seat anyhow looked like a tombstone, and we were quite happy to leave it behind us when we moved to B.H.

A little man called Thomas looked after us: a little man in the primary as well as the secondary sense, for he could hardly have measured more than five foot four. (His wife, our excellent cook, was on the other hand beautifully ample: her name was Nellie, but I always called her Flora in my mind.) Thomas had been third footman to an Earl, and he took it rather hard, I think, that I was a plain mister: anyhow, he always referred to me as 'Mr Gollanz-of-Brimpton-Lodge' (the z as in lozenge) even when ringing up my own secretary to give her some message—the idea being, I imagine, that a mister however plain could still be endowed with territorial status. At first we dressed for dinner to please him, even when quite alone; but soon he had to put up with our natural selves.

On frequent week-ends before the war, from mid-May to late July (the children's term-time), we gave parties. We could house up to twelve, ourselves included, provided we had only cohabiting pairs; and once even reached fourteen by making use of an annexe. It happened like this:

BRIMPTON

Mansell-Alinari

VENUS CALLIPYGUS

On a Thursday afternoon in high summer the great Yiddish-American novelist Sholem Asch, whom I was publishing at the time, rang me up at my office and announced that he and his wife had just arrived from America. "I am told," he went on, "that you give parties in the country. We should like to come this week-end." I explained that every bed in the place would be occupied, but offered to put the two of them up at the pub at Aldermaston, so that they could take all their meals and spend most of Saturday and Sunday with the main party. He acquiesced, and turned up on the Saturday morning dressed as for the City. Noticing how the others were dressed, he was dressed as for tennis when he turned up for dinner. On both occasions he seemed annoyed with his wife. After dinner he told a long story about someone called Basha, which was not as clear as it might have been, though I gathered that she was some sort of Chekhovian nurse (Alan Thomas, who was there, says no, it was his sister); and by the time we moved to the drawing-room everyone had gone to bed except my wife. There was something of a malaise between us all Sunday: he seemed upset with me, and I could not understand why. But years later we met again at Dick Simon's country place in Connecticut: it was Ruth's and my first visit to America, Dick was giving a party for us, and Sholem, who had grown famous in the meantime and lived in the neighbourhood, was brought in to make a speech in my honour. He was charming: he thanked me in detail, and in terms of the utmost generosity, for what, he was good enough to say, I had done for him. (Not that I had done anything for him in years: we had long since given one another up as publisher and author.) I felt considerably ashamed, and again I do not understand why. I would add that Sholem Asch was a great writer: his novels were long, but, in their own way, works of genius.

§ 2

Rose Macaulay was often at Brimpton, and one of our B.H. exhibits links her up with it in a particularly intimate fashion. It is the only gouache I have not yet mentioned: she gave it us, within a month of our settling at Brimpton, as a moving-in present.

Depicting 'Antient Rome in its Splendor and Magnificence', it juxtaposes seven typical monuments, which it lists, with identifying numerals, as follows: An Egyptian Obelisk (right in the forefront—there was a rage for Egyptian Obelisks at the time); The Senate House (stretching mile after mile to a distant horizon); The Temple of Fortune (which might be a Ziggurat); A Triumphal Arch and A Column Erected to Augustus (looking really rather like what they are supposed to look like); and A Temple Dedicated to Jove The Thunderer, up the steps of which hobbles a small hunchback. A couple of fountains are playing; three dozen or so figures are standing about, some in coloured togas; and in the middle of them, uncoloured and almost invisible, stands a dog. Rose adored this piece of fantasy, and so did I. It was "printed for John Bowles at the 'Black Horse' in Cornhill", Bowles being a famous print-seller of the beginning of the eighteenth century.

Not content with giving us one moving-in present, Rose gave us a second four or five months later: a Victorian glass-painting, with the legend in modern-ornamental "POMONA The Goddess of FRUIT", and painted "by W. B. Walker, 4, Fox & Knott Court, Cow Lane, London". (I prefer Fox and Knott Court even to Black Horse.) It forms no part of our museum, which is what I shall henceforth call our Bottom House shelves: it hangs above the lavatory seat, opposite Ruth's picture of Moses, about a million times magnified, at play with his gondola.

But back in the museum there are still a couple of Macaulay items to be recorded. The first is a small wooden cow with her calf, once brightly coloured but now rather spotty and subfusc: Rose had brought it back with her from somewhere out East, and gave it us at Brimpton one day for our two youngest children, Vita and Francesca. The second is a bird-in-the-box: a Macaulay item, not because she gave it us, but because we jealously bought it to rival hers.

This is how she described it herself: in her *Personal Pleasures*: a book of many delights, from which however she omits a special pleasure of my own, that of drinking a few sips of water after eating leaf artichokes.

"He lives in elegant retirement in a house of dark tortoise-shell, behind an oval china door on which is painted a blue lake, a blue and pink sky, three transparent pink mountains, a rocky shore, three red-roofed houses, three slim bending trees, and two sailing-boats. A small lake paradise, you think, and wonder what it does there, so sweetly, gaily set in shining gold-flecked dark-umber shell. Then you lightly touch a spring, and lo, a miracle. The door of lake and mountains springs back, opening wide, revealing its inner side, on which winds a broad reach of blue water (lake or river?) with more pink mountains, more small red-roofed houses on the shore. This tiny china land and waterscape springs up from over a golden floor, a broidered mesh of woven flowers and leaves, like one of those enflowered golden meads in Paradise where, it is said, the blessed saints walk in bliss; and simultaneously there rises from this shining bed a bird. You will not credit this most extravagant sight, and I myself, as Herodotus was wont to say, am slow to believe it, but it is, nevertheless, the truth. An iridescent bird, a bird of shining blue and green, peacock-hued, tiny, he springs up, he flaps blue wings, he opens a small beak, he sings, turning this way and that, like a prima donna, against the oval background of pink mountains and blue lake. A stream, a fountain, of sweet pure lovely shrillness cascades into the air, unearthly, celestial, like the songs of angels which the blessed saints, walking on the golden floor, doubtless hear. This (approximately) is the tune that he sings:*

* My thanks are due to Miss Livia Gollancz, who patiently and skilfully took down this tune straight from the bird's beak—no easy task, with so rapid a performer.

"And, having sung it, folds his wings and retires, lying suddenly, swiftly down on his side on the golden meadow, which opens to receive his small form, and the china door snaps shut on gold-broidered floor and vanished bird. The sweet echo of that piping cadence still lilts upon the silent air; I hold in my hand a mute shell box, dark umber, flecked with gold, inset with an oval door, the outside of a closed door, whereon blue lake and transparent pink mountains and slim trees delicately smile, lying firmly, reticently, over the strange secret within, over music fallen dumb and a blue bird sunk asleep beneath a flowery golden floor.

"A bird of pleasure indeed. Like Walton's nightingale, he breathes such sweet music out of his little instrumental throat, that it might make mankind to think miracles are not ceased. He that at midnight (when the very labourer sleeps securely) should hear (as I have very often) the clear airs, the sweet descant, the natural rising and falling, the doubling and redoubling of his voice, might well be lifted above earth, and say, Lord, what music hast thou provided for the Saints in Heaven, when thou affordest men such music on earth! And this makes me (as it made Walton) the less to wonder at the many aviaries in Italy.

"So much for the bird of pleasure, of which very much more might be said. In brief, how infinitely am I taken with this agreeable cheat! Like the phoenix, like the sun, he sinks into his golden bed only to rise again. Call him, and he will return, singing his carol before his opened door, turning this way and that, with flirting wings, against china lake and hills—tirra lirra sweet sweet sweet!

"But will there come a day when he does not come, when, though his door springs back, his gold bed holds him still asleep and stirless beneath its starry mesh? Or a day when he cannot get back, when, his song ended, he still stands poised as for flight, lacking power to fall sideways and sink into the floor, so that the little door shuts on him and crushes him as he stands? For at times he seems weaker, more tardy in his retreat, and you may glimpse him lying half sunk in gold, with the china lakescape resting lightly on his folded blue wing. Are he and the spell that bids him come and go immortal, or will the enchantment one day end, and leave only a box of dark and shining shell, with china door closed tightly over a golden mesh and a buried, songless bird?

"Come, press the spring once more; make sure that he will come. Rustle, flutter, tirra lirra sweet!"

Rose's bird-in-the-box was of the high aristocracy. It may even have come from the hand of Pierre Jaquet-Droz, the master-craftsman in this kind, and perhaps the inventor of the whole species, though singing birds of a larger type had been made in Germany as early as 1350. Jaquet-Droz had a fascinating career. He was born in Switzerland soon after the beginning of the eighteenth century, and at an early age became so famous that he was summoned to court by the King of Spain in 1758, and made such miraculous automata in his service that he was in danger of being condemned by the Holy Office as a sorcerer. But all went well, and his son, Henri Louis Jaquet-Droz, was received by George the Third when he opened a branch in London.

Our box can lay no claim to such ancestry: in comparison with Rose's it is almost austere, with not even the simplest painting on either the inside or the outside of the little door. But it may nevertheless be unique, for the covering is of shagreen, and I can find no mention of shagreen in Mr J. E. T. Clarke's exhaustive work on the subject. The classic boxes were of gold, silver or tortoise-shell (as Rose's was): the cheaper, more modern ones were of stamped or hammered brass or of black 'composition'. Ours, moreover, is not only of shagreen, but deliberately so. My wife bought it one day at the hairdressing department of Messrs Marshall and Snelgrove in Oxford Street. She was leaving after her hair-do, when she saw, set out as if on exhibition, several objects for a lady's boudoir, all in shagreen: two or three brushes, a mirror, a couple of bottles—and a bird-in-the-box. This had clearly been specially ordered to go with the rest. The Marshall and Snelgrove people were glad to let her have it at a bargain price, for the bird had lost its feathers: a defect we have often tried to remedy, with messy results.

You rarely see a bird-in-the-box nowadays (though they were still being made in France and Switzerland as late as 1948, and were even mass-produced in Germany and Austria after 1918). But the genus of which they are so precious a species, namely musical boxes in general, were once in considerable vogue among the leisured classes of Europe: they were specially favoured at various courts: and references to them can occasionally be found in contemporary literature. James Hogg, author of that masterpiece of terror, *Memoirs of a Justified Sinner*, shows himself in gentler vein when it comes to musical boxes:

Of all the arts beneath the heaven,
That man has found or God has given,
None draws the soul so sweet away
As music's melting, mystic lay.
Slight emblem of the bliss above,
It soothes the spirit all to love.

Fanny Kemble is clearly referring specifically to a singing bird when she writes:

Poor little sprite! in the dark, narrow cell,
Caged by the law of man's resistless might!
With thy sweet liquid notes, by some strong spell,
Compelled to minister to his delight!

So perhaps is Leigh Hunt, though what exactly is happening, with 'his pearl guitar' and 'just as if it knew the song' and 'as if 'twere fingering', is obscure:

Hallo!—what?—where?—what can it be
That strikes up so deliciously?
I never in my life—what? no!
That little tin box playing so?
It really seemed as if a sprite
Had struck among us, swift and light,
And come from some minuter star
To treat us with his pearl guitar.
Hark! it scarcely ends the strain,
But it gives it o'er again.

Lovely thing!—and runs along
Just as if it knew the song,
Touching out, smooth, clear and small,
Harmony, and shake, and all,
Now upon the treble lingering,
Dancing now as if 'twere fingering,
And at last, upon the close,
Coming with genteel repose.

Rose would have adored this: she would have listened, if you had recited it to her, with those dry little spasms of mocking laughter that so lovably revealed part of her character.

But best of all I take the following from Harford's *Life of the late Lord Bishop of Salisbury* (namely Thomas Burgess, who died, after a life of gentle piety, in 1837):

"His recreations were simple and innocent: religious and literary conversation: the perusal with a friend of some fine pieces of poetry: a pleasant walk: listening to the tunes of his musical boxes, of which he had several of exquisite quality.—Such were his favourite relaxations, and he enjoyed them with a keen relish. When his nights were, as they sometimes proved, wakeful, he would solace the time by a tune from one of these boxes, which usually stood by his bedside."

The bird-in-the-box was not our only musical toy. In the hall at Brimpton, on the serpentine-fronted gentleman's chest, stood a bracket-clock of English make but with Turkish numerals. Columns of tooled crystal ran up either side, with metal bases and metal caps of the Corinthian order; and the screen of the clock-face was decorated with a delicate array of coloured flowers. There were eight tunes, set on a brass drum, which you started by pulling a piece of string; and as one of the tunes was either 'Là ci darem' or 'Batti, batti', I forget which, the date must have been subsequent to 1787, when *Don Giovanni* was first produced. We bought this plaything for the price of a song, and sold it at Sotheby's twenty years later, when we had to give up Brimpton, for the price of an orchestra.

We still have our other musical toy in the sitting-room at B.H.

It is a work-box in the shape of a grand piano, made of mahogany and brass, with mirror lid and exquisite fittings in crystal and mother of pearl, and with the initials F.G., which are those of our youngest daughter, on a little gold tablet let into the rim. We bought it from Lee of Kingston, from whom we got a lot of our stuff when we were furnishing Brimpton. Lee had valeted Edward the Seventh when he was still Prince of Wales; and Queen Mary, who was a great collector of antiques, was a frequent visitor at his shop. One day we were looking round, and noticed a Sheraton table of small size, fine colour and exquisite workmanship. But Lee would not let us have it: "It is reserved for Her Majesty," he said. We did however buy it eventually, for Queen Mary let it go; and we always called it 'Queen Mary's table' till we sold it, with the Turkish clock and other treasures, when we left Brimpton. This was one of the three occasions on which Queen Mary came into our lives. The first had been when, as we were walking over the bridge in Kensington Garden just before we were married, swinging our hands and looking I suppose very happy, she waved to us from her carriage: the second was when she gave up the Sheraton table: and the third was just after the war, when she sent a messenger to my office in Henrietta Street for one of the forms you were required to fill in if you wanted to send a food-parcel to Germany. Her page was the first, that Monday morning, to arrive. Later I rang up some official at Marlborough House and asked if I might tell the press, as Her Majesty's example would greatly help the campaign. He said he would ring back, and did so half an hour later. "Her Majesty," he said, "would not wish to interfere in any way with your freedom of action: please do as you wish. . . . But if you felt inclined to refrain, Her Majesty would be very grateful."

B.H., August 13th

We have been listening to a performance, broadcast from a Prom, of Liszt's arrangement of the last movement of the 'Eroica'; and I am reinforced in a view that I have held on and off since my boyhood, namely that the slow variation is the greatest thing in all music. Now I con-

stantly have the itch to materialise with the exactness of language what it precisely is that particular passages of music mean to me: well aware that the attempt can never succeed, for music and words are without points of contact, can never get at one another, exist in separate and even mutually alien spheres. But I cannot help myself: I must make my attempt, by reason of an irresistible impulse to praise that I cannot satisfy by making music myself.

Two words come into my mind: solemnity and holiness. I do not mean that the music is solemn and holy, or that it conveys solemnity and holiness: I mean that, as it is played and I listen to it, solemnity and holiness a r e*: and that within that* a r e*, without distinction or separateness, are myself and the world and the universe and whatever it may be that comprises all these while itself it can never be comprised. And all this being so, I am engulfed in peace and joy inexpressible.*

§ 3

Three of Rose's presents to us—Antient Rome, Pomona and the bird-in-the-box—immediately reveal an essential element in her make-up: her connoisseurship of oddities. (If I include the bird-in-the-box among her presents, this is because she did spiritually give it us, ours being an imperfect terrestrial copy of her heavenly, perfect original.) For instance, she did not really love music. She 'liked' it, of course, and would always insist, when the matter came up, that her feeling for it went far beyond that; in confirmation of which she once told me that she wrote with particular concentration against a background of gramophone or radio music turned on low—"particularly Beethoven". (I was so furious at this insult that we might easily have had a row, if a row with Rose had been possible: but it was not: her sense of values, which derived, to be pompous, from her belief both in reason and in God, would always in the end have ruled it out.) She loved the bird-in-the-box, loved it with a special flavour in her love, not for any musical reason (in point of fact most people, unlike myself, get no specifically musical pleasure from musical boxes of any kind, they just mildly like the pretty tinkle), but because it was so outré in its tiny perfection. That a diminutive piece of metal should sing like that, and in such beautiful surroundings! That anyone should have had the patience to make it! How irrational, but how lovely! It was the irrationality, I think, that loomed largest: that is why, when the bird had finished, she would break silence with that dry mocking laugh of hers to which I have already alluded, a laugh in which mockery and affection were inextricably mingled.

It was the same thing with art, in the narrower sense of the word. I doubt whether she had more than any educated person's appreciation of pictures and sculpture: but her eye for curiosities was unfailing. The gravely self-satisfied gesture of the goddess and the crowned humanity of the lions in the one case, and all that delightful bogusness in the other, are what prompted her to give us Pomona and Antient Rome: the medium, in both cases, adding to the attraction.

By a lucky chance we have on permanent record the facial expression that went with her laughter. A number of people were down one week-end, and Stefan Lorant, the brilliant photographer of *Picture Post*, joined us on the Saturday with the idea of taking some pictures. At teatime I started groaning about my weight, and Stefan, I think it was, insisted that in spite of it any four people could lift me high in the air with a finger apiece. I was prepared to risk it, and let my wife, Alan Thomas, Reeve Brooke and Bertie Farjeon have a try. They succeeded, with Rose looking on, and opposite page 80 is a picture of her in the process. The performance really was, I suppose, rather funny, but not as funny as that; and I have always hoped that it was the scientific and therefore irrational element in it—something to do with leverage or whatnot—that explained her affectionate mockery. Science, after all, *is* rather outré!

By the same token, she loved ruins, without however any particular interest in architecture; and she loved beasts, though not, so far as one observed, an animal-lover even in the milder and less pejorative of senses. I do not of course mean that she hated animals, or, to be less absurd, was indifferent to them: she could never have been indifferent to a creature of any kind, and would have risked her life to save an animal in distress with the same sense of urgency as that with which, during the blitz, she would rush in her terrible car to succour the victims of an air-raid. (Not that it was only on occasions like this that she drove at several hundred miles an hour: this was her usual practice, and she could never understand why, when she offered people a lift, they preferred to walk unless positively crippled. She once arrived at Brimpton with one of her mudguards hugging the ground: a cow had sat on it, she said.) What I mean is that one expected to find a pet in Luxborough Mansions or Hinde House, but never found one. What she loved above all were extraordinary animals (hippogriffs, manticores, basilisks, amphisbaenas, phoenixes, Pegasus, etcetera—she would laugh as she talked of them almost as God might have laughed after creating them wrong) and stories of ordinary animals doing extraordinary things. She was gathering material for a book of such stories, and asked my wife in the meantime to do a book-plate for her with a boy on a dolphin for motif.

This was not to be just any boy on any dolphin, such as the one told of by Pausanias, who "had seen with his own eyes the dolphin at Proselene, which was mauled by fishermen, but had its wounds dressed by a boy, coming in answer to the boy's call, and gratefully allowing him to ride on its back."* Still less was it to be Shakespeare's 'Orion on the dolphin's back', for Arion was not a boy but an adult poet and musician. No, it was specifically to be the boy Pliny the Elder has immortalised (for the tiniest of minorities) in the following anecdote:

"The dolphin is a friend not only to man, but also to the art of music; it is charmed by the flute, and particularly by the sound of the water-whistle. It is not frightened by men as though they were strangers: it comes to meet ships, it leaps and plays around them, it even races them, and can pass them though they are under full sail. When the Divine Augustus was emperor a dolphin swam into the Lucrine lake and became wonderfully attached to the son of a poor man, who was going to school from Baiae to Puteoli [part of Naples]. The boy would call to the dolphin by the name of Simon, and often entice him with bits of bread he had brought for the purpose. It would be a bore to set the story

* Robert Graves, *The Greek Myths.*

down, if it had not been recorded by Maecenas, Fabianus, Flavius Alfius and others.

"At whatever time of day he was summoned by the boy, even though he was quite hidden from sight, he used to hurry up from the bottom; and when he had eaten from the boy's hand he would offer him his back to climb on, covering the sharp points of his fins as though in a sheath; and when the boy had mounted took him over the great sea to Puteoli. This went on for several years until, when the boy died of a disease, the dolphin came forthwith to the usual place, with a sad appearance as though mourning, and itself died of longing for him."

I have had some difficulty in tracking down this story, for everyone knows Arion and no one, it appears, knows anyone else with delphinous connections; and my wife, while determinedly rejecting Arion, could remember nothing except that the boy's name was Simeon or Simas or something like that. She was not far out, but was confusing the boy with the dolphin. According to Pliny all dolphins are called Simon. "Dolphins," he writes, "emit a sort of groan like a human groan; they have flat backs and snub noses. For this reason they all, amazingly, answer to the name Simon and prefer to be called it." (Simus is the Latin for snub-nosed.) I have just read in my *Oxford Dictionary* that, according to popular belief, the fish dorado, namely the dolphin, changes to many colours when it dies. I hope this may be true.

The stories of boys on dolphins are not myths. Dr J. C. Lilly, the dolphin expert, has recently made a movie of a boy actually riding on a dolphin at his experimental station in the Virgin Islands.

I do not think that Rose's choice of this particular dolphin story was accidental. She was always in Italy when a child, and, although she loved Venice, as she told me, more than any other place there, she must have loved Baiae second best, and chosen it for her venue because Venice has no dolphins, but gondolas instead. The bay of Baiae is indeed one of the loveliest in the world, as well as the neatest (my wife's word): we went there this summer, and though unfortunately we could find none of Keats's pumice, what we did bring back was a reminder or two

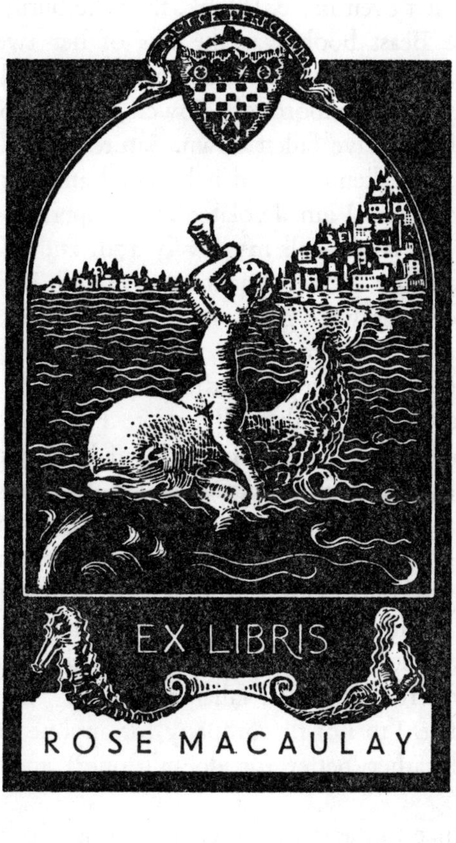
EX LIBRIS
ROSE MACAULAY

from the current excavation of a great Roman bath: several tesserae, and a pretty bit of light orange marble.

Rose feared that the block she had had made of my wife's bookplate had gone with the rest when Luxborough Mansions was hit by a bomb. The destruction of Luxborough was her dark night: and what she felt even more, I think, than the burning of all her notes for the Beast book was the loss of her twelve-volume *Oxford Dictionary*, for next after her family and her religion words were her passion. "Luxborough Towers," she wrote to us on May 18th, 1941, "have fallen down. Saturday night I returned there after the weekend to find it bombed and burnt to bits—*everything* destroyed. I am desolated and desperate—I can't face life without my books—all my lovely 17th and 16th and 18th century library, my Oxford Dictionary, my all. Incidentally, all my MSS and notes were gone, for my Animal Book and my current novel, my typewriter and wireless. I have no clothes, no nothing. I feel like jumping into the river . . .

"I've got some stamps that I'll send to Francesca soon (I got them from old letters at Liss [where one of her sisters lived])—a mixed collection, some no doubt worthless. I've taken a horrible furnished room in Manchester St. for a short time, and spend my days climbing up my Ruins—the stairs are gone, but (when the police aren't looking) I climb up by charred laths and beams to no. 7. And I found a pot of marmalade and some glass and china in my dresser—the one thing not destroyed in the building; it was protected by a roof that had fallen across it . . . I am looking for another flat. I'm not fit company for anyone yet, but soon hope to feel rather better (or doesn't one?) and then let us meet . . ."

The reference to the stamps is characteristic. To have thought of stamps at such a moment! But she had always been specially fond of Francesca ever since our baby was three days old, and Rose had been the first, apart from my wife and the nurse, to take her in her arms. She had given her and Vita that Indian cow, or wherever it was that it came from.

When we replaced the *Oxford Dictionary* her joy was literally unbounded—for the moment there was nothing else on her horizon. "What can I say," she wrote on May 20th from 35 Manchester Street, "and wherewith can I thank you? It's simply too marvellous—I came in rather jaded this afternoon, and there in the passage of this lodgment lay those divine packages dropped from heaven via Bumpus—my darling Dictionary again, in the same vestage and habit as I have always known it—and I was transported to Jerusalem the golden from the dreary limbo where I have been trudging lately. You *shouldn't* have done it—of course you shouldn't. It's such money, and you haven't such money, I know, none of us have. [Rose was in error here: the boom in books had just started, and I had far more money than I knew what to do with. Messrs Boots of Nottingham, who catered for a highly popular market, were to order at a slightly later date twenty-five thousand copies of a book called *Modern Islam in India*. They reckoned that, owing to rationing, we were unlikely to supply more than a hundred at most, but even so . . . Once we did supply a certain order in full, and there was a terrible rumpus.] But how grateful I feel, and how I love you both! I begin to feel I can live again. The O.D. was my Bible, my staff, my entertainer, my help in work and my recreation in leisure—nothing else serves. Bless you a thousand hundred times for angels! . . .

"My new flat already looks lovely in my mind's eye, its shelves abloom with those dark red vols. Oh God, if H. bombs it now! I thought I didn't care, but now I do. What hostages to fortune one gives. I was prepared to sit tranquil through the Luftwaffe's worst efforts, but not now.

"I had been going to ask you, Ruth, if you have still a rough draft of my bookplate, which of course perished, together with all copies of same. If you have, I think I shall have another block made of it—I can't not have my dolphin. But if you have no records of it, I shall do without a bookplate until happier days—I don't want any other, I loved that one so much. [The original drawing was found at Brimpton.]

"Today I hope to dig out those stamps for Francesca, from Romford, where I think I packed them in one of the suit-cases. Also, there is somewhere (I think still at Liss) my eldest brother's old stamp album, which she might care to have? It has some good ones in it, I think—he collected them over many years, then got killed.

"Well, I must catch a train—so much more gaily than I've caught trains of late . . ."

Shortly afterwards Rose gave a tiny party at Manchester Street, with the O.D. on display. I had inscribed the first volume with the word for 'Greetings' in a couple of dozen languages, all, except Hebrew and the otherwise obvious minimum, bogus. She recited the farrago gravely as if she thoroughly believed in my polyglotism, but gave her dry little laugh at the end. It occurs to me, however, that she may not have been mocking at my intended deception, but may have been thinking "How outré that one man should know so many languages!"

Rose adored parties: she was one of the best party-goers in London. She liked the glamour and noise: she liked the talk: but what above all she liked was that parties implied people, and people meant even more to her, now I come to think of it, than words. With a group of exceptions, which I shall come to presently, I cannot remember ever hearing her saying anything seriously unkind about anyone, though her wit and insight sometimes tempted her to a delightful cynicism only an inch or so deep: "I attended the unfortunate Hugh's [Hugh Walpole's] memorial service on Tuesday," she wrote in 1941. "It was a great gathering, and after it to Lynds and Priestleys: I lunched at the Ivy. X rather cross and sulky; Jane [Priestley] full of good works, Robert [Lynd] of whisky. What extraordinary obits. poor Hugh got! A new terror is added to death." Her very first letter to us that I have preserved—accidentally: I have always been terrible about letters, and often think with a pang of what treasures may have gone on the dust-heap—her very first letter to us was to thank us for a party in December 1932, given perhaps in celebration of my firm's fifth anniversary: "We talked a lot of nonsense last night, but what we all meant was . . . what fun we always have [at your parties]. It *was* fun last night, and thanks ever so much for it. [Before you began giving parties] life was much less like a circus!" And nine years later, when we gave a party in

ROSE MACAULAY
WATCHING THE
LIFTING GAME

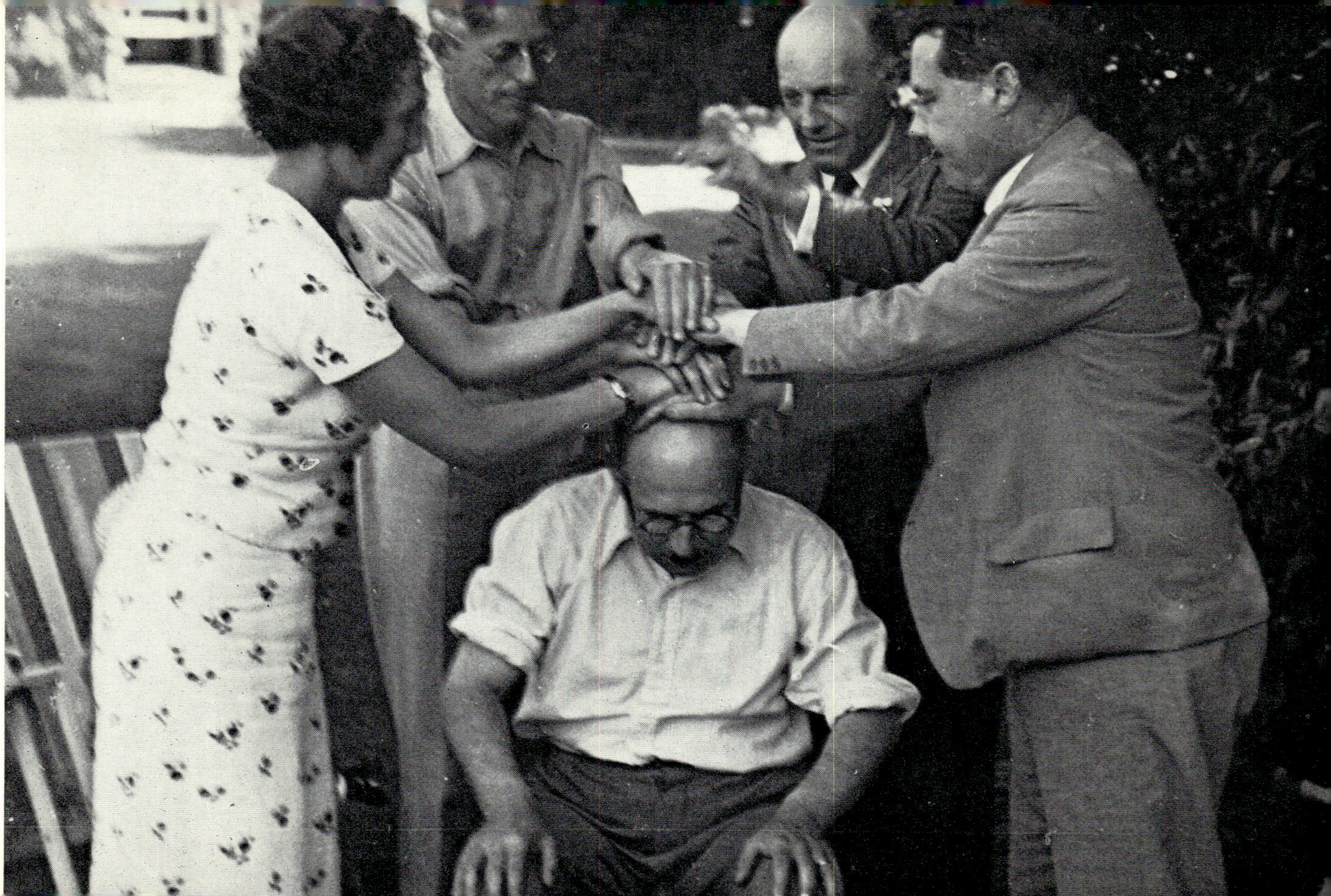

THE LIFTING GAME

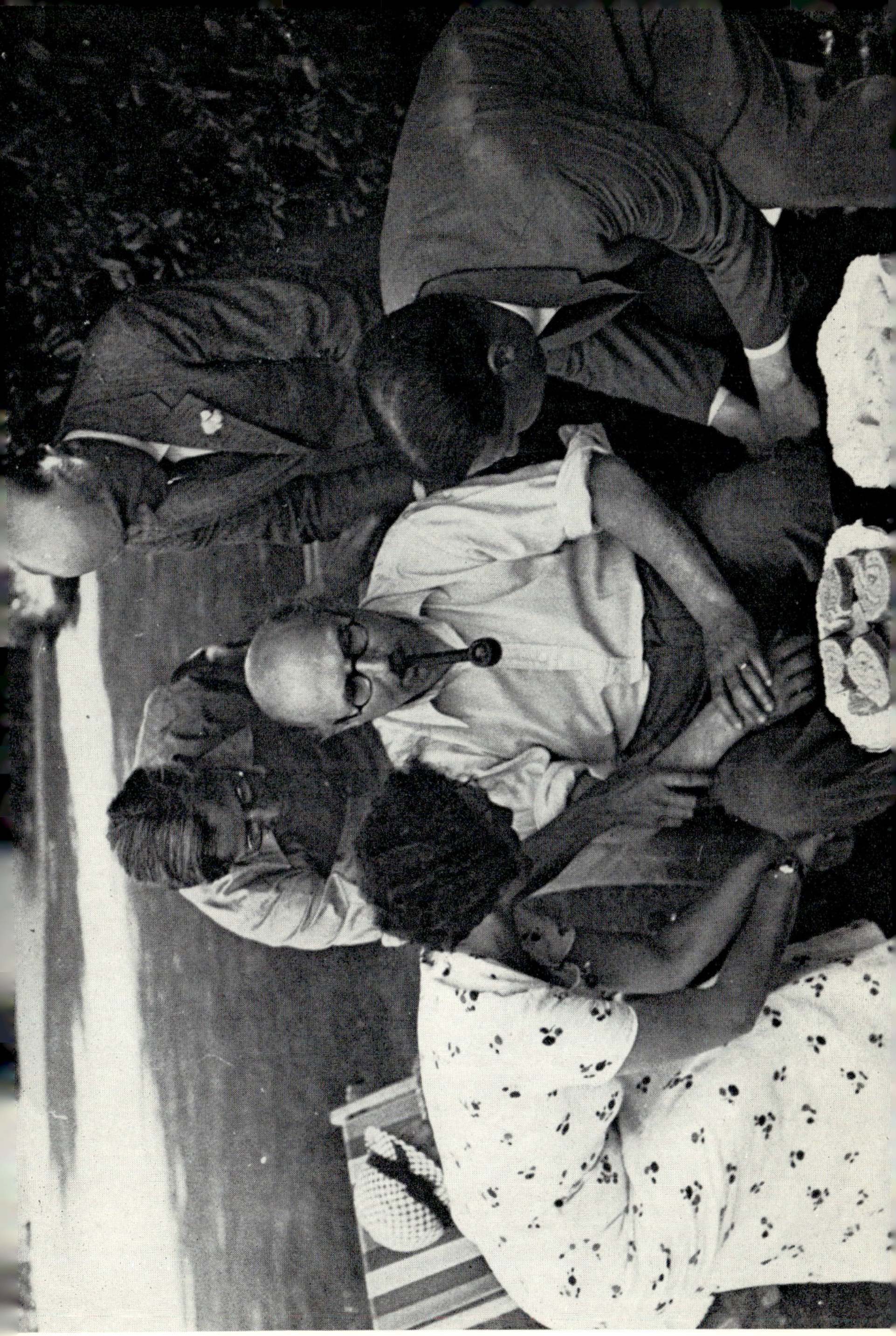

the middle of the phoney war at the Café Royal, "What a marvellous and lovely PARTY," she wrote; "an oasis in the wilderness—at times one felt it must be a mirage, but it wasn't! A grand opportunity for talk—and nearly everyone there one would wish to talk to (besides, no doubt, a few others). I had a *very* amusing evening . . . I do think it was a splendid idea—so did everyone. If you really want *gratitude* for a party, this is the time to throw a party, there's no doubt. I didn't see many drunks, but I suppose there must have been some towards the end. I had a remarkable conversation with Y.B. [Francis Yeats-Brown] about Europe! He seems to have married a Russian émigrée, whose father was 'murdered by the Bolsheviks' . . . You looked so lovely, Ruth (I don't mean V. didn't—don't get me wrong, will you?)." I was wearing a scraggy imperial at the time.

But though I fancy she liked not only the talk but the food at those parties, her regime at Luxborough and Hinde House was very different. My wife once went to see her when she was ill, and counted no less than nine dirty teapots: tea was almost all she lived on when alone, and her habits were as slovenly as even the most casual of her prose was elegant and well cared for. Years before her death she had begun looking so thin and transparent that her friends wondered how she could be surviving at all. Some thought she must be desperately poor, but her will disproved this: besides, she was so lavish in her charity that if I asked her for five pounds in some good cause, as I often did, she would usually send fifty.

Most people, essaying an estimate of her, would have given first place to her wit. This, in which she abounded, was of the genial kind, or one should perhaps use the word genialis, for the full flavour of the Latin original has hardly survived into its English equivalent. Her wit, that is to say, was a welcoming wit, not a rejecting one. Being witty, she was rejoicing: she was 'accepting the world', but not in the way that led Emerson to retort "She'd better!".

(Wit is a great reconciler. I was a friend of Douglas Jerrold's for the best part of my adult life: and it was his wit—a self-delighting wit, unlike Rose's, though there is perhaps an element of self-delight in all wit: his eyes would gleam, and he would chuckle in that almost prissy way of his, coughing a cigarette-and-whiskey cough meanwhile—it was his wit that primarily kept us together, that and our common memories of Oxford. And yet he was a fascist and I was a radical: he had brought Franco to the mainland or helped to bring him there, through his friend Hugh Pollard, and I did what I could, which was little enough, for the republic. I detested war, theoretically and emotionally, and he was all for it, theoretically and emotionally too. Once, when war was imminent, he gave me the Hitler salute at a public party: I thought it in bad taste but was otherwise hardly affected, whereas in nearly any other case I should have made a flaming rumpus. And yet—can it really have been nothing but his wit that united us: this, and his room in the Cottage and mine in Pandy? I only know that at his memorial service in Maiden Lane I felt for a brief moment that I had loved him. But the cause may merely have been that churches, silly though I know it to be, always affect me like that.)

Rose's politics were on the side of the angels (my angels) but hardly profound. She was conservative in her traditional Liberalism, or nearly so: "I have just been invited to join the Council of the Liberal Party!" she wrote in November 1942. "But am I a Liberal? I think not. Nor Labour. What am I? I think no party. All are so tiresome. Why is there no proper, Socialist, non-Communist, non-Transport-House, party? Anyhow, I hate party politics." Her pacifism went deeper. She wrote "An Open Letter" in 1937 for the Peace Pledge Union, of which she sent me a copy inscribed "to a non-Pacifist. (Victor and Colonel Moses, please read!)". It was printed and issued by her regular publishers, William Collins Sons & Co., who were at pains to point out that it was "set in Fontana, a new type face designed for the exclusive use of the House of Collins", but got her surname wrong with an E instead of an A: I was glad about this, for few things delight me more than other publishers' blunders. I refrained from reading this opus at the time, for I was in stays about pacifism, and could not have borne to; and I shall certainly not read it now, for I am sure I shall find nothing in it that is not as obvious to me, and ought always to have been as obvious to me, as the nose on my face. And yet I should hesitate to say that Rose herself would wholeheartedly have endorsed pacifism in the autumn of 1939 and thereafter: I fancy, though I never discussed the matter with her, that she wavered.

There were many things about Rose that I must pass over with a word, for this, I am sure to many people's disappointment, is not a book about her, but a book—I was going to say—about me. She was, for instance, the only completely honest author I have ever known: she would always pay back to her publisher any unearned remainder of the monies he had advanced. She was a mistress, too, of that prettiest element in punctuation, the colon, and would often discuss it with me. But I must write a few paragraphs (it would be unfitting to write more) about the two deepest things in her life, her love affair and her religion.

Her love affair (that sounds a horrid way of describing it, as if it were a mere excrescence, but I can think of no alternative) was the best kept secret in London. I doubt whether more than a dozen people, including ourselves, knew about it: my wife says half-a-dozen. Not that we really knew anything about it at all except the bare fact of its existence, Rose, for all her gregariousness, being far and away the most 'private' person I have ever known. But Rose did us the highest of honours, and I shall always be glad to remember it: she asked us to see her lover on his deathbed. I had not seen him since 1918, when, arriving at a London publishing house to launch a programme of general books, he accepted one of mine.

I must be even briefer about Rose's religion. It was with difficulty that I realised at rare intervals that it really *was* religion, basic to her life: I tended to think of it as an indulgence in the minutiae of theology, which must surely fascinate anyone with an addiction to intellectual gamesmanship. I was even offended or made queasy at times by her expertise in theological scholarship, as by the first page of *The Towers of Trebizond*, a book I never went on with. But occasionally, as I have said, some remark of hers, some action or attitude, made me wonder. I cannot recall examples: but a friend of mine, who had known her well for many years, gave me one the other day. They were in the theatre, and my friend, who had been visiting a sick relative, happened to remark that this duty had been prescribed by St James. "Someone else prescribed it too," said Rose: and she said 'someone', my friend told me, in such a way that Christ was there in the theatre, her living Master.

Apropos, I thought the publication of *Letters to a Friend* in dubious taste, though such a sensitive man as Raymond Mortimer, who knew and loved her well, applauded it. Rose, as I have said, valued privacy above all things: could she have borne to see herself paraded like that? I have heard the publication defended on the ground that it exhibits a highly intelligent woman obeying orthodox injunctions, and that to give currency to such an example is part of a priest's duty. It is not a defence that appeals to me.

I should be less than candid if I concealed that, during her last years, something happened between us. There was no hint of a breach: she dined with us within a week of her death: but the old careless days, when we had adored her and she had adored us, were over. I have searched my memory and my conscience, but have been unable to discover the reason. May it perhaps be that the more integral practice of her religion that her lover's death allowed her led to a certain lessening of her intimacy with, a certain withdrawal from, ourselves and maybe others?

I shall end, as I believe Rose would have wished, with a criticism. She was a snob: in relation not, God forbid, to the working class, but to tedious and uninteresting members of the middle one, and particularly to the wives of famous men and the husbands of famous women. "Poor so-and-so," she would say. "It's a pity one can't see him more often, but, really, his wife!" The chances were that there was nothing wrong with the lady, apart from her conversational inferiority to her husband; and the certainty was that Rose would have sacrificed a great deal to do her a service. The fact however is that, though she could never have been unkind to anyone face to face, in the privacy of intimate conversation Rose could never resist the promptings of intellectual snobbism. Moreover her desire for the company of the latest intellectual to arrive always seemed to me excessive.

But how we loved her! How I love her still!

§4

Rose occasionally came to Brimpton alone, but more often with the Lynds and a few of their circle. It was very definitely a circle. Many of their friends we may not have known, indeed did not know, at least with any intimacy: but there was enough common ground to make their circle our circle too (or one of our circles—I shall come to the Russo-Chinese one presently), with, for its core, Alan and Elsa Thomas, David and Madeline Low, Reeve and Dorothy Brooke, Norman and Sarah Collins, Humbert Wolfe and Rose herself.

Sylvia Lynd was the group leader. She was handsome, immensely energetic, ambitious, and a trifle ruthless and domineering. Under the influence of her great mother, N. F. Dryhurst, she had at one time been a devotee of such contemporary causes as Irish nationalism, socialism and atheism (for atheism too was a cause in those days); but by the time we were getting to know her her worldly ambition for herself and her daughters had become her dominant characteristic. She was a poetess, and had written a good novel. There was something of the grande dame about her.

(Not that she was a grande dame in the fullest sense. The only woman I have met, except casually, whom I should so describe is Violet Bonham Carter. I have known her since just after Oxford, though I doubt whether we have met a couple of dozen times in all, if as often; and invariably, not only when face to face with her but when hearing or reading her name, and whatever reservations I might have about what she was saying, I have felt (and I am not a conspicuous patriot, inclining rather to citizenship of the world) "Here is an England one can really reverence". I felt this particularly when I heard her speak in the House of Lords at the third reading of the Bill for the Abolition of Capital

Punishment. She had gone in a wheelchair (her heart was still bad after an attack) and she could hardly stand in her place: but, as she spoke, what had been a thrust-and-parry debating chamber became a temple. I have heard many attacks on capital punishment, but this was something far more than that: it was a hymn, spoken in a voice of passionate tranquillity, to the untouchable sanctity of man.)

I was very fond of Sylvia, and not only because she puffed me up and made me feel important. Some time in the early thirties she gave me a little box with an enamelled Napoleon on the lid. This was not for any special occasion, but by way of a general tribute; for to be immodest about it—after all, those days are long since over—I was carrying everything before me in the world of contemporary publishing, and was indeed recently described by an American lady as the George Weidenfeld of the nineteen-thirties.

It was as a *salonière* that Sylvia loomed largest in what were then our too crowded and emphatic lives. We rarely go to parties nowadays: for the matter of that we are rarely asked. A concert or the opera once or twice a week during the season, and a game of bridge whenever we can get one—that is enough not merely to content us but to make us happy during our five days in London. (It is extraordinary what a grip bridge gets on the unlikeliest of people, myself included. Gerhardt Adler, for instance, the greatest practising Jungian of our day, or so I am told, would give up everything for a game except his painting, which, like everyone else nowadays, he pursues with the other half of his fanatical devotion. He particularly likes doubling, an offensive procedure which rarely, I am glad to say, brings him profit—quite the reverse. He has never shown me his paintings, for fear, I imagine, that I shall start analysing him, for I am sure that his idiom is of the most modern. Gerhardt is a very good fellow: I like him enormously.)

But there was no bridge for us in Sylvia's day, and we looked forward eagerly to her Friday nights: these were almost weekly events when the season was right. There was a hard core, a crowd of casuals, and an occasional star: we were of the hard core, with

Rose, the Priestleys, the Alan Thomases, the Norman Collinses, Humbert Wolfe and others. There was no one you might not meet there—Mark Gertler, Peg Irwin and her husband, Margaret Kennedy and David Davis, W. J. Turner, the vastly entertaining Dulanty (who became Eire Ambassador) and Johnny Morton—but he was a regular. So, almost, was Sylvia's father, old Dryhurst (I never knew what his Christian name was: everyone called him 'old Dryhurst' by reason not so much of his age as of his pedantry). He was a dull dry antisemite: I used to call him 'the old goy'. When the Lynds' second daughter became engaged to Jack Gaster he was outraged: "Once you had decided," he said, "to marry out of your race I could have wished you had chosen someone financially better based." On which Isaiah Berlin commented "Something in it, yes, yes. It's the job of a Jew to be rich."

We had games, songs, recitations, charades, anything anyone might think up; and the astonishing thing is that one rarely got bored with it. Johnny Morton would recite that masterpiece of the bathetic, 'Blackwall Tunnel':

> Blackwall Tunnel, that's the place for me,
> Blackwall Tunnel, that's the place to be,
> And the only game I like
> Is a ride upon my bike—
> And fishing.

Dear Alan, now the oldest of our friends but one, and a man we greatly love, might be persuaded to do 'Young Albert' (my wife had a stick with an 'orse's 'ead 'andle specially made for him), or Herbert Farjeon's 'Thank God That I'm an Englishman':

> Thank God, thank God for the Englishman!
> Thank God for the pluck and grit he's got!
> You always can rely upon the Englishman,
> For the Englishman is always on the spot!
> Thank God the air I breathe is English air!
> Thank God the sod I tread is English sod!
> Thank God, thank God that I'm an Englishman!
> Thank God, thank God, thank God!

Thank God, thank God for Bulldog Beresford!
For the boys who march in red and those in blue!
For our little English home on its patch of English loam!
And thank God for all English mothers too!
Thank God the air I breathe is English air!
Thank God the sod I tread is English sod!
Thank God, thank God that I'm an Englishman!
Thank God, thank God, thank God!

or Eleanor and Herbert Farjeon's 'Victoria':

Victoria, Victoria,
Was England's pride and joy
When grandma was a baby
And grandpa was a boy.
And they can still remember
The happy days long fled,
When the penny stamp was purple
And the ha'penny stamp was red.

Then Salisbury and Gladstone
Were powers in the land,
And Dickens was an idol,
And the Albert Hall was grand;
And hostesses resorted
To Gunter's for a spread,
When the penny stamp was purple
And the ha'penny stamp was red.

Then saucy Nellie Farren
Was billed upon the boards,
And Grace sat in a growler
And bundled down to Lords,
And everyone repeated
What Mr Whistler said,
When the penny stamp was purple
And the ha'penny stamp was red.

Then Wolseley or whoever
Went forth to fight our foes
Was honoured by Lord Tennyson
As well as by Tussaud's,
And Watts and Ouida were alive
And Darwin wasn't dead,
When the penny stamp was purple
And the ha'penny stamp was red.

Now the penny stamp is scarlet
And the ha'penny stamp is green—
How different from the days when Queen
Victoria was queen;
The far off days when grandpapa
And grandmamma were wed,
And the penny stamp was purple
And the ha'penny stamp was red!

Rose and Jack Priestley were marvellous, on one occasion, in a charade, but I have forgotten everything about it except that they were marvellous. And, though people were sometimes reluctant to perform, Sylvia kept it all going by an ingenious combination of tactics, playing now a Papageno with his glockenspiel, and now an imperious Queen of the Night.

The two stars I remember were Max Beerbohm and James Joyce. Humbert and I were lucky enough to please Max Beerbohm with a little dialogue in our best Jewish accents that ran like this:

What sort of composer was Mozart?
Mozart? *Mozart*? Rotten! Why, he wrote Faust.
No, he didn't.
What, he didn't *even* write Faust? Didn't I say he was a rotten composer?

This was before 1933. I told no Jewish stories after that till one evening in 1950, when we dined with President Heuss at his residence in Bonn. Then everything came right: Jewish stories flowed between us, but through an interpreter who made an unspeakable mess of them.

But best of all was the James Joyce evening. Joyce, like so many Irishmen, was not only an operamane but a connoisseur of fine singing (which amounts to much the same thing); and we found ourselves in pleasurable agreement about the merits of Joseph O'Sullivan, who sang very high parts—Arnoldo in *William Tell* and Eleazar in *La Juive*, for example—at the Paris Opéra. "You will agree," exclaimed Joyce, "that the really important thing about a tenor is that he should sing *loud*" (which is at least half the truth). But Sylvia interrupted us, and ordered him, clearly by arrangement, to the piano. He sat down, and I shall always remember what followed as among the rare experiences of my life. Against his own low accompaniment he recited, though that is not the word, *Anna Livia Plurabel.* He neither spoke it nor sang it: he used something like the *sprechstimme*, or pitch-controlled speech, familiar from *Moses and Aaron* and other works by Schoenberg. And the sound of it was lovely beyond description.

Sylvia's husband Robert had points of resemblance with her: he had been fiercely devoted to Irish nationalism, and Roger Casement, a photograph of whom was to hang in his bedroom till his death, had been his greatest friend. But the Civil War wrought a change in him: though he never wavered in any aspect of his radicalism he became one of the gentlest of all the men I have known, and one of the most tolerant. I always thought of him as a man's man, even almost as a bachelor: while he greatly cherished his family what he liked best was pub-crawling with a few special friends of whom James Bone was the chief, for he was shy as well as warm-hearted, and talk with men came easiest to him.

He once celebrated Brimpton in the *New Statesman*: in one of his Y.Y. middles he suddenly asked, *à propos des bottes*, "Did you ever see the dahlias at Brimpton?" The dahlias were my speciality —great flaming purples and yellows, with a few pom-poms to give them scale: and the middle, if I remember rightly, was about pride in possessions.

Robert illustrated *à merveille* one of my favourite theses, namely that the essence of a man is revealed when he is captive to liquor. There was another man I knew who, I will not say normally but on and off, is as civilised as you or I: but when he has drunk too much becomes an evil and vituperative monster. With Robert I cannot say it was the other way about, for even when out of liquor, a comparatively rare occurrence, he was far more than merely civilised: but at the Lynd parties he became gentler and gentler as more and more whiskey passed through him, until at midnight he just looked at you with faintly quivering nostrils and a smile like a Seraph's. But on occasion, with a determination that a casual acquaintance might have thought beyond him, he drank nothing at all. This was when Sylvia was ill: abstinence was his substitute for prayer.

I only once drank with him away from the house in Keats Grove, and then somewhat, I am afraid, to excess. A few of us suddenly decided one evening to go and hear Frank Buchman, of whom there was much talk at the time. We managed to get in, and listened to a few confessions, one, I remember, from a plumber with a Lancashire accent, and another from a multi-millionaire. Then Robert suggested drinks, and we acquiesced.

He was very fond of Brimpton, but what I chiefly remember about his week-ends with us was that urinating in the garden gave him special delight, above all after midnight, when a primal smell as of the sea hushes one's spirit, even in the heart of London. Not but that all men prefer the open air to a lavatory for this purpose, possibly because the open air *is* the open air and a lavatory is 'the smallest room'. (I am told that ladies also prefer it, and that it is only the unfortunate posture they are compelled to adopt that inhibits them.) I cannot help feeling, however, that the natural explanation, namely pleasure in the open air as such, or the mere convenience of greater speed in reaching one's objective, is not the sole one. May it not be that satisfactory urination is as liberating as anything in bodily experience, and that one instinctively seeks the freest of earthly environments to enjoy it in?

The practice has, if not royal approval, at least one royal association. The following is quoted in John Nichols' 'Progresses of Queen Elizabeth' from Sir John Cullum's *History and Antiquities of Hawsted*:

"Immediately upon your peeping through the wicket, the first object that unavoidably struck you was a stone figure of Hercules, as it was called, holding in one hand a club across his shoulders, the other resting on one hip, discharging a perennial stream of water by the urinary passage into a carved stone basin. On the pedestal of the statue is preserved the date, 1578, which was the year the Queen graced this house with her presence."

If the normally lengthier and more troublesome of the evacuatory functions is performed *al fresco* less often than the other, this is no doubt because some permanent equipment is called for, or at any rate some temporary equipment not at all easy to come by. Permanent equipment was forthcoming in classical Ostia, or so I believe; for on our first visit there, long before the ruinous over-excavation—it was February but might have been August, and there were wild flowers everywhere—we saw what looked like a great open hall, lined with lavatory seats of gleaming marble, and this, we were told, was where the students spent part of each morning, chatting and arguing in the usual undergraduate way. My wife thinks that the hall may have originally been at least partly covered.

As to temporary equipment, I read in Mr Wright's learned and invaluable treatise, *Clean and Decent*, that William Hawkins of Fleet Street, who had previously been selling pretty lavatory bowls with delicate pictures in willow-pattern style, was advertising in 1824 a newly invented self-acting *portable* w.c.; and I find it hard to believe that when Louis the Fourteenth gave audience to kings and princes from his *chaise percée* this was always within the palace and never in the gardens of Versailles. I daresay there is evidence on the point, but I have as yet lacked the leisure to ferret it out.

I often accompanied Robert on his nightly pilgrimages, for in this matter, as in very few others, two are better than one: and twice I was lucky enough to witness a curious and fascinating sight. On our way back to the house Robert shone his torch on the lawn; and as a wriggle of worms incontinently popped back into the earth a gentle, sad, contemplative and benevolent smile appeared on Robert's face. He particularly liked, too, the fireflies that used to come out in great numbers on Crookham Common.

The only other thing I remember about Robert is that he invariably put off doing his Y.Y. articles till the very last minute; but this is perhaps not worth recording.

III

THE LOWS AND THE LYNDS

THERE IS A third Lynd who must come in with Robert and Sylvia: their daughter Sigle, as I have always called her, for she liked her name to be spelled in the Irish way and pronounced to rhyme with giggle (she now prefers Sheila). "Your favourite Lynd" is how she described herself to me, and this was exact.

But first I wish to write about David and Madeline Low, who were in the Lynd circle, and of course in many others as well.

Men of integrity, and in particular men of supreme integrity, are not always lovable: David was a man of supreme integrity, and was supremely lovable. And, what is not necessarily the same thing at all, he was supremely likeable too. It is more enviable, I think, to be likeable than to be lovable. You may love a man, and still not want to spend a great deal of time with him: I cannot imagine anyone not wanting to spend as much time as possible with David Low. To say "everyone liked him"—that is surely the happiest epitaph any human being could have, and I cannot think of a more fitting one for David.

Let me say a few words about this integrity of his. It was not the comparatively easy type of integrity, the integrity, I mean, of a man who has accepted some absolute, accepted it once and for all, and tries his hardest, in thought and speech and action, never for a moment to deviate from it. I am thinking, for instance, of the integrity of the best kind of pacifist, or of a man who, in all circumstances, thinks it wrong to take any form of life, human or animal. Now, David's was not that kind of integrity. Let me put it like this. There have been many in the world's history who have served the relative, to the degree that their weakness permitted, by fixing their eyes on the absolute: David served the absolute by the closest and most scrupulous attention to the relative. By the same token, there are men whose concern for the good of humanity makes them dubious about people who calculate, who weigh up possibilities and practicalities: David's equal concern for the good of humanity made him dubious about fanatics. He was passionless on the surface, but passionless of set purpose, passionless, one might say, by the exercise of discipline: for David's outer restraint had its roots in a deep moral passion for the good and the true. He was a man of profound feeling, but not of easy enthusiasms: for all his inward fire, he was *careful*. If I wanted to sum him up in a word, I think I should call him Socratic, the most Socratic of men, it may be, since Socrates himself. Like Socrates, indeed, he would even play the Devil's advocate on occasion—strictly in private—a little by way of teasing but above all to arrive at the truth. But it was always a temporary alliance: I never knew a man who hated the Devil more.

I remember, in this connection, a little dinner party my wife and I had arranged round about 1952. Only the faithful had been asked, and we fell to discussing Malaya, and the destruction, or threatened destruction, of a village there as a reprisal. Somebody asked David whether he was going to do a cartoon about it, and suggested as the underline "Lidice": that village, it will be remembered, had been horribly wiped out by the Germans, also as a reprisal, during the Second World War. Immediately you saw in David's eye, in the pose of his body and in his shy and slightly mocking smile, a whole complex of reactions—and if anyone objects that a man's eye and pose cannot exhibit all this much then he did not know David. A sense of responsibility about the comparison he was being asked to draw between British action in Malaya and German action in Czechoslovakia; a dread of haste and over-simplification; a distrust of emotionalism, on his own part or anyone else's; a determination to weigh up pros and cons and not be rushed, by himself or whoever it might be; a gentle wryness, a charitable irony—impossible to imagine a more beautiful counterpoint. And then, after some humming and hawing, he came out with his Ace of Trumps: Wasn't it *possible*, he asked, that in the British case the end justified the means? I was horrified: could this be David? Yes, it was David, and he eventually answered his own question in the negative. He was of course teasing us a bit, but what explained it all, apart from that, was a determination to be solidly based before agreeing with our comparison.

David was Socratic in another sense too. Like Socrates, he was a man of the highest intelligence: his book of cartoons, *Years of Wrath*, is devastating in its critical insight, besides being one of the best histories of our time. But like Socrates, too, he was far too honest to be, in the bad sense, a highbrow. He couldn't abide humbug. I met him once at a fashionable exhibition of extremely modern paintings, and shall never forget the smile on his face as he stood looking at a particularly pretentious and meaningless specimen. If you called him the plain man, with ten times the plain man's intelligence and a hundred times the plain man's wisdom, you would not be far out.

Some might say indeed that, as a critic of art, he was the plain man to excess; that he was incapable of getting away from the ideas in which he had been brought up: more, that he made no effort to do so. This last is untrue. Thirty-five years ago, when such things could be got for comparatively little, we bought a Modigliani: a picture of great and even classical beauty. David would look at it from time to time at Brimpton or Ladbroke Grove, where we lived till the war; and always, after a brief examination, he would shake his head. Then one day, about a dozen years or so after he had seen it for the first time, he smiled and said to my wife, "Yes, I think there's something in it". But he could never have said the same about an abstract. In matters of art, it must be confessed, he was of conservative mind: with the new rubbish he rejected some new excellences.

He was quietly devoted to the masters of his choice, of which the chief was Velasquez, and one of his favourite pleasures was to go down to the Wallace Collection and sit gazing at the Laughing Cavalier. He had the ambition to be a painter himself, but was always dissatisfied with what he was able to do: he would show his paintings to no one, and they were all destroyed after his death as he had wished them to be, except a self-portrait of himself at the age of thirty-five.

I am not competent to assess the artistic merit of his cartoons.

DAVID LOW · SELF PORTRAIT

The immense popularity in Russia of the newly discovered revolutionary writer Charles Dickens is inspiring the Left Book Club to publish his works here. The Home Office may take steps

That his line was superbly bold cannot be questioned; and if his draughtsmanship was not so much great as greatly expressive, that is because it was put at the service not, like Michelangelo's, of an artistic concept, but of a social or political idea. The fact is that he was a commentator first, and an artist second: if he thought Daumier the best of all cartoonists, and Gillray the best of all British ones, this was not so much because they were great artists as because they didn't give a damn.

I should like to write a very few words about another facet of his life. There is nothing of better repute than a perfect marriage, and David's and Madeline's was perfect as I have known few others to be. These were more than loving companions, more than quiet playmates: they were workmates too, for Madeline co-operated with David in a way few were aware of. And their marriage kept its freshness to the end.

But yet another side of him was almost as strong. People who did not know about his home life might have taken him for a typical clubman of the very best sort. I do not in fact know if he even belonged to a club, but if he did he certainly could not have spent much time in it. And yet somehow, for all that, he was very much of a man's man: if you went to an all-male dinner and did not find him there you were greatly surprised—and greatly disappointed.

Finally, David was a man of exceptional benevolence: for all his acute penetration into human foibles and pretences and wickednesses, he wished everyone, or nearly everyone, well. It was a benevolence unqualified by self-regarding considerations: many of us have to fight our way up to benevolence through resentments egoistic in origin, but not David—it came naturally to him. And yet even his benevolence was in a sense Socratic: there was on occasion a flavour of irony about it that robbed it of sentimentality and made it all the more genuine.

His hatred of poverty and war, of injustice and oppression, was uncompromising: it is true to say of him, as d'Annunzio said of Verdi, that he suffered with and for his fellow-men. His compassion was infinite. We have two of his cartoons at Eaton Place that illustrate this essential of his nature. The first was done just after Buchenwald was opened up to a horrified world: a black-suited young man crumbling up a newspaper is crying "The whole German people should be wiped out for this!", and rising in front of him from the bones and ashes are four gaunt figures, with the legend, "Don't forget some of *us* are Germans, friend." The second was done to raise money for the relatives of concentration camp victims. High up at the top of a wall and behind barbed wire, you see a mother's hands clasped together: below, looking up at them, is a group of three little children with retroussé noses. In the tenderness of the line with which those Germans and those children are drawn the deepest compassion impinges on one like a living presence.

People used to say that David had no feeling for religion. Certainly you might have expected him to be, if not an atheist, at the very least an agnostic, for must not agnosticism have been part and parcel of that Socratic make-up, must he not have felt that to judge of things no human being could know about would be in the highest degree improper? I do not know: Madeline once told me that a couple of years before his death he said to her, "Sometimes I think—I have always thought—that there is a Superior Being". It would be easy to retort that he was suffering terribly at the time. Anyhow, everything depends on what you mean by religion. There is a poem by Leigh Hunt that everyone knew in the good or bad old days of my boyhood but probably no one knows now, and I should like to set it down here:

Abou Ben Adhem (may his tribe increase!)
Awoke one night from a deep dream of peace,
And saw, within the moonlight in his room,
Making it rich, and like a lily in bloom,
An angel writing in a book of gold:—
Exceeding peace had made Ben Adhem bold,
And to the presence in the room he said,
'What writest thou?'—the vision rais'd its head,
And with a look made of all sweet accord,
Answer'd, 'The names of those who love the Lord.'

'And is mine one?' said Abou. 'Nay, not so,'
Replied the angel. Abou spoke more low,
But cheerly still; and said, 'I pray thee, then,
Write me as one that loves his fellow men.'
The angel wrote, and vanish'd. The next night
It came again with a great wakening light,
And show'd the names whom love of God had blest,
And lo! Ben Adhem's name led all the rest.

§ 2

Sigle Lynd. A freshness comes into my mind when I think of the beginnings of our growing together, a sense of the world being young. She must have been about twenty when I first met her, at a Lynd party: 'splendid for the day', she was of an eager beauty (but her younger sister, Moira, called B.J., was perhaps even lovelier), of a wit and gaiety and intelligence that touched the mind. She asked for a job in my firm, and of course I gave her one: we got to know each other well, often lunched together (at the Ivy, where everyone lunched in those days), and found a special bond in our common love of music. I can hear her humming about the place things I particularly liked, such as the dance *alla tedesca* from Beethoven's opus 130.

She was a Liberal (even, I think, with a big el) to begin with, and I spent a lot of time, in and out of the office, trying to make her a socialist. I got nowhere: "If everyone was as good a boss as you," I remember her saying, "socialism would be unnecessary." But one morning she came and told me that she had joined 'the Party', meaning of course the C.P. A young man in a train coming from Oxford had been talking to her (his regular Party job, I believe, was the conversion of young intellectuals); B.J., already a communist, had been working on her for some time: but above all she had been outraged by what she had seen when the hunger-marchers arrived in London. Her communist practice was at once exemplary: she explained things to the men in the office, sold them *Daily Workers*, tried in every way to win them over.

She was deeply religious by nature, and had got herself baptised (Sylvia and Robert both being atheists, as I have explained) at the age of sixteen. Her passionate loathing of injustice, her fellow-feeling with the poor and underprivileged, her horror of war, all these took their origin from a Christianity central to her make-up: and a Christian she remains to this day, though she will loathe me for saying it—she will think it starry-eyed and sentimental, and these are of all things the ones she hates most. When she went to Oxford, three years after her baptism, credal religion rapidly lost its hold over her: but it was not till she joined the Party in 1933 that she spoke of it with hostility and contempt. The habit of thought at King Street confirmed a growing conviction that Christianity as practised, and then as a thing in itself, was pie-in-the-sky, a cover for cheating the working class and for everything reactionary, in fact the opium of the people. This affected, though at first only slightly, her relationship with me: she disliked, and made it plain that she disliked, my allusions to the Sermon on the Mount in Left Book Club speeches. Her doubts about me grew stronger when I published an editorial in the *Left News* called 'Thoughts after Munich', for this was openly liberal-Christian in its outlook, and as far removed as could be imagined from Party ideology. But there was no hint of a breach between us, or even of any real coolness, till the Nazi–Soviet Pact.

I am glad that Sigle joined the Party, whatever unhappiness she may or may not have suffered at certain periods (I know nothing of this, for I completely lost touch with her between the outbreak of war and Hungary, and have never discussed with her what life was like at that time, and do not intend to). I hate the type of ex-communist (mainly American) who beats his breast and cries 'peccavi' whenever his doings in the thirties come up: and it follows that I must equally hate non-communists who beat their own breasts about such doings on the part of their friends. I shall not say that any young person who loathed social conditions before the war, realised what Hitler was about, and was concerned to do something about it—I shall not say that any young person of the kind was a scoundrel, or careless and selfish, or a fool unless he joined the Party, for he might well have seen that no possible solution could inhere in a Marxist or supposedly Marxist organisation directed from Moscow: what I shall say is that anyone who did see such a solution, and drew what seemed to him the necessary conclusion at never mind what cost to himself—in discomfort, or cold-shouldering by family or friends, or dislike of renouncing his power of individual judgment and submitting to discipline—was the salt of the earth. The craze is or was to play Freud with young middle-class communists: this one was looking for a father and found him in Stalin, that one was in morbid revolt against society, this other was sexually frustrated. A few, if they had submitted to an actual analysis, might have agreed five years later that such was indeed the obvious reason for their joining the Party: but in the vast majority of cases young intellectuals joined it out of idealism. And idealists, I repeat, however little 'with it' I may be in saying so, are the salt of the earth.

The break came with the Nazi–Soviet Pact. I furiously denounced it: she furiously denounced me. She ended by saying, "You're as bad as Norman Collins".

I must break off here to write a few paragraphs about Norman.

When I first got to know him he was a pacifist and Tolstoyan (that was the word used by one of his intimate friends); he was also extremely brilliant, had 'worked his way up' from small beginnings, and so could hardly have failed to be ambitious. He was at the time assisting Robert in the literary editorship of the *News Chronicle*: he asked to join my firm: Robert agreed: and he arrived at Henrietta Street almost simultaneously with Sigle.

We were not very successful with one another, though he remained with me for close on ten years. I thought him a good businessman but not a superlative one like myself (how wrong I have turned out to be!). I was particularly sceptical about *Anthony Adverse*, which he bought for us on a business trip to America: it proved one of the biggest best-sellers we have ever had. It was indeed the business side of him that Sigle was referring to in her outburst; for while no one could have been more scrupulous in his dealings, the Tolstoyan was being submerged in the man of commerce. Something else, too, was drawing him towards the moderate Right. I objected to his writing novels, which I felt to imply a lack of concern for the firm: this was unreasonable of me: and the effect was, in a subtle way, to estrange him from my politics. (When in the summer of 1939 we built a hut on the meadow at Brimpton and moved half our staff there, I objected to his writing novels in the country office, which, apart from anything else, I thought bad for morale, as in the absence of partitions everyone could see what he was doing: this was not so unreasonable: but really, now I come to think of it, I wonder, for no one had much to do anyhow, business was so flourishing. Anyhow, we parted company, on my initiative: and the present Norman was born.)

After an interval, I see quite a bit of Norman nowadays. Often, when we both happen to be lunching at the Savoy, he will beckon me over, introduce me to the invariably interesting if sometimes politically uninstructed friend he is sharing his table with, and offer me an excellent brandy and the sort of cigar I feel rarely inclined to allow myself. The Tolstoyan Norman has by no means vanished. He is the most generous of men, and whenever I beg from him he invariably sends several times what I expected by return of post, as in the case of the Campaign for the Abolition of Capital Punishment.

So that was the end, for the time being, of my friendship with Sigle Lynd. The breach was complete, for though I tried more than once to make it up with her by letter she would have none of me. I believe now that the fault was more mine than hers, and that she was right in thinking that I had treated her badly in a way it would serve no useful purpose to record: but the fundamental reason, of course, was political incompatibility in a given situation. Anyhow, she resigned from the Party after Hungary, and we saw one another almost at once; and now I feel as close to her, though I cannot hope she feels as close to me, as ever.

§ 3

Sigle is all mixed up in my mind with three journeys my wife and I made with her in the first half of the nineteen-thirties: we were always taking people abroad with us at that time, for we tended to be a good deal better off than our middle-class friends, and like Croesuses in comparison with our working-class brethren. (But how I detest the words middle class: to call myself middle class would never for a moment occur to me, or to any Jew, I rather think, for the matter of that. My father was typical in this respect. He thought of all goyim as middle class, except the exceedingly rich ones, and all Jews as aristocrats, except m'shummeds—people who had apostasised—and a few who were excessively *link* or lax in their religious practices. These were in an abysmal class by themselves. I rapidly became a member of it myself: long before I left home I had declassed myself. But even the very linkest might rehabilitate themselves by making enough money: though I doubt whether he would have included our modern property magnates, except the few orthodox ones, in the real aristocracy.)

But if we took several people abroad in the early and middle thirties (Viola Garvin, for instance, who was always very close to our hearts—and still is—in spite of her atrocious procrastinations when keeping, or not keeping, an appointment for lunch or dinner), Sigle was in a category that included only herself: if you had looked up 'abroad' in our private dictionary, you would have found a subhead 'taking people abroad' with the reference 'see specially Lynd, Sigle'. For I was unwilling to confine my pleasure in her gaiety and wit to a few brief moments in the office or an hour or so at lunch or dinner: I wanted to have it for days or weeks on stretch; and my wife acquiesced, though she would far sooner have been alone with me. The fact is—and I may as well say it frankly, for this is a record, among a lot of other things, of a perfect marriage—that my wife has a beautiful charity, or say a sane common sense, in sexual matters: on the first of the very few occasions on which I have slept with another woman (early in the war: my wife was living at Brimpton, and I was often in London, where I had rented a flat) she gave me a copy of my favourite poem, *The Excursion*, beautifully small on hand-made paper and bound in morocco, with the inscription 'for a very special occasion'. I had told her in advance, as men of the world will think cruel as well as half-witted, for we both believe that of the many sins that damn married people deception is almost the worst: I hasten to add that Sigle and I were never lovers, otherwise Sylvia's ghost might draw false conclusions from this narrative and be horrified, for though a woman of exceptional brilliance she proved herself an intolerant puritan of the narrowest kind, not perhaps because she really felt like that but from fear of public opinion. Robert was a puritan too, but a tolerant one—about homosexuality as well as about marital irregularities and extra-marital pleasure (at any rate as touching others): not only had Roger Casement been the dearest of his friends, as I have already mentioned, but he cherished the memory of Oscar Wilde, as I do almost nightly, when reading, in the best of all bedside books, his letters. Already when still in life Sylvia had had a scare about Sigle and me. We once went out to Venice together, each in a separate *wagon*, but communicating: my wife had been staying with Stella Churchill at a little pension, the Seguso, next on the Zatteri to the one Ruskin used to live in, and was to join Sigle and me on our arrival at Danieli's. Sylvia was dismayed, not because she thought it likely that we had cohabited in one or other of the *wagons*, the least comfortable procedure imaginable, but because she was sure other people would think so.

The longest journey we made with Sigle, or maybe the longest but one, was from Paris to Aix, where she was to leave us and take the train on to Salzburg. Our daughter Diana was with us, and we were driven by a man called Breakwell, whose clientèle had mainly consisted of fashionable gamblers and men of the turf, whom he spoke of by their nicknames and described as class. He despised us as milksops, and obviously poor ones at that, for we would have nothing to do with the nightspots he so ardently recommended. Breakwell did not survive with us long: he sacked us within hours of our return, and was replaced by a man who appeared, for about six months, to suit us admirably.

This man, whose name I have forgotten, was imposed on us—I say impose, for she was rather insistent—by Rose, who told us what is called a hard-luck story about his merits and miseries—something about a family and a piano and other details I have long since forgotten. Rose believed hard-luck stories: this was one of

LOWS TOPICAL Budget
BOOK CLUB WAR
A fierce battle is now taking place on the Reading front, the Blimp Book Club advancing strongly against the Left. Heavy casualties are reported including 29 unconscious and General Gollancz's spectacles blown up.

DINING IN ROME WITH THE FLEGS

the most lovable as well as one of the sanest things about her, for if they are factually untrue, as in my experience they rarely are, they are spiritually and psychologically exact; for to be the sort of man who tells bogus hard-luck stories is itself hard luck, and so worthy of compassion. Now I should have said that this man suited us not admirably but more than admirably: he drove so slowly that even I, who still find sixty miles an hour excessive, occasionally got restless. He was very quiet too, and he had the curious habit when driving, a habit I often discussed with my wife, of staring, not straight ahead, but with his head a bit inclined to the right. I thought he might be astigmatic, as I am. This continued for six months, until on a Sunday night, when we were all at Brimpton, we sent for him to take us to London. As he failed to turn up we asked Thomas, who had given him our message, to find out what had happened, and he told us, when he came back, "He's in the hedge". The garage was practically on the road, and he had driven right across into the hedge that faced it: he was wildly racing his engine, and getting deeper and deeper involved. "You're drunk," I said. "Of course I'm drunk," he replied, smiling quite gently. "I've been drunk for a year . . . I suppose this means the sack?" "I'm afraid so," I said. "Quite right," he replied. "But let me take you to London first." We declined, and asked Thomas to put him up for the night. Nellie told my wife afterwards that Thomas had a terrible row with him: "To treat Mr Gollanz-of-Brimpton-Lodge like that!" I can hear him saying.

We covered a lot of lovely ground in that journey with Sigle from Paris to Aix: Saumur, Poitier, Angoulême, Cahors, gloriously burnt-sienna Albi, Carcassonne, Montpellier, Nîmes, the Pont du Gard, Orange, Avignon. Two episodes remain in my mind. When we got to Montpellier I asked a gendarme in the main street where to find a good restaurant. He directed us to an inn a few miles away, and we drove there. It was a quite unpretentious sort of place, and no one seemed about; but we were told after a few minutes that if we sat on the balcony above a stream and waited a bit they would cook us something. They first brought us bread, and we amused ourselves by throwing little pellets of it into the water and watching the fish play polo with them. Then the feast began to arrive: an omelette first: fish, chicken and cheese: and we were very happy. Opposite were some Utrilloish houses. (Or am I mixing up this visit to Montpellier with another? I think I must be, for I suddenly get the strong impression that my wife and I were alone.)

Our time at Carcassonne started with a couple of disagreeablenesses. My wife, just before we got there, was visited by an extreme exaggeration of that monthly occurrence which impels pious Jews of the other sex to say daily "Blessed art thou, O Lord our God, King of the Universe, who has not made me a woman": and next day, as we were examining the ramparts, we were deluged by the most violent rainstorm I remember ever experiencing. We had no coats, no umbrellas, nothing for our protection at all; and no shelter was in sight except a few holes (gun-emplacements? receptacles for the emission of boiling oil?—which was not as bad, I imagine, as napalm) in the ramparts. So we made for them, and must have looked like university students on the lavatory seats at Ostia. We did not much care for the place, anyhow: the mediaevalism seemed so bogus, the whole ensemble a Hollywood set. I was reminded of the Schrager tribunal in St James's Park, when Macquoid, in opposition to Cescinsky, defended a chair as genuine Chippendale because one arm of it was.

As for Aix itself I fell in love with it, and like it still, though the charabancs and growing bustle of tourists have greatly diminished its charm. But the double Boulevard remains, and as you wander under the arches of this you are given, for simultaneous pleasure, country freshness and city grandeur.

When Sigle left for Salzburg the three of us motored on to Les Baux, where the cats turn into ladies or the ladies turn into cats, I forget which, and an Englishwoman had just been murdered in her bath or perhaps someone else's. We approached from the south through vast desolate quarries, and the sloping sides of the entry so vividly recalled Aïda that we bellowed the triumphal march from Act Two, Egyptian trumpets and all, as we clattered over the cobblestones. An Englishwoman there made pottery tiles and was showing them off: not the Englishwoman, I think, who had been murdered, though she may well have been, for everything was out of order in Les Baux. We bought a couple of the tiles, and sent them home for the children.

We revisited Les Baux in 1961. We were again staying at Aix, and approached this time by the north-east, stopping at Cavaillon on the way. The synagogue there, of the early eighteenth century, is quite beautiful, resembling a large French room of its period: the *Beemah* (reading-desk) is, or rather was, in the middle of an exquisite balustrade of wrought-iron, with the Ark of the Covenant opposite. But the chief feature of the place was its museum. This was crowded with the ceremonial trappings of *Siphre Torah*, or Scrolls of the Law: rich stuffs, finely worked, to cover them with, crowns or clustering bells to give them splendour on top, and pointing fingers in silver or gold to guide the rabbi's hand and guarantee a correct reading. Then there were *menoras*, or seven-branched candlesticks; marriage-contracts; *shofars* or ram's horns for blowing, on New Year and the Day of Atonement; and such a rarity as a ritual scourge, like the one they used for Baruch Spinoza, when the beadle gave him '40 stripes save one' as he lay, face downwards, on the floor of the synagogue at Amsterdam.

We were only a few minutes at Les Baux. The cats had mostly vanished or were temporarily away, and I shouldn't have been frightened of them anyway, having advanced in sophistication since our previous visit, thirty years before: so we dropped down a few paces to lunch at Baumanière.

This may be the best restaurant in France. Michelin gave it the very maximum of forks and stars, an exceedingly rare occurrence, and without being connoisseurs, like Alfred Knopf, we certainly liked it better than the world-famous Point at Vienne. The room itself was a delight, with a great deal of space between the tables, so that one never felt, as one feels even at such a super-restaurant as the Caprice, that one was sharing a communal feast. As for the feast itself, I fear that even nowadays, when I am trying to be a vegetarian, to forgo it, if I ever had the chance to eat it again, would seem sinful. The heart of it was *gigot d'agneau en croûte*: not so much a dish as a celebration of the third primal day, when God created the herbs of the field. We took away the recipe, which we have lost; and because I should like it to embellish this record with it I wrote a flowery letter, full of the most distinguished sentiments, to the management, requesting a copy. Here it is, exactly as it was sent to me:

RECIPE

GIGOT D'AGNEAU EN CROÛTE

Un gigot d'agneau	*Madère*
Rognons d'agneau	*Herbes*
Champignons	*Pâte feuilletée*

Select a leg of mutton less than 2 pounds in weight. Remove the centre bone with a fine, sharp point-bladed knife. Clear the meat off the bone up to the joint. Cut off at this joint and take off.

Brown in a frying pan, with some butter, fine-diced lamb kidneys. Clear the grease with some Madeira wine, add mushrooms, thyme, rosemary, tarragon.

Put this dressing in the hollow place left by the removed leg bone. Restore the leg of mutton by nearing the meat together, and fix by two or three stitches.

Rub the leg with some butter. Put it in a brisk oven to make the meat hold and have its water out. Let stay some fifteen minutes.

Take out of the oven and cover with fine-rolled puff paste. Glaze top side with yolk and put back to the oven for 15 to 20 minutes to complete the cooking.

ET SON GRATIN

Advice: A gratin of potatoes is the real vegetable trimming for mutton-leg pie.

Cut potatoes as you would do for chips. Wash in running water and dry with a linen.

Put in a fire-proof dish a small layer of cream, then one layer of potatoes, salt, pepper, grated Gruyère, and again cream, potatoes, etc. Complete with a layer of cream without Gruyère. Cook in water bath. When the dressing is cooked to three quarters, take off the dish and replace the cream with raw cream. Put back to the oven to complete the cooking.

Before serving up, dust with Gruyère and gratinate in a brisk oven, keeping still the dish in water bath.

BAUMANIÈRE

Particularly memorable was the *sommelier*, a giant of a man with a huge leather apron diversified by brass. He gave us a Châteauneuf du Pape from the neighbouring vineyard, and it was worthy of him.

The other long journey Sigle made with us was from Salzburg to London. I shall mention it in the chapter I propose to write about Salzburg, where it belongs.

IV

MORE PEOPLE AT BRIMPTON

I WANT TO mention, with as much brevity as I can manage, and always for some special reason, a few of the others who came down to Brimpton before the war, in most cases for one visit only. There was for instance Stanley Spencer, my wife's oldest friend, an even older one than Reeve Brooke: and I bring him in for the purpose of quoting two letters he wrote to her, for they might perhaps be considered of some minor historical interest. The first, dated July 10th, 1911, refers to a drawing, 'Jacob and Esau', that he had done the same year, when they were fellow-students at the Slade: she had bought it for five pounds, and had asked him to sign it. "Many thanks," he wrote, "for the cheque. I am much to [*sic*] modest a kid to sign my works, nevertheless I will sign that." In the event he didn't, and nothing we have by him is either signed or initialled, whatever his general practice may have been. The second letter, dated November 28th, 1919, is about another drawing, the one he gave us that year for a wedding-present. My wife must have asked him to give it a name: "I do not know," he replied, "that my picture is called anything. The lady on the waterlily leaf is a Fairy if you please, and of course the boy on the bank is Edmunds, but honestly I do not know what the picture is all about. You might give the persons depicted a different name for every day in the week with special names for High days and Holidays."

It was Stanley who proposed my wife's health at the party we gave for her sixty-fifth birthday; and just before his death he asked me to go down to Cookham, for he wanted to discuss a particular kind of 'ghosted' biography that we had previously talked about. He was already dying of cancer, and was afraid that a biography might be written after his death that would fail to interpret correctly the spiritual and artistic ideas that he set such store by. His wish was to have a series of talks with a local journalist whom he admired for his integrity, and who could be trusted to reproduce what he had been told with a minimum of editing. But I was very busy at the time: it was two or three weeks before I felt able to go down: and then it was too late—Stanley had gone back to hospital, and was in such agony that any attempt to discuss the matter, I was told, would be useless. Stanley died: and a biography appeared.

I must not omit Gerald Gould, who came down with his wife Barbara Ayrton, the fiery-headed Labour politician, in very early days—I think 1934 or 1935. He had been my reader at Ernest Benn's, and had followed me, without a moment's hesitation, when I started on my own: and the letter he sent me when I told him of my decision was more heartening than any other of the many I received. I searched for it a few weeks ago, and found it in an ancient suit-case bursting with accumulated rubbish, but have now lost it again (as I have already said, I am terrible about letters: even one from Winston Churchill, recommending me to General Marshall in delightfully flattering terms, has vanished, not to mention many others). But I remember the general import. My decision, he wrote, might turn out to have been commercially mistaken (though he did not think so) but was morally and spiritually right, and he was overjoyed that I had made it.

My intended move was indeed welcomed by almost everyone who knew me well enough to comment on it at all. Most enthusiastic of all was Garve—J. L. Garvin, at that time editor of the *Observer*, and weekly author of those huge double-page middles, complete with three or four headlines in diminishing sizes of type, on the slopes of which, someone remarked, you could pleasurably take your Sunday repose. But to his congratulations Garve added a warning. "Bravo!" he said, with his famous exophthalmic intensity. "I couldn't be more pleased. But you must call yourself The Victor Publishing Company, and leave Gollancz out of it. People are prejudiced, and the name Gollancz does sound . . . foreign. I don't want to see the whole thing come to nothing for the sake of a name."

The only dissident voice to put against this chorus of approbation was my father's. He had always thought me, not only m'shuggah, but quite incompetent in matters of business—he was right about this, though few will believe me; and when I told him my plans he showed himself, not merely shocked, but personally aggrieved. "What," he said, "leave Benn's? *Benn's*? Don't you know how solid Benn is? And such money you are getting!"

To continue with Gerald Gould, I have never understood why we were not closer to one another. I admired him immensely: I admired, in particular, what I once dared to call the Christianity of his reviewing. By this I meant his invariable fellow-feeling with the author, any author, he was writing about: he always praised what he could, and if he could praise nothing (for his mind was finely critical, whatever some may have thought) he left the man or woman alone. There was doubtless a defect in this virtue: he could be over-enthusiastic. But when I think of reviewers who go to the other extreme: when I detect, in this reviewer or that, a patent inability to get into the author's skin; then I snap my fingers at the people who used to jeer at Gerald for discovering a masterpiece every week.

Nor was he generous only in his reviewing. He was generous to and about particular people, all particular people, and he was generous in his abiding attitude to humanity as a whole. To myself he was always gracious and helpful. He was a good poet, too, and a witty versifier: when *The Sleeveless Errand* was prosecuted for obscenity, he wrote a many-stanza'd poem with the happiest of refrains, "You may say bloody but may not say bugger, You may say bottom but may not say balls". At a party he gave at the time we roared it in chorus. In other words, he was excellent company.

What, then, came between us? I think he liked me: I more than liked him. We were always writing to one another, as our professional relationship required: we met with reasonable frequency: we never quarrelled, indeed I cannot remember even a mere difference of opinion: and yet we at no time really got at one another, as I got at Rose, Sigle and Alan and many others, and they got at me. I have often wondered what the reason could have been for our comparative remoteness to one another, and have never found the answer.

I would add that underneath his gaiety and wit there was a profound sadness: and the reason, I think, was the same that made Vicky commit suicide. Vicky may have been a depressive, but there was more to it, I am certain, than that. He could not bear the sorrows of the world: and Gerald, similarly, felt in his own person the pangs of the unemployed and the agony of the concentration camps and what others would suffer in the imminent war.

It was in 1924 or 1925 that we first met Edmond and Madeleine Fleg, and it was not till 1952, when the place was long past its prime, that they came to Brimpton. We were intimate with one another, in a peculiarly tender way, from almost the start, and remained intimate, without any lessening of tenderness, until Edmond's death at eighty-nine two or three years ago; and although circumstances have prevented us from seeing her since, we still feel as close to Madeleine as we ever did, and she feels, I cannot doubt, as close to us.

Our friendship might very easily never have found itself at all. We were dining one night at the Villa Montmorency with Doris Orna, daughter of Siegfried Strauss, one of my father's greatest friends; and sister of Frank Strawson, who became a founding director of my firm, of Eric Strauss, who became one of the leading psychiatrists of the day, and of Otto Strawson, who became nothing in particular except an excellent and witty friend. The Flegs were there, and we left together: Doris having whispered to me, as she took us to where the coats were, "They're terribly difficult to know; they don't like letting new people into their circle." In a sense this was true, but not out of any exclusiveness: though he always gave the impression of infinite leisure Edmond was a man of great and varied activity, and both he and Madeleine had large families, to which they were devoted. To Doris's open astonishment, however, they almost immediately asked us to dinner, and so everything began.

Edmond was a type of Jew I had never met before, and, I am persuaded, shall never meet again. He was not a Frenchman by birth, but a Swiss: his name had been Flegesheimer, and he had changed it to Fleg when, after fighting for France in the 1914–1918 war, he became a naturalised Frenchman. (The architect Flegesheimer, who built the railway-station at Geneva—"c'est magnifique, mais ce n'est pas la gare", as Humbert Wolfe used to say—was his cousin.) He loved France with a quiet and unselfconscious intensity: and he loved, as naturally and inevitably, the Jewish people, everything Jewish, and, when Independence came, the Land of Israel. I have never read the book, *Ma France, Ma Palestine*, in which he deals with this duality of devotion; but, whatever he may say in it, I am certain that there was never any question, in his case, of a 'conflict of loyalties'. He was a complete Jew, and as good a one as could be: and that was the end of the matter.

His Jewishness was, in my experience, unique. I have met Jews who are versed in, and fascinated by, Jewish lore; who are glad they are Jews and feel very Jewish; but who do not 'believe in' the Jewish or any other religion, or in religion at all. I have also met Jews who are religious in the best sense, but have no interest in, and still less a liking for, the old Jewish practices, and whose attitude to their own Jewishness is more or less neutral. And I have of course met many Jews who detest being Jewish.

Edmond was like none of these. He was a very religious man, a man of great spirituality: he was a close student of traditional doctrines, which fascinated him and in which he often found a valuable significance: but he was totally unorthodox in his way of living—it would never have occurred to him, for instance, to keep the dietary laws. He was intensely liberal, with a passionate and sympathetic interest in orthodoxy.

A Jew of Jews though he was, Christ and Christianity meant almost as much to him. He loved Jesus, but with a love that confirmed him in his love of Judaism; and this, coupled with his tolerant liberalism and his understanding of orthodoxy, brought him into lifelong contact with the Catholic priesthood, with which he eagerly collaborated in the cause of Jewish–Catholic harmony. As war grew nearer, he felt it his special duty to hearten and inspire the Jewish youth: but he eschewed, as a matter of course, any narrowness in matters of race, nationality and religion. He was a Frenchman, a Jew and a universalist.

His singular sweetness was such that to quarrel with him even for a passing moment would have been unthinkable, a single harsh or sarcastic or even overemphatic word out of the question. You can tell people by the way they laugh or smile, and Edmond's smile was the gentlest I have ever known. He was witty, too. I once asked him if their new President, Coty, was the parfumier. "Même pas," he replied.

He was devoted to literature and music and painting, and while primarily a writer and anthologist, almost exclusively on Jewish themes, he was a good casual pianist, and often played for us, always from memory. Many musicians and artists were among his friends, and one evening, after we had dined together in his flat on the Quai aux Fleurs overlooking Notre Dame, Georges Enesco strummed for us, well into the early hours, part of the score he had been writing for Zeus, to Edmond's libretto, on the subject of Oedipus. (The work was produced at the Paris Opéra in 1936.) I will not say that he was a patron of artists, for that sounds too pompous, and Edmond was less pompous than anyone I can think of; but he was always trying to help them. He took us once to Chagall's studio, hoping we would buy two or three pictures, which were then to be had for the equivalent of a few pounds apiece: but with financial though I do not think artistic stupidity we refrained, for I do not care for Chagall's self-conscious Jewish whimsicality, though there are exceptions, including his magnificent windows for a synagogue in Israel. He begged us to commission from Chana Orloff, who was struggling to support an invalid son, a portrait-bust of my wife (and we did so: but we have always detested its perverse angularity, my wife's face being essentially broad and Praxitelean, and it lies hidden away at Eaton Place in a dark cupboard under the stairs). And he often talked to me about young French authors, and invited me to meet them.

We could have no contact with Edmond and Madeleine during the war, and were fearful of what might be happening to them:

I kept in touch with them, so to say, by translating and publishing a proud and humble little book, *Pourquoi Je Suis Juif*, which Edmond had written in 1927 and dedicated to his grandson "who is not yet born" and who was never to be born. But almost directly the war was over we got a telegram to say they were safe: they had been hidden near Grenoble by a Catholic farmer at great risk to himself and his wife. We subsequently met them: they were charming simple folk.

We went over as soon as we could. Conditions in Paris were very bad: people had to shop at the *marché parallèle*, as they called the black market, if they wanted to eat decently, and Madeleine had clearly put herself out to provide, that first night, a repast worthy of the occasion. The first course was a prawn cocktail. Now I cannot eat shellfish: my ancestral stomach, and not anything to do with religion, rejects the very idea of putting it into me, not to mention its look and its smell. My wife feels similarly . . . We glanced at one another: I gave a slight nod: and one by one I forced the things down, and my wife did the same. I am a great coward, I regret to say, but that night I felt like a hero, and was one. I was sick in the small hours.

It would be easy to say that they had lost everything, but it would not be true. Both their sons were dead: Maurice had been killed in the war, and Daniel, a manic-depressive, had thrown himself into the Seine when he was *réformé*—'excused' military service. Many of their friends and relatives had gone to Auschwitz and Buchenwald, including Léonce Bernheim, Madeleine's brother, and his wife Renée, the prettiest and gentlest of creatures: and somehow it seemed particularly dreadful in her case, just as the axe seems particularly dreadful in the case of Anne Boleyn, whose neck was very small. Paris was desolate. So they felt lonely, of course ("nous sentons une solitude, que rien ne comblera plus"): Edmond, for the time being, "feels deceived as regards his idealistic view, so distant from reality": "Happiness is awfully rare in our daily life, and joy has become an exception": and yet what neither of them had lost, it seemed to us, was their inner serenity. They grieved, they were disillusioned: but still they were at peace.

We had always wanted them to spend a week-end at Brimpton, but they had never been able to manage it. Then Edmond had to come over for a conference, and they fitted in a couple of days with us. The visit was a great success. On the Saturday morning, when I came down to breakfast, I found Edmond at our dreadful upright in the nursery, playing the Invitation to the Waltz, and Madeleine told me afterwards that this was the first time he had touched a piano since the war. She also told me, in a bread and butter that I do not care to quote, what that couple of days had meant to Edmond; but what specially pleased my wife and me was the adjective she applied to Brimpton: *Quel merveilleux souvenir, maison fleurie.*

I should like to round off these paragraphs about a very good friend of mine by setting down the conclusion to *Why I am a Jew*, which illumines not only his fidelity to Judaism but his Jewishness:

See this sublime design, which is revealed at the very beginning and which, from age to age, is realised. Did the Greeks declare to the world in advance that they would show it Beauty? The Romans, that they would show it Law? See this people, paltry and sinful, announcing what will be its history at the very beginning of its history; see it choose the mission which chooses it, and walking with it in the way which it has foretold. See it, this people of eternal sinners, banished twice and surviving two dispersions; and, as commanded by its prophecies, bringing back from its first exile the divine unity, and preparing, by the second, human unity. See it driven over the face of the earth, always near to dying, and always finding some providential shelter to save it from death. See it bearing its truth, and, to keep it pure, suffering it to spread through the world in the light of the blazing stake. See it, incarnating in its flesh the two loves that torment it, and, at the very moment when it gives itself, with them, to all the nations of the earth, reconstructing, for its own survival still, the home of its memory and its hope, which is the universal hope. And tell me if, in this unique history, you do not feel the eternal presence of a thought and a will which have dictated its task to this people and have made its accomplishment possible, trying it by suffering, saving it in its trials, and guiding it step by step from its grievous past to its triumphant future. For me, my child, who have so long sought the proof of the existence of God—I have found it in the existence of Israel.

I am a Jew because, born of Israel and having lost her, I have felt her live again in me, more living than myself.

I am a Jew because, born of Israel and having regained her, I wish her to live after me, more living than in myself.

I am a Jew because the faith of Israel demands of me no abdication of the mind.

I am a Jew because the faith of Israel requires of me all the devotion of my heart.

I am a Jew because in every place where suffering weeps, the Jew weeps.

I am a Jew because at every time when despair cries out, the Jew hopes.

I am a Jew because the word of Israel is the oldest and the newest.

I am a Jew because the promise of Israel is the universal promise.

I am a Jew because, for Israel, the world is not yet completed: men are completing it.

I am a Jew because, for Israel, Man is not created: men are creating him.

I am a Jew because, above the nations and Israel, Israel places Man and his Unity.

I am a Jew because, above Man, image of the divine Unity, Israel places the divine Unity, and its divinity.

Sometimes, my child, when I wander through a museum, and stand before all the pictures and statues and furniture and armour, the faïence, the crystals, the mosaics, the garments and the finery, the coins and the jewels, gathered there, from every place and every age, to hang on the walls, to stand on the plinths, to line up behind the balustrades, to be classified, numbered and ticketed in the glass cases, I think that one or other of my ancestors may have seen, touched, handled or admired one or other of these things, in the very place where it was made, and at the very time when it was made, for the use, the labour, the pain or the joy of men.

This door with the grey nails, between two poplars, in a gilded frame, this is the Geneva synagogue where my father went in to pray. And see this bridge of boats on the Rhine: my grandfather crossed the Rhine, at Hüningen. And his grandfather, where did he live? Perhaps as he dreamily calculated the mystical numbers of the Cabbala he saw, through his quiet window, this sledge glide over the snow of Germany or Poland? And the grandfather of his grandfather's grandfather? Perhaps he was this money changer, in this Amsterdam ghetto, painted by Rembrandt.

One of my ancestors may have drunk from this wine goblet, on returning home from the lesson of his master Rashi, at the school of Troyes in Champagne; one of my ancestors may have sat on this jade-incrusted armchair as he felt a sultan's pulse; one of my ancestors may have been led to the auto-da-fé by a hooded monk who carried this cross of Castille; one of my ancestors may have seen his children trampled down by the horse of the Crusader who bore this armour.

These feather head-dresses, did another get them from an American savage? These African ivories, these Chinese silks, did another buy them by the banks of the Congo or the Amur, to sell them again on the shores of the Ganges or on the Venetian lagoons?

One of them drove this plough, tempered in the fire, through the plain of Sharon; one of them went up to the Temple to offer, in these plaited baskets, his tithe of figs.

When this marble Titus was in the flesh, one of my ancestors was dragged bleeding at his chariot wheels in a Roman triumph; beneath the feet of this bearded image with the fringed robe, flanked by two winged bulls of human profile, one of my ancestors smelt the dust of Babylon; at the breath of this porphyry Pharaoh, with the two flat hands on the two flat thighs, one of my ancestors bowed himself down, before girding on his girdle and taking up his staff to follow Moses across the Red Sea; and this Sumerian idol, with spherical eyes and angular jaws, is perhaps the very one that Abraham broke when he left his Chaldean home to follow the call of his invisible God.

And I say to myself: from this remote father right up to my own father, all these fathers have handed on to me a truth which flowed in their blood, which flows in mine; and shall I not hand it on, with my blood, to those of my blood?

Will you take it from me, my child? Will you hand it on? Perhaps you will wish to abandon it. If so, let it be for a greater truth, if there is one. I shall not blame you. It will be my fault; I shall have failed to hand it on as I received it.

But, whether you abandon it or whether you follow it, Israel will journey on to the end of days.

* * *

There are many others I should have liked to commemorate, if only to the extent of a few paragraphs. There was Adam von Trott, who spent a couple of days with us before returning to Germany: his intention, he specifically told me, was to join the Nazis and 'bore from within'. (The book he chose to read in bed the second night, I remember, was Swift's *Satires*.) There were Dick and Naomi Mitchison. We had a camp on our meadow for the children of Dick's Labour Party constituents at King's Norton, many of whom had never seen the country before: they flew the Red Flag, and this smashed us with the neighbourhood. There was Noel Brailsford, as much a 'passionate pilgrim' as Henry Nevinson himself. There was Gilbert Harding, rather later than the others, and I am not sure that he actually stayed. And there was Clennell Wilkinson, highest of Tories and adored by everyone. He was once dining with us in London at the time of a General Election and during a lull in the conversation was heard to remark, in tones that seemed to mimic the traditional Colonel's, "Extraordinary country, what? I was dining with some people the other night, and they told me they were going to vote Liberal. They were perfectly normal people. There you are! Everything seems all right, and you suddenly realise that the whole place is seething with revolution, what?"

But I must content myself with these brief references, for Brimpton has had a good share of attention, and I am anxious to press on.

I cannot, however, finish this chapter without recalling the most poignant of all my Brimpton memories.

Ernst Toller, who had written the 'Schwalbenbuch' in prison (he had fought very bravely for the oppressed in the early nineteen-twenties), was staying with us: he had just married a slim young girl who looked very gentle and happy. Well, we were sitting that blazing forenoon on our lawn overlooking the Berkshire Downs when someone suggested champagne; and as we sat sipping it Toller asked us whether we would like to see the girl dance. So we brought out the gramophone and put on

BRIMPTON (*l. to r.*): Nye Bevan, Jennie Lee, Quo Tai-chi, Mme Maisky, Maisky, V.G., Julia, Francesca, John Strachey, Vincent Sheean, 1937

BRIMPTON, in front of the Eric Gill seat (*l. to r.*): Sigle, David Granville, Mollie Pritt, Ruth, Gilbert Harding, V.G., 1936

MOSES

the Dance of the Sylphs: and the girl took off her sandals and danced, and that was that. Shortly afterwards they sailed for America, where he committed suicide. He was terrified by the Nazis (spiritually, not physically), felt sure they would win, and couldn't face it. I never knew a man who loved his fellow-creatures more. "The words 'I am proud to be a German', or 'I am proud to be a Jew'," he wrote in his autobiography, "sounded ineffably stupid to me. As well say 'I am proud to have brown eyes'. Must I then join the ranks of the bigoted and glorify my Jewish blood now, not my German? Pride and love are not the same thing, and if I were asked where I belonged I should answer that a Jewish mother had borne me, that Germany had nourished me, Europe had formed me, my home is the earth, and the world my fatherland."

V

RUSSIANS AND CHINESE

SIGLE CAME INTO this narrative as a member of the Lynd group at Brimpton. But she was a member of another group too, namely the Russo–Chinese–Spanish–Republican one: on which I shall now launch a chapter by mentioning three little presents, two of them given us by Pearl Binder, a porcelain figurine and a pottery figure, and the third by Maisky, a small box.

The three were once four; the figurine is one of a pair that Polly brought back for us from the Soviet Union in 1936. The other was unfortunately stolen.

By 'unfortunately' I mean simply that I cannot reproduce the pair of figurines as an illustration: in no other sense was its theft 'unfortunate'. Unfortunate for whom? For the man who stole it? Certainly not: he got something he wanted, whatever his reason for wanting it may ultimately have been. For society? By no means: why should society care a snap of the fingers which of us has it, he or I? For me then? For me least of all.

As people are no doubt already beginning to tap their spacious foreheads I shall cite here a few Hasidic stories dealing with thieves, and illustrating the Hasidic attitude to them and to one's own possessions: first explaining that Hasidism was a religious movement that sprang up among the Jews of Poland early in the eighteenth century, under the leadership of Rabbi Israel ben Elieser Baal Shem Tov, called the Baalshem (which means 'Master of the Name') because, so rumour had it, he could pronounce the unpronounceable Name of God. Hasidism was a Christianity without Christ: a religion of joy in God and love of one's fellow men: a way of life that took more stock in original virtue than in original sin, laid more stress on the good people thought and did than on the bad, 'people' being indifferently one's neighbour and oneself. It was at the opposite pole to Calvinism; and the Baal-shem, I suspect, is the only religious teacher in the history of the world, or at any rate of the West, who has never caused a moment's unhappiness.

Here are the stories:

Rabbi Wolf of Zbarazh once saw thieves robbing his home. He remained still and murmured: "I do not wish to cause you to be guilty of a sin, and therefore I make you a gift of everything you take."

In a moment he noticed that they were taking a jar containing medicine. He then approached them and said: "Do not fear to take away whatever you can place in your bag, for I am presenting these things to you as gifts; but, I beg of you, do not consume the contents of the jar you have included. It is medicine and may harm you."

A thief in his old age was unable to ply his trade and was starving. A wealthy man, hearing of his distress, sent him food. Both the rich man and the thief died on the same day. The trial of the magnate occurred first in the Heavenly Court; he was found wanting and sentenced to Purgatory. At the entrance, however, an Angel came hurrying to recall him. He was brought back to the Court and learned that his sentence had been reversed. The thief whom he had aided on earth had stolen the list of his iniquities.

A Rabbi ordered his Warden to get together a quorum to chant Psalms for the recovery of a sick man. When they entered a friend of the Rabbi exclaimed: "I see among them notorious thieves."

"Excellent," retorted the Rabbi. "When all the Heavenly Gates of Mercy are closed, it requires experts to open them."

Rabbi Shmelke once had no money to give to a beggar. He ransacked his wife's drawer, took from it a ring and gave it to the destitute man. His wife returned, saw that the drawer was open and that her ring was missing. She raised a hue and cry, and when her husband explained his action she asked him to run after the beggar, since the ring was worth fifty thalers.

The Rabbi ran swiftly in pursuit, and catching up with the beggar, said: "I have just learned that the ring is worth fifty thalers. Let no one cheat you by giving you less than its value."

These are not pretty, quaint, sentimental (sentimental!) stories, as I have heard them described by the spiritually illiterate: they illumine a way of thinking and feeling directly opposed to the unregenerate one that is leading the world to disaster.

We are property-mad. We think more of holding on to a farthing that is 'ours' than of loving the neighbour who, sinning with the sin of covetousness (which is a real sin, and one we all share), would have it for 'his'. And how, in any case, can there be an 'ours' or a 'his'? In what way, except by law (and law has nothing to do with spiritual reality), can anyone own anything except himself, and even this he cannot really own, for it belongs to God or humanity or life in general or the whole? And yet I have known people who have deliberately condemned their neighbour to long years in a noisome prison because he has deprived them of the tiniest fraction of their vast fortunes.

I am not to be misunderstood. I am not praising or commending thieves (though you can sometimes love one, as in the case of my third Hasidic story); and there are thieves who, for their cruelty and rapacity, rank far lower than the least worthy of those multi-millionaires they occasionally resemble in point of their business organisation. Nor am I suggesting that, with the world unhappily organised as it is, we can dispense with laws against thievery. What I am suggesting is that, if a few of us felt like the Hasidim, and carried what we felt into practice, property madness, that ungodliest of evils, might begin to show traces of a modifying sanity.

But I must not leave one of my ends loose. Why did I say that the theft of my figurine (only of trifling value, anyhow) was unfortunate 'least of all for me'? Well, our doctors say that to be enabled to do a *mitzvah*, or religious duty, is the happiest thing that can befall a man. And to be content with a misfortune, however trivial, is a *mitzvah*.

The figurine is a product of the Imperial factory, and is marked with a hammer and sickle. The base had previously been plain. This absence of an earlier mark, in conjunction with the Soviet stamping, might equally mean one of two things: either the piece is an old one that had never had a mark (as was often the case) but was stamped by the authorities, or it was made at the old factory, which had now become the State one, in revolutionary times. I wish someone would write a treatise on this subject: all I have been able to discover is that there was no break in continuity between the two factories—the legendary resources of the Czarist establishment were put at once at the service of the Revolution.

Some of the new wares were artistically barbarous: instruments of propaganda at its crudest. But others, to judge from our figurine, were of high merit, not only artistically but as propaganda too. For there can be no doubt, I think, that our harvester was made after 1917. Her vanished mate was a worker, a woman with a black coat or hood and manacled hands: and such a pair, worker and peasant, can have nothing but a revolutionary origin. I cannot assess the quality of the porcelain, because I know only about pottery: but it seems to me admirable: and the peasant's face is lovely—there is the serenity of good earth in it.

Polly's second piece is a clay doll with arms akimbo: rough, primitive-looking, rather like an English bell-woman of the early salt-glaze period, but less self-consciously naïve, and therefore more satisfying. I can say nothing about its origin and date, except that it is clearly quite modern. Polly has the idea that she got it at Zagorsk in 1936, when she visited a toy museum there, with toys from every part of the world: including the enormous dolls about six feet high dressed by Worth and laden with jewels of immense value that the last Imperial family used as their playthings.

Maisky's present is a piece of contemporary Pàlekh ware, such as you see everywhere in Moscow and Leningrad, or did when we were paying our only visit to Russia in 1937. Pàlekh is the name of a village where the Cheremételfs, who owned it, started an industry, in Catherine the Great's time, for the manufacture of what we now call Pàlekh ware: for a tradition was established, which has been maintained to this day.

§2

As memories have come to me of Polly and Maisky and a host of others whom these three objects evoke I have been vividly aware of a growing sense of contrast: between friends, friends as such, and occupational friends. By friendship as such I mean friendship that depends on nothing at all but the selfness of the people involved: on a 'pre-existing harmony' between two human beings. Chance, it may be, brings them together: they respond to one another: a sense of union grows: and unless something comes between them, their special relationship endures to the end. Even if their friendship breaks up, they have been pure friends while it lasted: nothing can affect what they have been to one another. Nor do they become any the less friends if they meet but rarely: circumstances are such that my wife and I see Alan Thomas far less often than we used to, and Elsa hardly ever, but our friendship remains what it was, living and intact.

In married friendship something is added. In the secret citadel of everyone's being there is a core of ultimate loneliness: if one did not know it from one's own case one would know it when reading letters from X who is in prison or Y who is suffering in this way or that. And the magic of married friendship is this: that within it the loneliness is shared. One is not merely intimate with one's husband or wife, as one is with every other sort of friend, however great: one is in a unity, despite one's ultimate and inevitable loneliness, with him or her. That is why my wife and I, for all I have said about our propensity for taking people abroad, prefer to share our holidays alone.

Occupational friendship is widely different from friendship as such. It depends, not on the selfness of the people involved, but on their common occupation, their sharing of common activities or, at the least, a common point of view. It is true, of course, that what originally brought them together may have been one or other of these things, and that then a pre-existent harmony—in respect of their selves, not merely in respect of the systematic ideas or habits of thought or emotion that constitute a part of their selves—may have been found to inform them; in which event I call their friendship true in essence and occupational only in origin: but my experience is that friendships occupational in origin rarely develop into true ones. And of course there are degrees, in this as in everything else: the line between friendships-in-themselves and occupational friendships is not a hard and fast one.

Now all the friendships I have so far described have been friendship-in-themselves; but I am now coming to the most political part of my life, the second half of the nineteen-thirties, when many of our friendships, based on political unanimity (more or less) and common work for common objects, were occupational. All the more precious, in retrospect, are the exceptions.

The friendship between Pearl Binder and ourselves was and is a true one. When we first met her, in the late twenties, she was sharing a flat with Liam O'Flaherty's wife—I was publishing him at the time; and, apart from something almost fairy-like in the look of her, my heart was touched and my mind encouraged by the compassionate humanity that was the basis of her politics. At no subsequent time have we met often; but she has faithfully kept in touch by sending us, Christmas after Christmas, an enormous piece of paper covered with painting in the gloriously posterish style she goes in for. I always pounce on it and stick it up on a shelf as a centre-piece for lesser offerings.

I had a sudden memory of Pearl when her husband, Elwyn Jones, was made Attorney General recently. During the thirties my wife, our daughter Livia and I were driving through France on our way to Salzburg, and stopped for a few days at Venice, where the Pritts had a holiday place with Polly and Elwyn (who was in Pritt's chambers) and Charles Cundall as their guests. One evening we went over to San Juan for a spree. The Pritts, Elwyn and Polly ate lobster (I remember calling Polly a goy), she waltzed with me and I broke my braces, and Johnny and I won a prize at the coconut shy. But what I chiefly remember is the smile on Elwyn's benevolent but meaningful face as he 'courted' Polly. The date must have been 1935 or thereabouts, for the Lambeth Walk was the dance of the evening, and it was at that time that everyone was singing it. Elwyn sang it, as he danced with Polly, *con moltissimo brio* with great whoops at appropriate places.

Our friendship with Mollie and Johnny Pritt, which is alas as though it had never been, was purely occupational. But I hate to say that—there must have been *something* more in it, or perhaps *no* friendship can be purely occupational if it can be called friendship at all. The story is a wretched one, and it grieves me to tell it: but tell it I must, for to leave the Pritts out of this narrative, as I can leave out so many others, would be to falsify it.

We saw the Pritts as often as we saw anyone from about 1933, when Hitler got going and I became active in left-wing politics, till shortly before the outbreak of war. They lived at Beech Hill, near Mortimer, seven or eight miles from Brimpton, and we often motored over to see them in their beautiful Priory and they often motored over to see us, particularly if Maisky or Azcarate or some English left-winger was down for the week-end. I must mention, *pietatis causa*, that among the people we met at the Priory was Gilbert Harding, who stayed with them a lot: he was a schoolmaster at the time, young and pale but already rather vivid, and I believe that they were very good to him. What had originally brought them together, I imagine, was his Catholicism and a certain rebelliousness already beginning to show in him: for Mollie was and is a Catholic, the only one I have ever known whose pro-Sovietism was apparently based on that way of thinking. I grew to love Gilbert Harding: we met occasionally for lunch at the Savoy when he was living at Brighton, and went into things. He was, as everyone knows, a very unhappy man, and, as most people know, an exceptionally good one.

Johnny and I spoke on common platforms: he wrote and edited books for the Left Book Club: we co-operated in a dozen ways. But the whole thing went wrong. He was the most rigid Sovietist, if I may use the word in that sense, that I have ever

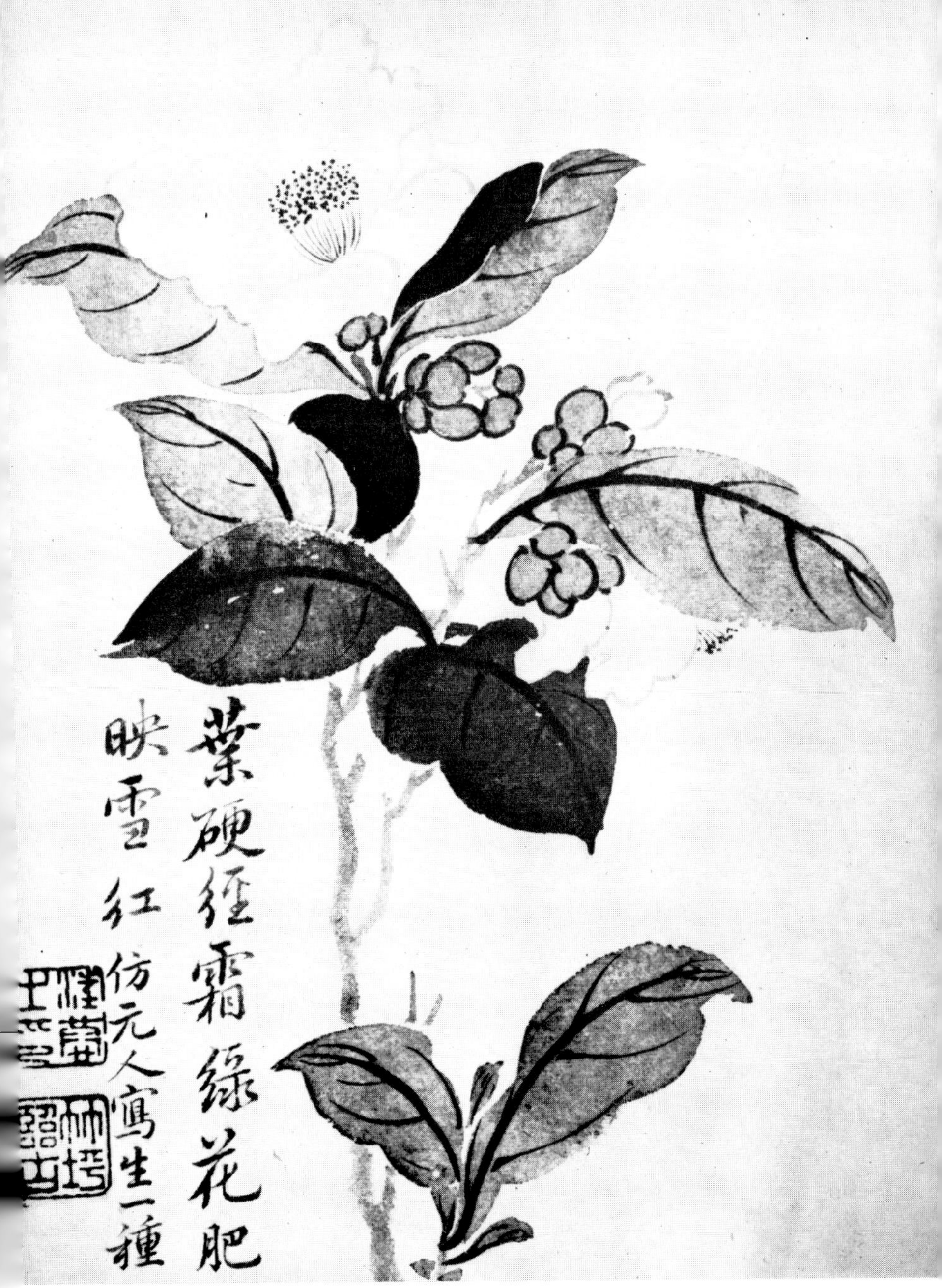

FLOWER PAINTING FROM SHELLEY WANG'S BOOK

LANDSCAPE FROM SHELLEY WANG'S BOOK

known: more rigid even than Raji, for I am certain he would never have permitted himself Raji's "*this* is an exaggeration". He was Chairman of Voks, of which I was a member: and there was something about his "I must ask the friends" (meaning Kensington Palace Gardens) when a suggestion was put up that raised my bristles. There was something resentful about his Sovietism too. I said earlier that the analysis of communists is, in my opinion, usually misplaced; but I sometimes wonder whether it would have been misplaced in Johnny Pritt's case. It passed my mind on occasion that his political attitudes may have had something to do with Westminster, where he was educated.

Anyhow, a malaise developed between us; and after the Nazi–Soviet Pact, and what I said about it, there was no question of his having anything more to do with me, or of me, for that matter, having anything more to do with him. The last, remote contact between us was when he made a derogatory reference to me in the House of Commons. I do not remember what the occasion was, but I should not be surprised if it was some plea of mine for decent behaviour towards Germany after Germany and Russia had become enemies.

And yet—we *did* have some gay or interesting or amusing moments together; and Johnny's inflexible devotion to the Soviet regime had its admirable side, for devotion to anything at all, for whatever reason, is better than social and political carelessness. Moreover he has always been willing to appear for the oppressed, both at home and abroad: he has never cared about money: and there must have been much excellence in a man whom no one ever dreamed of calling by his surname or his Christian name, Denis, but invariably called by his nickname Johnny. So I send him and Mollie my belated love through this writing, and hope they will accept it.

With the other great socialist advocate of the time, that odd combination of genuine Christianity and Messianic ambition, Sir Stafford Cripps, my friendship was less occupational. We were fairly close to one another: directly he was sacked by the Labour Party in the late thirties he rang me up from his Chambers and asked me to come round, and when he returned from Russia just before Hitler's attack he saw me, owing to some difficulty about fitting in times with far more important associates, even before he saw Churchill. But our relations did not go deep. He was a very good man: I admired him, if I did not love him (lovable though, according to his intimates, he really was): what he felt about me I cannot know, but I doubt whether we should have been more than close acquaintances but for our common political ground.

Stafford was a man of poor judgment. He told me, the time I saw him on his return from Russia, not only that the Germans would attack almost immediately (which was right) but that they would be in possession of the Caucasus oil within a fortnight (which was ludicrous). His barrister's brain, on the other hand, with its power of assimilating and grasping the significance of the most varied material, was miraculously quick and clear. With half-a-dozen others I was sitting with him one afternoon in a committee-room at the House of Commons: it was the time of our association on *Tribune*, and a point of policy, which could be decided only on sight of a document not yet in print, was being discussed. Someone went off to get a proof, and the report, or whatever it was, turned out to consist of thirty-two large pages, or say ten to fifteen thousand words. Stafford, who was not looking for anything in particular, rapidly glanced through it page after page, and said to us, not more than five minutes later, "Now here are the points: first, A; second, B; third, C . . ." and so on. And everyone knew that he had missed nothing.

Nor can I claim much more than occupational tie-up with Harold Laski, one of the three (with John Strachey and myself) who selected choices for the Left Book Club. This was a man who awed me in all intellectual contexts, but the darting speed of his mind, his ability to concentrate, and the range of his reading in politics and its allied disciplines were daunting. He was said to be a very great teacher: of this I can know nothing, but that he was devoted to his pupils, and always doing them kindnesses, is beyond question. Equally certain is his passion for liberalism in the broadest sense on the one hand, and for socialism (which he saw as involving support for the Soviet Union) on the other. He was aware of a clash between the two sides of his nature, and was concerned to bring into harmony the competing claims of those systems of thought and complexes of feeling that caused it: but he failed, and was unaware that he had failed. *Thoughts on the Revolution of our Time* was eagerly awaited by many who, like myself, shared his trouble; but most of us, I think, found no comfort in it.

There were critics who called him a liar by reason of remarks he would make, and stories he would tell, about his intercourse with the great. One wartime afternoon he came into my office (if memory serves, during an air-raid). "I won't keep you a moment," he said. "I thought you'd like to know that I've been lunching at Downing Street, and that Winston promised me Palestine for the Jews." But his critics were wrong. The great did in fact think a lot of him, and would often ask his advice: he was not a liar but an exaggerator, and who am I to condemn him for that?

His happiest story is this: "I was sitting one day in my room at Harvard when the telephone rang. It was Woodrow. 'Harold,' he said, 'I am in a bit of a mess, and I want you to help me. I have undertaken to draft fourteen points, and can only think of eleven. Do please come to Washington the moment you can'."

My other partner in the Left Book Club, John Strachey, had little in common with Harold Laski except a secularism which, in both cases, was of the naïve, taken-for-granted variety: how could an intelligent man of the twentieth century believe in God? Laski was a Jew from Poland by way of Manchester, a man of the people whose socialism cum liberalism was of the kind that comes naturally to those of his origin and environment who abjure money-making: Strachey was an Anglo-Indian highbrow, an English gentleman with a passion for efficiency and a strong feeling, albeit slightly de haut en bas, for social justice. Laski was a citizen of the world: Strachey, for all his loyalty, over a period of many years, to the Soviet Union, was essentially a patriot. Laski was a pacifist by instinct, whatever (I really do not know) he may have practised or professed: Strachey had no slightest objection to war as such—but it must be the right kind of war, a war that the dialective demanded. Strachey wanted open power, Laski the subtler role of *éminence grise*.

John Strachey, a party communist without a card for four or five years, I suppose, was never remotely a socialist in my sense of the word. He did not think capitalism wrong, as I do (such a proposition, indeed, would have been all but meaningless to him): he thought it inefficient and historically doomed. The crux of the matter, of course, is the profit motive. Strachey favoured it: to me it was and is anathema, as basing our communal lives on selfishness and greed.

Less occupational than some was our friendship with the Maiskys, but strongly occupational none the less. We took to one another from the start: we were often at the Embassy, whether for lunch or dinner or at their huge official parties, and they were occasionally at Brimpton, coming down on the Saturday or Sunday rather than staying the week-end. On these occasions Maisky, a subfallstaffian figure, was usually central: Quo Tai-chi, the Chinese Ambassador, once sent us a snapshot he had taken, with the words, "The enclosed snapshots will remind you, as they do me, of a very delightful afternoon. Maisky appeared to be 'holding court' with a haughty American critically looking on!" The American was neither haughty nor critical: he was the highly sympathetic Vincent Sheean.

Ivan and Agnes Maisky (not that we ever called them that; we stuck to 'Maisky' and 'Madam [not Madame] Maisky', though Ivan called me 'Victor') were of strongly contrasting temperaments: she was gay, confident and an uncompromising revolutionary, he was quiet, with an occasional air of apprehension, and, though a loyal and devoted ambassador, rather liberal in his outlook. (People used to say, by way of a joke—God forbid anything else!—that Madam Maisky was 'in charge' of Maisky: or perhaps I invented that one myself.) Not that Maisky was gloomy or solemn: he used to tell wonderful Jewish stories, which he called Armenian, and loved listening to mine, which he called Armenian too. I do not know whether he called them Armenian because he thought they *were* Armenian, or because he did not wish to appear antisemitic; or maybe they really *are* Armenian, and the whole Jewish joke business is a myth. I should hate to think so.

The Maiskys did us many kindnesses. When indeed we wanted to go to Russia in 1937 he refused to take a hand in the matter: I had asked him to facilitate our visa, but he insisted that we must leave him out of it, and apply in the usual manner. When however everything was in order they came to see us off on a Soviet boat at the London docks, and Madam Maisky gave my wife a superlative bouquet. It comforted us a lot on the voyage, which was a hideous one.

The last time I ever talked to him, and of course to her, was just after the Soviet attack on Finland. They had asked us to lunch with them, all by ourselves, at the Embassy. Madam Maisky was as gay and confident as ever, indeed even more so. But Maisky was subdued. I had to leave early, and he saw me out. We exchanged a few words on the doorstep.

The Maiskys gave excellent dinner parties, and I remember one in particular that made me very happy, for Bernard Shaw and Charlotte were there. I was devoted to Shaw (I should use a stronger word if I could find one) and had several amusing encounters with him. I wish I could tell the story of how he sent me down to Dartington to find out whether it was really the Venusberg Aldous Huxley and some others seemed to think it was (it wasn't); and of how he rewrote Frank Harris's life of him, changing for instance "our first words resulted in a disagreement" to "we had a very enjoyable afternoon", deleting the "shabby" from "shabby-genteel Shaws", commenting in red ink "A frightful lie, but let it pass", slashing away two whole chapters and adding many thousand words of his own. But things like that must wait for my publishing memoirs, on which I hope very soon to get going.

Our friendship with the Maiskys came to a sudden and almost terrifyingly complete end. The occasion was a speech of mine at some bethel in Hampstead about the Nazi–Soviet Pact, and Maisky was of course acting under instructions. We continued to meet from time to time at other people's parties, but all that passed between us was a nod or a 'good evening'. Our mutual friend Pablo Azcarate reported Maisky as saying, "We like the Gollancz's as much as ever, but we hate their politics". Nor did Maisky's departure from London, or the end of the war, make the slightest difference. From that day to this an efficient filing-clerk has seen to it that we should never be asked to the Embassy, not even to those enormous crushes at which the Tories of the extreme right and the most hyenaish capitalists rub shoulders with the social-fascists of the Labour Party.

I have mentioned Pablo Azcarate. He was Ambassador in London of the Spanish Republic, and he and his wife were the Maiskys' greatest friends. They were our friends too, friends-as-such, and we were as close to them as to anyone from the time we first met, in the late thirties, to the day she died, in 1943, and he left London. There is little I can say about the Azcarates: we loved them and they loved us, and that is the end of the matter. They were aristocratic in what I imagine, though I know nothing of Spain, to be the best Spanish manner: they were also very quiet and very gentle, which is perhaps the same thing. I can think of no episode in our intercourse that would interest anyone: nothing we saw or did together, nothing they said to us or we said to them. They were just part of the permanent background to our lives.

Of course we met in their company most of the prominent Republicans in London, and got to know some of them extremely well. Early in the war a letter was delivered at Henrietta Street—with the loss, I was afterwards told, of only a single post—addressed to "Señor Negrin, c/o Gollancz, London".

§3

So far as affection went, the heart of our left-wing lives during the middle and later years of the nineteen-thirties was not the Soviet Union or Republican Spain, but China: and it was with a Chinese that there developed at this time one of the truest friendships we have ever experienced.

It started with the Japanese attack on China and our formation of the China Campaign Committee, the purpose of which was twofold: to enlist public opinion in support of the Chinese Republic, with its United Front of the communists and Chiang Kai-shek, and to raise money for the International Peace Hospital that was being set up in South Shansi. Chinese suffering was terrible: a trite word, and perhaps worse than useless, for the only thing to do about suffering is to suffer it, so far as one can, in one's own person, to feel or rather realise ("for we are all part of a common whole, like the upper and lower teeth") that it is happening, here and now, to oneself. The hospital was to serve a vast area, in which medical services were non-existent: the wounded had to be carried thousands of miles in lingering agony. Mission buildings already in existence were being taken over and equipped. Surgeons and nurses were ready. Money alone was needed.

I remember only a percentage of my colleagues on the China Campaign Committee. The Vice-Chairman was Margery Fry, a quietly great Englishwoman in the Eleanor Rathbone mould: the Honorary Secretary and fulcrum was Dorothy Woodman, as dedicated a human being as you could find—she was later to pursue, with a knowledge that equalled her devotion, many other Eastern and Far Eastern causes. Then there was Reginald Bridgeman, one of those aristocrats with a conscience that seem more English, even, than aristocrats without one; Kingsley Martin and Billy Listowel; my wife; and one or two Chinese, whose names I could never remember except in the most general sort of way. But the member of our Campaign that remains clearest in my mind is Arthur Clegg. He was a pale and, you would have thought, an ineffectual sort of man; and yet he epitomises the Campaign for me—more than that, he epitomises the quiet, unpretentious, devoted middle-class section of the left-wing England I knew. John Allen, who ran the Left Book Club theatre group, was another such. When I hear people sneering at the communist and fellow-travelling youth of those days, I always think of Arthur Clegg and John Allen.

The Campaign ran the usual meetings, and it was in connection with one of these that we first met Shelley Wang. A 'rally' was to be held at the Queen's Hall, and someone suggested that we should decorate the place, not merely with Chinese flags, as would be taken for granted, but with something special and, if possible, unique. The Embassy was consulted, but nothing happened for days; then, only thirty-six hours before zero, my wife was asked to meet two or three Chinese outside the Embassy in Portland Place. Between them they thought up the idea that the balcony should be draped with a great long piece of paper on which an appropriate message should be painted in Chinese calligraphy. Lining-paper was obtained in neighbouring Newman Street, and the message was up within twenty-four hours. Shelley Wang had worked for eighteen hours on stretch to get it ready in time.

Shelley Wang was a poet, with a love of English poetry passed down to him by his father: that is why he was called Shelley (and this immediately endeared him to me, for during a lifetime of changing fashions I have never ceased to rejoice in the poet of more abundant life). Whether he was an expert calligrapher I cannot say: I thought his calligraphy entirely beautiful, but perhaps it is almost the rule for a Chinese gentleman to write like that. Anyhow, he gloried in calligraphy, as he gloried in everything truly Chinese; and one day, out of love for my wife, he produced a great roll on which he showed how certain ideographs to be found on oracle-bones of the Shang Dynasty—tiger, turtle, deer, etcetera—developed into letters for various scripts: seal script, official script (for notices), regular script (for books), running script (for writing one's own letters), and grass script (for poetic composition). I hesitate to call him a great patriot, for the ring of the word is as offensive to me as it was to Dr Johnson: but he loved China with a gentle and non-exclusive love that I found very moving.

Shelley Wang was a short, thick-set man who wore glasses with heavy black rims; but I remember little else about him, or of our intercourse with him, in detail, except that he once stayed at Brimpton for a month or six weeks when he was writing a book. But what I retain with the utmost vividness is the general picture of a gracious and gentle presence that was part of the background to our lives.

Before he left England he gave us something to remember him by: eight portfolios, reproducing dozens of Chinese masterpieces, that he always carried about with him, "to remind him of China". I have chosen two of these for reproduction. The flower painting that faces page 128 is by Yün Shou-p'ing, the great seventeenth-century master.

Shelley was very fond of the children and loved to tell them celestial stories, a particularly celestial one being the Old Man and the Mountain (something about an Old Man who moved a Mountain or for whom a Mountain was moved by his neighbours or God: whenever Shelley appeared Franci, who was five or six at the time, used to cry out "Olmahn"). He also gave them their own special present: a couple of dozen pieces of rice-paper with flowers, leaves, birds and fruit (particularly strawberries) casually painted on them. I recently found them but could not remember what they were meant for, and have had great difficulty in finding out. After drawing a blank with several possible informants I looked up 'Chinese Chargé d'Affaires' in the telephone book, and found a subhead 'Cultural'. I gave them a ring, and asked "Are you Cultural?" "Oh yes," someone replied. I explained my business. I had a couple of dozen very ordinary Chinese objects, clearly mass-produced, and more or less contemporary, that looked like handkerchiefs: could they tell me whether they *were* handkerchiefs if I brought them round? "What is your name, pliss?" the voice asked. I told him, and then repeated my query: had he understood? "Oh yes," he replied. "How do you spell your name, pliss?" I told him. "One el or two, pliss?" he asked. I told him. "Who are you, pliss?" he asked. "A publisher," I told him. "Publisher?" he asked. "Yes," I told him. "Now might you be able to help me?" "Oh no," he replied. "Do you know anyone who could?" I asked. "Oh no," he replied. I suddenly wondered whether I had made a mistake, and got on to a suspicious Chiang Kai-shek man instead of a Mao man. But whichever side they may have belonged to, both my non-informants seemed reluctant to talk. However I have cleared the matter up. These are not handkerchiefs, but pieces of notepaper: you do your calligraphy all over them, ignoring the fruit or flowers. What a contrast to those acquisitive societies where to produce beauty for throwing away would be unthinkable!

§4

Another of our Chinese friends was a boy of eight. It happened like this. My wife had been asked to organise an exhibition of Chinese art in support of the International Peace Hospital, and it had been a remarkable success. Everyone had rallied round: the R.I.B.A., who had just vacated their premises in Conduit Street, but still owned them, let her have them for nothing; the builders we used for our house in Ladbroke Grove cleaned and white-washed them for a nominal ten pounds; Sidney Bernstein took care of the lighting; and Gage provided the show-cases, again for nothing. Almost every well-known collector sent pieces, taking out their own insurance. And many friends volunteered to assist, notably Peter Floud of the V. and A., Dorothy Brooke, Billy Listowel and Edmund Dulac.

(I want to write a belated obituary here of Edmund Dulac, who died more than twenty years ago. If a man who is expert in nothing may dare to judge, he was among the greatest polymaths of our or perhaps any other time. He built one of the first receiving sets, if not the first, in England, and used to fiddle with it for our amusement at his studio in Ladbroke Road. He knew a lot about music, so much, in fact, that he now interested himself mainly in the remoter folk-songs, and cared to play only the nose-flute. Himself an atheist, he was an expert theologian, and even, in the early thirties, could discuss logical positivism skilfully with professional philosophers. His reading, in several languages, was extremely wide. But greatest of all was his *expertise* in many forms of art. There was almost no painter whose style he could not counterfeit: and his statuette of George Moore in wax was an amusing miracle. One night we introduced him to Moses: twenty-four hours later he sent us a model of our friend in wood, complete with eye-glass (of mica), removable topper (of thin grey cardboard), beautiful little spats (of white leather, also removable), aeroplane wings (of plastic), and of course a separate scooter, the basis of which was a couple of thin wooden buttons that couturiers make use of, covering them with velvet or whatnot, when at work on a dress. Impossible to imagine anything more faithful. (A photograph of the model faces page 121.)

Nor was there anything bogus about Edmund. When a man hears that you are going to Mexico, and begs you to stay, not at what everyone has told you is the best hotel, but at the second best, and when you have arrived to ingratiate yourself, not with the maître d'hôtel, but with his assistant, you may feel inclined to take his advice; but when he informs you half-an-hour later that 'little X' is a better conductor than Giulini, and you happen to have heard 'little X', you begin to wonder whether your know-all (who is often in fact a near-genius *manqué*) has ever been in Mexico at all. You never felt anything like that about Edmund, apart from tangible proofs to the contrary: if he ever touched on anything that you knew, by exception, something about, he always convinced you. The fact is, he had an omnifarious curiosity, combined with a scholar's equipment and power of application; and learning at once came so easily and meant so much to him that already by the age of forty he was beginning to suffer from *taedium vitae*.

Withal, he was a man of great affection and great humility, and was wholly devoid of pretentiousness. He might have hobnobbed with the élite: he chose as his friends the very ordinary and on occasion rather peculiarly unsuccessful people he happened to love. And his friends, in their turn, loved him greatly.)

Well then, the Chinese art exhibition was a conspicuous success: overheads for the whole three weeks amounted to only five hundred pounds, and something in the neighbourhood of fifteen hundred was sent to Shansi. In the meantime Plato Chan, an artist aged eight, his sister Christina, also an artist, aged ten, and their parents had arrived in London. I do not recollect where they arrived from, but I rather think from Paris: certainly among the paintings Plato brought with him were a portrait in oils of Léon Blum and a water-colour drawing of the Moulin Rouge, which he had done at the age of three. For, naturally though so many children draw and paint long before they go to school, Plato was far more precocious than most: he had begun to draw when he was only eighteen months old, and thereafter poured his stuff out with an alluring combination of spontaneity, technical dexterity and imaginative vision. His delight in rapid movement, his keen sense of the ludicrous and his genuinely childish conception of what was going on around him quite carried one away. His range was remarkable: from 'Christ' and 'After Seeing Some Works of Michelangelo' to 'Ducks warning a Soldier that the Water is poisoned'.

The Chans quickly attached themselves to the Campaign, or the Campaign to the Chans; and my wife was asked to follow up the Conduit Street exhibition with a Plato Chan one. As a result they were often at Brimpton, and we got to know them, or rather Plato, very well indeed. (I remember nothing of his mother, and of his father only that we heard him sing Chinese songs at the Embassy in a European frock coat.) Plato was often gay and often serious, and always affectionate: his face could take on a beautiful serenity.

VI

FLORENCE AND VENICE

MORE OF OUR bits and pieces were picked up at Florence than anywhere else, for we went there year after year during the earlier part of our married life, and it came to have the feeling of home for us, just as Venice was to have later. Our first visit was in 1924, when I was trying to build up a major publishing business, but not my own. I had been working with the Wee Free Liberals as a sort of assistant to Wedgwood Benn, and he told me one day that his brother Ernest had a vacancy in Benn Brothers Limited: would I like to apply? Now ever since 1916, when I was sacked from my schoolmaster's job at Repton for radicalising the youth, I had wondered whether it might not be a good idea to become a publisher and radicalise the world; so I asked for an interview, and was granted it and got the job. Sir Ernest and I undoubtedly misunderstood one another. He ran a chain of 'trade' papers, with a few 'trade' books hanging on to their coat-tails: and Sir Ernest's idea was that the books should be freed from the coat-tails and, in greatly increased numbers, should go their own way. I, on the other hand, while happy to do what I could in the matter, had no intention of confining myself to *Modern Gasworks Practice* and *Automatic Telephone Systems*. Moreover, our social and political ideas were not of a piece. I was much as I am now: while Sir Ernest was a proselytising money-man (as well as a teetotaller), and was just finishing an exposé of his creed, entitled *Confessions of a Capitalist*, which the bawdy shops of Soho, misreading its title, were to order in great numbers.

Anyhow, by 1924 I was plunging into 'general non-fiction' (by way of 'art books', which after all might be thought of as 'semi-technical') with apparently a casual by-the-way but really with feverish intensity, and we went to Paris one week-end for a breather. My wife suggested that we should go on to Florence, and I wanted to, very badly: for we had had no holiday for three years, and I knew nothing of Italy except Taranto (where I had been held up for a fortnight, enjoying only the sun, when exiled to Singapore after Repton) and Rome (where we had spent a deferred honeymoon in 1921, not too happily, for we had to be over-careful, and I was selfish, not having learned how a married man ought to behave). But I was torn (as I still am, though with increasing rarity) by a hideous conflict between an essential laziness, an almost ecstatically breathless delight in ease and comfort, and an obsessional drive not merely to work but, as I had been in the habit of calling it in my schooldays at St Paul's, to work 'extra'. If, for instance, we had a hundred lines of Vergil to prepare for homework, this job, being compulsory, possessed no reality for me: I did it as something meaningless, and then went on to the real thing—an 'extra' hundred. I used to psycho-analyse myself in respect of this idiosyncrasy, and inevitably discovered a guilt complex; but when released from my enthralment to Freud I found a more feasible explanation, namely a hatred of external authority and a passion for self-direction. By the same token, I do not think I attended more than two or three lectures all the time I was at Oxford; and I refused to buy a gown—when I was summoned to the Warden I borrowed one.

So when my wife kept pulling me to Florence I fought against the temptation for several days, hanging about indecisively, standing by the hour at the entrance to Cook's near the Madeleine and then walking away again; for the obsession to be back in London, to be watching the orders, to be building up the list, had me in its grip. When at last I found myself in the wagon lit ("*sous le lavabo se trouve un vase*"), I was furious.

We descended at the Grand Hotel, which I remember—the Grand Hotel of those days—with the utmost affection. It was quiet, rather dingy, but clean and spacious; and it had a charmingly old-fashioned winter-garden, where we used to meet, on this or a slightly subsequent occasion, my friend Jamie Hamilton (one of the only four publishers I have ever admired, the other three being Jonathan Cape, Geoffrey Faber and Rupert Hart-Davis: as to the last, what a publishing world it is that could do, in the end, without a man so brilliant, so honourable and so humane, and so devoid of the contemporary lack of scruple that will publish anything, however filthy or worthless, for the sake of making a little money!). The proprietor was a famous German-Swiss *hôtelier* called Kraft, a great figure of a man who always used to say "Yeses" instead of "Yes", intending a translation of "Si, si": and had the habit, when playing bridge in the winter-garden, of smashing the table with his fist and shouting "boom-boom" when he wanted to double, as he did every few minutes—rather exasperating, if one was reading the later Henry James.

The hotel had got itself a new top floor, all white and agleam with unpolished woodwork—a thing to fall in love with: but best of all was the little balcony from which my wife used to paint, early morning and late afternoon, in her dressing-gown. What are Italian holidays without a balcony? To sit with face upturned to the sun, and then drowse a bit, read a bit—this is of the essence.

I was often about for hours before breakfast. I would get up while it was still dark and go down to the Duomo. As the sun rose, the tower became lovelier even than Giotto had made it: all airy and transparent, it glowed like a piece of the rose-quartz that had given me so much pleasure when, as a boy of nine or ten, I had formed my little collection of minerals and rocks. The steps of the Cathedral itself had disappeared beneath the hillock of flowers, brought in by the market women, that rose against the marbled façade to the height of a man. The smell and the look of them in the morning air were as sweet to my senses as anything I had experienced before or have experienced since; not even sunrise in Venice, or flying into London on a summer night when all the lamps are lit, has seemed more beautiful.

And when I got back to our balcony, itself still grey with the earliness of the dawn, the houses on the opposite bank would be a long unbroken stretch of flaming brown.

Almost invariably we spent the fine mornings in our own special way. We would take our newspapers and books to a cloister, and sit reading there till it was time for lunch. I always chose books that it was necessary to read very slowly, for to be at one, in peace, with the subtle beauty of words and phrases, and to turn the leaves with a quietness of remembrance and expectation, was to experience a suspension of the fever and fret that had characterised, and was again to characterise, my daily striving. Our favourite cloister was the *chiostro verde*, because there, sitting on the little parapet, we could dangle our legs towards the grass below. The first time we went there an old keeper picked a rose and gave it to my wife,* who must have been looking very beautiful and happy, with a movement of the most charming gentleness and courtesy. It was one of those roses that you see in the Botticelli Venus, and that Walter Pater calls 'embrowned'. I searched for it a few days ago, and luckily found it, pressed in a book.

We refused to fatigue ourselves with sight-seeing. Eventually, of course, we saw more or less everything that anyone could reasonably want to see; but our habit, year by year, was to stand quietly for five or ten minutes before the things we specially loved, and to leave it at that.

These included the Boy with a Simon in the courtyard of the Palazzo Vecchio (maybe it is another sort of fish, not a Simon, but no matter); the other Verrochios, the Donatellos, the Desiderio di Settignanos, the Mino da Fiésoles; and the Botticelli Venus, which always reminds me, with the pang of her longing, of Berlioz' 'Voici des roses'. We would go often to the market by San Lorenzo, and buy little leather objects for our friends and ourselves; and we liked to wander towards evening in the Cascine, feeling like Florentines. Occasionally, too, we took excursions in a hired car (being ourselves, at that time, carless) to such places as Max Beerbohm's 'little Lucca' with the straightness of its Roman roads, just the two of them (or is this an illusion?), intersecting at right angles, and those encircling ramparts that seem as vast, when you walk on them, as the double boulevard at Aix; or Siena—we would perambulate those dark and narrow and rather sordid streets, until suddenly we found ourselves, with dazzled eyes and a sudden catch of breath, in the enormous blazing square, and dreamed that Pegasus might at any moment appear. Most days when we stayed in Florence we would drop in

* Referred to in the poem on p. 7 of this book.

for a glass of sack at Doney's in the Via Tornabuoni, revelling in what I am sure are its English eighteenth-century associations, like Florian's in Venice: we might even lunch there—in 1962 it was still the most agreeable restaurant in Florence. And we would wander down the Lung'Arno, and cross the Ponte Vecchio, and take a cloppety clop back: or drive up to San Miniato, our favourite church, and speculate on how, when we were rich, we might buy a villa just this side of the Piazzale Michelangelo (then devoid, if memory serves, of garish restaurants). This was a young Florence, an innocent Florence, a Florence sleeping in the sun, though I daresay I am indulging in an extreme of subjectivity when I say so.

My wife returned for a few days with Franci soon after the war: she had been unable to get me there, for I had heard that the little houses on the left bank had been ruined or destroyed, and I could hardly bear to think of it, still less to see it. They stayed at an hotel I should not have cared for, as the sewage made a regular practice of bubbling up into the wash-basins: my wife however sees fit to economise whenever, as occurs rarely, she goes alone, happy though she always is to change over to my own hotel if I should turn up half-way through. Many people are grotesquely wrong-headed, by the way, in their choice of an hotel. They choose the most expensive out of snobbism, or reject it for the same reason; or choose the most stylish of the moment, whether the most expensive or not. But neither fashion nor price, unless you are bound to consider price, should come into the matter at all: nothing should weigh with you except comfort, food (if you mean to live *en pension*), location and such amenities as the presence or absence of a balcony—unless, to be sure, the alpha quality of everything else is counterbalanced, or more than counterbalanced, by the omega quality of the company. As to price, it is surprising how deficient people are in any sense of proportion, like my wife, who when partnering me at bridge will risk the loss of a thousand when there can be no question of game, but shrink from risking a hundred when the rubber is at stake. In point of fact, the difference between an hotel of the first and an hotel of the second class is commonly, say, a pound a day for the two, half pension; and you will find people who would rather spend a hundred pounds a week in lousy conditions than a hundred and seven in attractive ones. The rule is, choose the best hotel: that this is usually the most expensive is in the unfortunate nature of things.

(My thesis is illustrated by the case of Cipriani in Venice. If friends of yours are going to Venice, money being no consideration, and you ask them where they are going to stay, the chances are that they will answer, with a lift of their eyebrows as if they are wondering how you can ask, and a wistful look in their eyes, "Cipriani". But the food at Cipriani is no better than at half-a-dozen other places: and if it is quiet and solitude that you seek, why go all the way to Venice for it? I could give the names and addresses of half a dozen country hostelries in England that would serve as well as or better than these. Moreover you have to clamber on to a ferry whenever you want to go to or depart from the city you profess to adore: whereas if you stay at the Gritti or Danieli you can walk straight out on to a little piazza or the molo. Nor is Cipriani either cheaper or even dearer than these; or so I imagine. It all comes down to chic.)

I shall pass over the few days that the three of us, my wife, Franci and I, spent at Florence one autumn in the early fifties, when my wife was having spells of vertigo (this was the time of my adventure with the dentist), and go straight on to 1962. I was just recovering from a broken thigh, and we thought it an excellent idea to hire a car for a longish spell abroad, with Florence for our main centre (Venice, now our home when out of England, was ruled out by my tedious walking). As things turned out, one of the best things about that trip was the evening that preceded it, when we listened, with a mixture of nostalgia on the one hand and excitement at our coming freedom on the other, to a marvellous performance of *Tristan* with Birgit Nilsson as Isolde. (I cannot refrain from passing on a story about this lady that Neville Cardus, doyen of music critics and intellectually most elegant of men, recently told me. She was singing Brünnhilde, and she was either fond of or less than fond of her Siegfried. When he arrived at her sleeping-place on the rock, and was bending down to awaken her, he found confronting him on her mail-armour a hotel notice that read 'Nicht stören'.)

Now I am embarrassed at what I am going to say, but really cannot see how I can avoid saying it. Careless talk about other nations is the most damnable thing in the world: 'the French are mean and charge you for sneezing', 'the Germans are sadistic brutes, not to mention their vile manners', 'Irishmen drink'—how often I have sworn that I will never be guilty of such rubbish or acquiesce in it, however sorely provoked, particularly in the first of these cases! Besides, many of my best friends really are Americans, like the beautifully heroic Hazel Rice, and they have treated me, en masse, with exceptional courtesy and warmth. Finally, how can any individual American be responsible for the inevitable march of history? Yet I am going to say that the Florence of 1962 resembled no more than palely the Florence that had meant so much to us in the nineteen-twenties. The Americans had all but ruined it. Everything was glossy, and smelled somehow of indiscreet dollars: calm and peace had to be looked for, instead of being ready for one anywhere without the asking. And the Grand Hotel had sadly changed. Ciga—the Compagnia Italiana Grandi Albergi—had bought it up: and this too was an example of that trustification of business in which America had been in the lead, with England and Italy itself and the rest of Europe so closely behind. The old individuality, the informal, I was going to say, grace, was no longer there: the Grand Hotel was just a Grand Hotel, immensely polished, immensely efficient. Even old Kraft was not to be seen, or at any rate we never heard his 'boom-boom'.

And yet, although we nodded to many, the only friend we made there, however transitorily, was an American. We had noticed a singularly beautiful young girl at dinner by herself and looking miserable: and one evening the māter dee, as the Americans call him, said to us at coffee, "Will you perhaps speak to Miss Gloria? She is very unhappy". So we asked her over (who could resist a name like that?) and had a lovely time in her company until she left. She was indeed unhappy. She had been for a year at Gaza on U.N. work, and had fallen in love there with a young Norwegian doctor: she was going home now, and feared she would never meet him again. We showed her a few places, which we should hardly have revisited alone: and before she left Florence she gave us each a little present—my wife a silver Boy-with-Simon, which she still uses as a key-ring, and myself a gay reproduction of a Persian miniature. A couple of years later we got a wedding invitation from Minnesota: Gloria was marrying her Norwegian.

Our car—the first we had ever had in Florence—took us about to neighbouring places; and this compensated to some extent for our general disappointment. We were told one day, by the concierge, of the Villa Medicea on an eminence near Artimino, about three-quarters of an hour to the north of Florence, so we sought it out. Its situation, up there by itself, exalted the spirit, and we spent a happy hour going over the place. I specially remember in that array, doubtless accumulated by successive owners, 'first editions' of Mozart and Beethoven, as well as some magnificent Hogarths. According to a leaflet the caretaker gave us: "The legend goes that Ferdinand I of the Medici, Grand' Duke of Tuscany, on a hunting day came to rest on the hill of Artimino. He called out for Bernardo Buontalenti and told him: 'Bernardo build a mansion on this hill, wich will be sufficient for me and my court. Do your best and hurry.' 1594 Ferdinand I came back to install himself and his court in the castle, which alread that time 'possessed in abundance all the amenities a nobleman can expect from a summer residence'" [*sic*].

But best of all was the meal we had at the old stables, which had been converted into an informal restaurant run by the gardener and his wife. There was no menu: we were just asked whether we would have the chicken or the veal. The woman insisted that it would be too hot in the open, but we laughed at this and lunched wonderfully at a table outside for almost nothing. I fear, however, that the place may already have become fashionable: for when we went a second time an English-speaking party had taken possession of the little restaurant upstairs, equipped with their own hampers and champagne.

We went also to S. Andrea in Percussina, near San Casciano, half-an-hour or so from Florence in the opposite direction. Machiavelli lived here when writing *Il Principe*, and his house is almost intact. History, if not 'the bunk stuff', is a very queer affair. I detest Machiavelli, whom I regard, in spite of all the encomiums nowadays lavished on him, as an extremely wicked man; and yet I went through his house, and little garden, not only with interest but with considerable emotion. Afterwards we went across to the little inn where he was in the habit of drinking. They gave us a glass of the local Chianti, with a crust of bread and some cheese, 'for free'; but we bought a flask of the wine, as we were expected to, and carried it home with us. Its label bears the stamp of S. Andrea.

Monday evening, September 12th

At twelve o'clock today there was a quiet little memorial service for John Barclay at St Martin's-in-the-Fields. This was a good man, and I say nothing more extravagant than that because anything beyond the bare statement would somehow put one out of harmony with him. I did not yet know him when he was working with Dick Sheppard in the Peace Pledge Union, but his devotion these last years to International Aid for Children, which he founded, brought us into fairly close contact, though my support for that blessed activity has been far smaller than it should have been. The idea was simple enough, even obvious: he would bring over to England from anywhere abroad, indiscriminately, parties of children who had never known the happiness due to them, and would give them a holiday in the English countryside. Simple and obvious, but no one else had thought of it. And he was, I will not say astonishingly, but obviously (I mean one ought to have foreseen it) successful: money was never lacking, nor was a friendly or loving welcome for the children by foster-parents all over the country. The secret lay in his persistence, and in that of his closest associate, Margaret McEwen: an intense persistence but a gentle one, with no trace in it of self-reference and little even of self-awareness. No one could have known better than John Barclay how wicked men can be, for the suffering their wickedness caused, particularly to children, was always with him; and yet he took goodness, or call it decency, for granted when appealing for aid. He was not exactly an optimist, which is too emphatic a word: he just believed in people—or just believed.

It was an appropriate service this morning. The obvious things—'To be a pilgrim' and 'Bring me my bow'—did not seem obvious: they seemed final and inevitable: so did the two lessons that Sybil Thorndike spoke in that specially living voice of hers, Christ's 'Suffer the little children' and the familiar chapter from first Corinthians. And at the end, as after a moment of hush we were going about our business, a trumpet 'voluntary' rang out with an affirmation of triumph (just as at this moment the reiterated triumph in the last movement of Schubert's ninth symphony rings out on the wireless).

When I first heard of John Barclay's death, only a few days after gossiping with him outside a restaurant in the Strand, grief took over: one would miss him, his place would never see him again, there was a blank where there had been life. But I began to wonder. When a good man goes from the earth, may not the earth be richer rather than poorer? At first thought a nonsensical question: that presence gone, that work at an end—how can this mean anything but loss? But I am not so sure. A moment of perfect goodness has intervened in the world: and that goodness is now forever in *the world, forever enriching it. It is not a question of personal survival, of personal immortality: goodness—human living in harmony with spirit and truth—*is*, and can never be destroyed, whatever may be the fate of the physical universe. Henceforth there is something* there *that was not there before.*

'Call no one happy till his death'. What may not happen to a man at the last? However fair his previous life may have been, what weariness, what loss of ideals, what positive selfishness, what impulse, even, to wrong-doing may not intervene before the end? This did not happen to John Barclay: the goodness he has added to the world is a humanly perfect goodness, not a marred goodness.

So I think we should be happy when a man leaves the world in his goodness, just as we should grieve when he leaves it in what, though we ought not to judge, we cannot help but judge to be his wickedness. Or perhaps we should neither grieve nor be happy, but simply say Amen.

I shall mention here, while my mind is on John Barclay, a man who somewhat resembled him in the way Christianity informed his whole life, Bell of Chichester; and another in whom I saw it at work in his later years, Cyril Joad. Cyril showed a fortitude during his last dreadful illness that might have been thought humanly impossible, and it was his recently acquired Christianity that lay behind it. He used to send one away when 'the little pains' were developing into 'the big pains', and he knew he must scream and scream; and yet when he thought that there would be a sufficient respite (from the big pains, not from the little ones) he put on a dressing-gown and got himself taken to Birkbeck, so that he might talk to some pupils in special need of his help. And he gave up the chance of ameliorating his condition because he was unwilling to treat his neighbour in what he thought an unchristianly manner.

§2

Though we had been to Venice at least three times before the war, it was not till 1947, when we stayed for three weeks with Giuliana Foscolo and Mario Sonino in their place near the Carmini, that she began to be a home for us, as Florence had been; and she has remained one ever since.

The generality are great humbugs where foreign travel is concerned: when they are expected to like a place they say they like it, and may even believe they like it, irrespective of their genuine reaction, just as you may see earnest tourists, when told in a famous gallery by their bear-leading expert "Now this is one of the world's supreme masterpieces", gaping in wonder at a neighbouring target. We first went to Venice in March 1926. The weather was wretched—cold, hazy and wet; and our room at the Europa fronted a passage so narrow that our choice was between shivering outside in the gloom or shivering inside (there was no *chauffage* in those days at the Europa) in artificial light. I shall not say that we detested Venice, for apart from the awful blasphemy involved I doubt whether it was true: but we certainly did not enjoy it. The greatest *déception* of all was our first gondola ride: such smells, such decay, such unseemly floating refuse in 'the world's fairyland'! Of course there were compensations: the Piazza was in its way rather fine, the clock-tower amused us for all the brevity of its performances, and there were some magnificent pictures in the nevertheless terribly fatiguing Accademia. By the third day, anyhow, we were dying to get away, and I was biting my nails (literally—I used to do this) at the idea of telling the manager that we wanted to leave, for we had booked for a fortnight. At last I collected, hour by hour, the necessary amount of courage, and went to see him; and was half-way through a painfully rehearsed story of why he must really release us when he interrupted me with a show of irritation, and said, in perfect English, "By all means go if you want to". So we fled to Florence, with which we were already in love: the weather was superb, and we had one of the best holidays of our lives.

By the time of our second visit, in April or May 1929, we had already repented *in absentia*. How ludicrous, after all, to judge by a single short visit in shocking weather! And we had hardly seen anything! To wash the place out was surely fantastic: we must have another try. And then I suddenly remembered that my Aunt Minna, a great traveller in her day, had raved about Danieli's: "Stay nowhere else, my dear," she had said to me (I must have been about ten), "when you go to Venice. Yes, my dear, it's historic." So we worked out a plan.

I had only a few days to spare, for I had just started my own publishing business: my wife, on the other hand, was in need of a longish rest, Franci being only three months old. My wife, then, would go with our friend Stella Churchill to Florence, and then on to Venice, where they would stay at the Seguso: a fortnight later I would go out with Sigle Lynd and stay at Danieli's, where my wife would join us, while Stella went off to Greece. (This was the time Sylvia Lynd was so fearful for Sigle's reputation: people might think that our *wagons* had communicated, or even, God forbid, that we had shared one!)

The plan worked *à merveille*. The weather was lovely: and our rooms in the Danieli annexe were adequate and comfortable, if lacking the period atmosphere of the palazzo itself or the welcoming freshness of our present quarters in the then non-existent new building. Above all, there was a plenitude of windows, two of them looking over to San Giorgio opposite and a third to the Lido away on our left. And as we explored a little we began to fall in love with the place, without as yet becoming wholly committed.

But what will always mark this visit for us is that, before I arrived, my wife had made her first contact with Giuliana Foscolo, and thereafter lifelong friendship was born.

Giuliana, whom it gives me special pleasure to celebrate, is the great-niece of Ugo Foscolo, the poet, and it is perhaps from him that she inherits her radicalism. (I haven't really the faintest idea, as I know nothing about him, and think it little worth while to enquire: I just have an instinct in the matter, and if it turns out all wrong, or even directly opposed to the truth, what matter?) Their contact happened like this. Sir Alan Napier was our Consul in Venice: he had worked under Stella Churchill's late husband in Palermo or Naples: so she went along to see him, and took my wife, of course, with her. There they found Giuliana, who was seventeen at the time. Napier had constantly run into her, chattering English with a friend, in the neighbourhood of his consulate, and had asked her home: they got to know one another well, and Stella, he thought, might like to meet her.

The basis of my wife's attraction to Giuliana, and of Giuliana's to her, was, I suspect, their common feminism (apart, that is, from a freshness and charm they were blessed with in almost equal measure). My wife had been a passionate supporter of the women's suffrage movement, and only her youth had prevented her from following her mother and elder sisters to prison: her family did dreadful things, I am afraid, such as pouring corrosive acid into letter-boxes. The same general attitude to her sex was characteristic of Giuliana when we first knew her; and though coupled with a delight in men's company (as, for the matter of that, was my wife's) this is predominantly the mark of her still, both for better and for worse. Even today, at the age of fifty-four, she is very much the forceful, independent, managing woman, as well as one of the kindest and most affectionate: and this can occasionally be tiresome, even to a man who loves her as I do.

(I hope I do not appear to be having a go at 'old-fashioned' feminism: I detest the neo-reactionary mystique that derides it.)

A little later Giuliana came to London, being anxious to perfect her English, and stayed at Brimpton; and I took to her with nine-tenths of my heart—for her candour, her liveliness and her young sensuality—though she was never one of my *innamorate*. But it was during our last pre-war visit to Venice, in about 1936, that our friendship was sealed. We were staying this time at the palazzo itself, in a room with long Gothic windows coming down to the floor; and after the happiness of that fortnight to have gone anywhere else than Danieli's when holidaying in Venice would have been unthinkable. Leslie Hartley was living at the time in one of the palazzi on a side canal, and we spent an entrancing evening with him: Jimmie Smith was there, and he sang German Lieder in what I remember as a charming *petite voix*. A few days later we asked Leslie Hartley to dine with us at Danieli's, with Giuliana as our only other guest: she looked lovely in a frock of pale flame-colour with a sprig of gerbera pinned to it. My wife's passion for growing gerbera dates from that evening.

Giuliana's outspokenness against fascism enraptured and alarmed us. Before all those waiters, and at the top of her voice—was it safe, wouldn't she find herself on one of those horrible islands? But she didn't give a damn, any more than Ongania had done when we bought our Guardi from him; nor it seemed, for the matter of that, did the waiters, and I am not in the least surprised, for the present lot, whom we have known a full decade or more, are as kind, decent and humane as you could imagine. The servants, indeed, are among the important if minor reasons for our continuing to frequent this hotel: the concierge, for instance—how embarrassed he is by my title! He doesn't like to call me Sir Victor, for he thinks the Christian name disrespectful: he knows Sir Gollancz is all wrong: Sir might be only the common-or-garden Sir, besides sounding unfriendly: and he hasn't yet tumbled to M'lord, as the Eden people at Rome did this spring, to my enormous delight, it made me feel so eighteenth century—the concierge, I was saying, gave us pleasure every morning as he took our instructions. Someone ought to write a book on 'The Great Concierges of Europe', for concierges, after all, are the lynch-pins of the whole business. The fat fellow, with hat aslant, who used to see to every last detail for us at the pre-Hitler Adlon, would figure largely in it: but the chances are that he became a Nazi—political complaisance is an occupational disease of such people—so I had better say no more about him. Any-how there are concierges and concierges. "Now, as in old days," wrote Oscar Wilde in one of those last terrible letters of his, so sordid and yet, in spite of everything, still so witty, "men rob the pilgrims in Rome. The robbery is chiefly done by hotel porters, or rather by real robbers disguised as hotel porters." I know those hotel porters very well, particularly the Roman ones: they pillage hirable chauffeurs so outrageously for introducing them that the chauffeurs, in their turn, must charge you double the job's value.

If I were writing such a book, as I still may do, I should enlarge it to cover hotel servants of other kinds as well, and should consecrate a whole chapter to the Savoy: giving special mention to the man (also fat, also with hat aslant) at the main entrance; to the maître d'hôtel in the restaurant, so nostalgically from Venice itself; to his confrère in the Grill Room, whom I always call Charles, but whose real name somewhat resembles Vermicelli; to Basil, the best and most courteous head waiter in the world; and to that masterpiece among managers (who must forgive me for talking about him with the servants—not that he will mind: he is a great gentleman, and considers himself everyone's servant), our friend and fellow music-lover Peter Stafford. But I feel ashamed to have omitted so many: two or three *chefs de rang*; the tall, handsome and enticing cigar-man in the restaurant; his confrère in the grill room; nearly all the cloakroom attendants; the girl in the grill room lounge; and so on and so and so on, selah, amen.

We of course lost sight of Giuliana after Italy had come into the war, but in 1940 (if my dates are right) she had done us a great but unhappily abortive service. My wife had been at school for nine months or so in Wilmersdorf before the First World War, was still greatly attached to the headmistress, Fraülein Zichel, a Jewess, and made every effort in 1939 and 1940 to engineer her escape to England. Unsuccessful, she thought of Giuliana: couldn't Fraülein Zichel be got away, despite all difficulties, to Italy, which was neutral? Giuliana immediately responded, arranged everything, and had just sent Fraülein Zichel her tickets when Italy came in. Fraülein Zichel was sent to Auschwitz.

(How I hate writing those words, as I have written them so often during the last twenty years! To do so, 'period' as the Americans say, seems a callous and cowardly evasion. 'She was sent to Auschwitz', as you might say, of a woman picked up with a broken leg, 'She was sent to Charing Cross Hospital'. It is as if one shrank from engaging oneself or others, from committing ourselves to the agony of recollection; or as if one couldn't bother, had no time to remember in the press of daily life. But one *has* to remember, for these were our brothers and sisters; one should say 'She was sent in lingering fear on a disgusting journey to an obscene death—with Viennese waltzes for accompaniment—in the gas chambers or burning-up machines of Auschwitz', and be damned to triteness or repetition. We shall never advance from our present inhumanity until we realise past sufferings as present and other people's agony as our own.)

Meanwhile Giuliana had got herself married to Mario Sonino, an able—and clever and witty—Venetian-Jewish advocate, and still, despite their separation, our excellent friend. He got away to Switzerland when Mussolini copied Hitler's antisemitism, bogus, in the Italian case, as it always was (who could ever tell a Jew from a really good-looking Italian, or want to?); and Giuliana went to live by herself at Casteldardo, the Foscolos' Renaissance farmstead up above Venice on the site of an ancient castle, which Giuliana owned in common with a brother and sister; but the Germans soon occupied it, leaving Giuliana enough living-space for her needs. Here she hid a couple of Allied parachutists, with the Germans next door; and here she received wireless instructions from Resistance H.Q., in the neighbourhood, on the basis of which she told Allied or Resistance airmen what places to bomb. It is to Giuliana, I like to think, that we owe the continued existence of those marvellous Giottos at Padua, so much finer, at any rate in point of preservation, than the ones at Assisi. She had passed on instructions to bomb the Padua railway-station, and as a result of her message the Hermitage, with its Mantegnas, was totally destroyed. A few days later she should have ordered a second bombing. But she remembered the Capella Scrovegni ('the Madonna dell'Arena'), and its Giottos next door to the Hermitage, and forgot all about her instructions.

Directly the war was over she begged us to take a good long holiday with her and Mario at their place near the Carmini; and we arranged to go for three weeks in the autumn of 1947, taking in the Flegs on our way. (This was that first post-war meeting with Edmond and Madeleine that I referred to earlier.) Those twenty-one days were full of warmth, joy and light-heartedness; and it was then, as I have said, that Venice became, as it has remained ever since, our European home when away from our English one.

The greatest thing about it, apart from our hosts' comradeship, was that we had our own gondola. People talk a lot of nonsense about gondolas; saying that public vaporetti are just as good, that gondolas are a stunt, a mere tourists' attraction, and that it is silly to waste money like that. Such chatter is to be dismissed. To bask in the sun as one travels slowly, with a single companion, down the Grand Canal (the slowness and aloneness are of the essence); to turn corners, the gondolier halloing, in the side ones—I can imagine no more gracious balm to the spirit than this, except listening to music: and that I can no longer board a gondola, owing to my damaged thigh, is nowadays a major disappointment to me when in Venice. And touching the side canals, for most of which a gondola or private speed-boat—a very poor substitute—is of course essential, these suffer a literal sea-change as you get to know the place better. The smells become ozone.

Our gondolier was a good old gentleman, who had once been employed, if I understood him aright, by Baron Corvo; and he spent a lot of time trying to teach me Venetian, in which he was wholly unsuccessful, for the only words I could retain were the ones Giuliana had taught me already, such as coccolona, which means more than a darling, commoma, which means more than a silly ass, and sbrindolare, which means more than to stroll. My wife was troubled when our man was below, and he was below every morning before breakfast: she thought it wrong, capitalistic, to keep him hanging about at our service. My wife's socialism is spiritually all but perfect, but a bit muddled in respect of some of its practical application. This—the spiritual perfection—is one of her greatest virtues.

Our gondolier is associated with the most beautiful of all our experiences during our visit to Giuliana and Mario. The fact is that, for all my loyalty to Venice, which is utter, I have never been able to live for more than a limited period without grass. I will have been strolling about or sitting at ease in a gondola, when I have seen, as if with sudden rediscovery, a green plant or two on the roof of some building, or the shrub in the courtyard of Peggy Guggenheim's palazzo on the Grand Canal. Then I have longed for Torcello, and when the desire has become painful we have gone there. The island, to be sure, has lost a good deal of its attractiveness: Cipriani runs a *restaurant de luxe* in place of the old drinks-and-snack place, a vaporetto is always arriving with crowds of noisy tourists, and somehow, though this may be an illusion, there has been a general poshing-up. But in our earlier days hardly anyone would be about: Santa Fosca and Santa Maria at the far end, grass, a sort of canal, a few uninteresting cottages with women outside at their bead-work—that was all, and enough. Torcello was a beautifully satisfying desert.

We had been there several times in the twenties and thirties by one of the occasional vaporetti, but now our gondolier suggested something different; he would impress a mate, and they would take us there by gondola. We set out soon after lunch, and sat with faces upturned, between waking and sleeping, as we skirted the guiding buoys. Arrived, we wandered down the footpath, bought bits of work from the women, rested here and there in the Cathedral, had a drink and strolled back to where our gondola waited. Then we made for Burano and dined at that restaurant, with pictures crowding its walls, where the artists forgather. The moon came up on our way home, and the men sang their songs as the lights of the Piazzetta appeared. Just before we got in we saw a vortex of seagulls gleaming white against the illumined darkness of the sky.

Another event when we were staying with Giuliana and Mario was the première—the first performance ever in Italy—of *Idomeneo* at the Fenice. Merely to look at the posters, with a great strip '*Novita in Italia*', pasted across them, was a happiness to me. I remember nothing about the performance, except that Gui conducted excellently: and as to the work itself, I thought it, for beauty, second among Mozart's operas only to *Figaro*, and, for the musical-dramatic technique of its middle act, most satisfying of them all. But what thrilled me most was the sense of sharing, entering into as my own, the traditions of such a place: the Fenice, where *Traviata* was first given to the musical world, and *Ernani* and *Rigoletto* and *Simone Boccanegra*! Not only did I insist, as was natural, on arriving by gondola at the water entrance instead of going by foot from the Piazza in the commoner fashion, but I thought, with a momentary pang, what a pity it was that I couldn't be wearing a white tie and a cloak with scarlet linings, and be carrying a gibus and a gold-headed ebony cane. I have a great feeling, doubtless inherited from my father, for even the stupider opera-house traditions. When I had an office in Paris and was going a lot to the Opéra, in spite of such appalling performances that I always swore I would never go again but always did, I used to look with a pang like my Venetian one at the old roués in *tenue de soirée* who traditionally sat in the first three or four rows of the stalls the more easily to ogle the ballerinas: and I once actually sat in the middle of the front row myself—not for a like purpose, but at the first performance there of *Parsifal*, conducted with the aid of a metronome. I always have the instinct to dress for Covent Garden, or at any rate for 'big' nights there, though I never do: and I felt savage when at the première of Zeffirelli's *Don* I saw a man lounging in a box without coat, waistcoat or tie. Another example of this eccentricity is the regret I used to feel that I had never gone to the opera in St Petersburg in the old Tzarist days. I still occasionally feel it; and this is the more odd in that I abominate the Russian *ancien régime* and anything remotely connected with it.

For the rest, we really 'did' Venice in the course of those crowded three weeks, packing in a visit to Maser, with its grand Veroneses over against one another and Castelfranco, where the famous Giorgione disappointed us. We 'did' Venice, once and for all.

Nowadays, far from 'doing' Venice, we live in it whenever we can get there. We have a room on the fourth floor of the new building, white, spick and span and almost undecorated, and with a decently wide and broad balcony that looks across to San Giorgio opposite and to the Lido on our left and the Salute on our right. Just above us is the roof-restaurant, very precious indeed when they first installed it, however commonly you may lunch at one now. It is our height that gives us tranquillity. We were sitting outside Quadri's one summer night, listening to the brass band, when Dick Mitchison came up: he was on his way to Bologna, with the intention, no doubt, of sampling its gourmet restaurants. "You can have Venice," he said. "What crowds! It's like Margate" (which I would wager he has never been near). We neither see nor hear crowds up in our eyrie: we see nothing but the lagoon and its buildings and shipping (and sometimes a tiny fishing-boat with yellow or orange sails on the blue or green waters), and hear little but the occasional hoot of a passing liner or the tolling of a bell on San Giorgio. But often we *want* crowds, native or tourist, we want to mix with them, share their life and populous movement: for crowds suit Venice as surely as they do not suit Florence. And the adjuncts to any holiday crowd please us, in Venice, hardly less than the crowd itself: the man just across the bridge over the molo with his silly little toys that go wrong the very moment you get them home; the stalls where you can pick up a model gondola with a ballet-girl pirouetting on its bottom to the tinkle of music; the postcard vendors, and the newspaper men who cry 'Heute' or 'Inglispaper' as you sip your drink in the Piazza. Everything is grist to the mill of people who like living in Venice.

Our days are fairly uniform. Sometimes, until a few years ago, I would get up before anyone was about and stroll over to St Mark's, where I would spend a few moments on my knees: the golden background to the mosaic Christ in the lunette over the west entrance would be aglow with the rising sun, and this made me prayerful. But my thigh is too bothersome now at so early an hour to make the enterprise feasible: it takes time to get going.

After breakfast we remain on our balcony for as long as we care to: my wife paints and I read (always, for part of the time, *Don Juan*: I invariably reread it in Venice, where I find its cadences as irresistible as the chiming of bells). Then we go for a walk, beginning, as often as not, with the Merceria, which is nowadays almost as chic as Bond Street, besides being far more pleasurable; and ending at Florian's, where we listen to the band music and watch the sunlit parade of parents and children and sip at our *Ice Caffé*, after a row with the waiter who insists on telling me, morning after morning, that *Ice Caffé* is not what I think it is. At half-past twelve or thereabouts we stroll back to Danieli's, with the prospect of a dry cocktail on our balcony: this usually makes us both a bit tight, whereas a couple in London of double the size and double the strength would not affect us in the slightest. We sleep after lunch for as long as we can, and when we have pulled ourselves together may take one of my two favourite walks. We may either wander about by the Arsenal, with its quartet of ancient lions, and conspicuously the long thin one allegedly from Delos, a regular dachshund of a lion; or we may make for the far side in the opposite direction and start out from the Madonna dell' Orto. In both places one gets a feeling of unusual spaciousness, of a holiday-within-a-holiday remoteness from everyday Venice. Back for dinner we go up to the restaurant, and watch tinges of green creeping over the waters after the flaming of San Giorgio at sunset: one of the final lovelinesses of this our world, at once so holy and so wicked. Afterwards, we may go off to the Piazza and listen to the band if it happens to be 'on', or sit and read, or do more or less nothing. Nights before bedtime are unsatisfactory in Venice, as on almost every sort of holiday except festival ones: festival ones, on the other hand, can be boring (but not at pre-war Salzburg) by day.

We never sight-see in Venice. That is over and done with: we would no more think of revisiting the Frari or a dozen other churches and show-places than of making an excursion to the Tower of London. But there are places and pictures that have become an integral part of our Venetian life, and these irresistibly call to us on every visit. I think of the Carpaccios in the Scuola San Giorgio, and particularly of St Jerome's dog; of the marble pilasters, with their translucent interweaving of arabesques and birds, in my favourite Venetian church, the Miracoli; of Carpaccio's so-called 'Venetian Courtesans' in the Museo Correr; of the Scala dei Giganti in the courtyard of the Doge's Palace, such a coincidence of delicacy and strength, with the oleanders hard by; of our neighbouring San Zaccaria, with its festoonings of Gothic lace; of the Ca' d'Oro and its miniature rival Desdemona's House; and better perhaps even than these, of the Tribune at the Accademia. I mean by this the little room a few steps up from the first floor: I have always called it the Tribune, I do not remember why. I used to think of each picture separately—the Tempesta, the Memling, the Piero della Francesca, the Mantegna, the Bellinis, and that marvellous fragment of a Giorgione just on your left as you come in, the sprig of a tree with the artist's signature as if on a panel; but now I see them, not as many beauties, but as a single many-faceted beauty of the purest water. We stay there for half-an-hour, for an hour, then go home by way of the Zattere and the Salute; to our own heavy loss (there can be no doubt of it) we have denied ourselves the rest of the Accademia for many years.

Just as I cannot live without grass for more than a limited period, so every now and again when in Venice I long for *terra firma*, being in the end not a Venetian but a land-animal. I want to sit in a car with the sun on my face and watch the hedges go by: I want roads and villages and hills, want to be involved with them, know them as part of me, greet them as my own. My wife does not feel quite the same, for having driven since girlhood she does not greatly care for cars, other people's in particular: but she happily acquiesces when I want to go off on an excursion, for she likes chicken sandwiches in the sun as much as I do. Our favourite termini—we pick up a regular man at the Piazzale Roma—are Aquileia and Asolo. At Aquileia you may lunch in the shadow of the Cathedral, with the blaze all about you: at Asolo, avoiding Cipriani, high up by Duse's tomb. Two or three years ago, before she moved houses, we looked in on our way back at Freya Stark's, and talked to her and strolled in her garden.

But nowadays we see very few people in or around Venice. We have met a number of Venetians, of course, have hobnobbed with them, been to parties and dinners; but our only real friends, after so many years, are still Mario and Giuliana, and Giuliana is mostly in Rome, where she teaches English and looks after her three young people. She is as intense as ever, but what concerns her most now is her daughters' intellectual progress, as measured by how they 'do' in their exams. Italian women with Giuliana's type of background worry about such things more than their English equivalents.

An island ought to come in here, somehow connected with all this—I don't mean with Venice or Florence, with something more—but I cannot remember its name nor where it is. I have been half awake on and off for I do not know how long or how often, and I have wanted to ask my wife what it is called, but I have not been able to put on the light for that would disturb her, and I mustn't wake her up anyhow, and then I have gone to sleep again and half woken up and so on several times, but I now simply must find out what it is called, for it is a wonderful island and thank God I have paper and pen here by my bedside, certainly not the Lepari islands which I've never been near and none of the regular ones but somehow quite different. But now my brain is clearing and it is obvious that the whole thing was a dream, and yet so real to me that I must try to describe the place, though I get surer every millionth of a second that it will turn out a vague and commonplace jumble.

It is ruined—I am wide awake now, but will speak of it in the present—and yet the ruins are not ruins, but perfect classical architecture of rather small size. Some sort of trial is going on, but somehow it isn't a trial either, it is more like an investigation with one or two people on one side and a lot of people on the other. The whole thing is very slow and everyone wears Isadora Duncanish clothes. There is autumnal sunlight all about, and I think of the words 'a sunlit glade', and wonder, now that I am fully awake, whether the whole thing might not have been a vague memory of the last play in *Back to Methuselah*. But that certainly was not my impression at the time: there kept coming into my mind a Christmas card a girl of six did for me, the grand-daughter of one of my authors, or perhaps she did not do it for me but for everyone, and I got a copy.

And now, as I read this through, I find that it sounds like an allegory, particularly in view of what I am determined to write next. But it honestly isn't an allegory. The place was so vivid to me when I dreamed it, and gave me such utter happiness, that I think if I could get back to sleep now I should dream it all over again.

Wednesday, September 21st, Eaton Place

Last Friday night, a few minutes after the choral movement of Beethoven's ninth symphony had ended at the prom, it was announced on the wireless that a young man had been ordered six strokes of the birch for taking part in a prison riot. He was nineteen and was serving a life sentence for having hit a prison officer with an iron bar, and killed him, when trying to escape from a borstal. If the Home Secretary confirms the award, this will be the first flogging in an English prison for four years.

According to a report in the 'Sunday Times', "Mr Jenkins, Home Secretary, said yesterday that he was unlikely to decide whether to confirm the birching sentence . . . until he returns from the United States. He spoke before leaving London Airport on a two-week trip to look at American police and prison methods . . .

"'I shall make a decision as soon as all the facts are available,' Mr Jenkins said. 'I will need the whole history of the case, including the medical record. But I don't want to keep people hanging around for longer than necessary.'

"He said it was 'quite wrong' to think, because he was normally against corporal punishment, that he had made up his mind. He said his decision would be 'something of a judiciary nature'.

"Asked whether he thought prison warders deserved this protection against convicted murderers, Mr Jenkins replied: 'They must be protected, but that begs the question of how big a deterrent corporal punishment is.'"

I have no doubt at all that Mr Jenkins will refuse to confirm the sentence, and that, being the man he is, he was talking politically, with an eye to the public, and not as a human being from the heart: more's the pity, for today it is politicians and not men of religion who have the ear of the public, and so can influence them in the direction of decent living. There is nothing 'judiciary' about the matter, and Mr Jenkins knows it as well as I do: it is not a question of 'the whole history of the case', 'the medical report' or deterrence: the choice is between right and wrong, good and evil, the men of Galilee and the men of Rome.

Judicial birching is not like birching at Eton and similar establishments, as a lot of people thoughtlessly assume. School birching is painful and disgusting: judicial birching is an extreme form of torture, I repeat an e x t r e m e *form of torture, and I say it on the authority of a doctor whose duty it has been to attend one. He had to examine the man after each stroke. You understand why? The man's heart may give out, you may kill him: and while torture is O.K., murder isn't. So you flay and examine, you flay and examine, you flay and examine . . . Yes, flay: for in terms of the pain inflicted—the subject is so disgusting that one can hardly go on with it—there is little difference, for the time being, between birching a man and flaying him—the two processes, indeed, are not dissimilar. Nor is it a question of a few minutes, and finish: the man is an invalid for months to come. Birching, the doctor said, is worse even than the cat.*

And pain apart, what is the object, or if you like the result, of a birching? Degradation: and to degrade still more thoroughly a man already degraded enough is the meanest, wickedest, stupidest thing I ever heard of. If you're going to make anything out of him, for the good of his own soul and of the society he menaces (and will continue to menace if he emerges from prison unchanged, not to say worsened), your object above all must be to give him, or give him back, self-respect.

Why, I have been asking myself, was this particular man picked out for torture, cruel as well as silly though the other sentences were? Perhaps because he had led the riot—though it appears that he was a joint leader and not the sole one. But I cannot but suspect that the reason was in fact something quite different: he was a murderer, and this was an act of revenge. May not the sentence, I mean, be mixed up with the recent murder of three policemen, and the agitation to 'bring back hanging'? And, apropos, I want to say something that has been on my mind for weeks.

The Campaign for the Abolition of Capital Punishment relied overwhelmingly on arguments tending to show that fear of the death penalty is not a unique deterrent. This was probably good tactics, and anything that resulted in the abandonment of this obscenity, if only for a period of five years, was perhaps justifiable. But, though I do in fact believe that little or nothing can be claimed for the death penalty on the score of its preventive value, I was always critical of such emphasis on what in any case, in view of varying circumstances, can never be proved. I wrote at the time, and shall now repeat, that if I believed the opposite of what I do believe; if I believed it established, beyond the possibility of a doubt, that the death penalty is preventive of murder as nothing else could be: I should still be passionately opposed to capital punishment. Capital punishment is wrong, and that is all there is to it; and the defence of it on any "practical" grounds whatever—and irrespective of whether those grounds are well or ill taken—is not an atom more relevant than the defence, on similar grounds, of the practice, a couple of centuries ago, of executing little children for the theft of five shillings.

I do not rest my case on the sacredness of human life, though I do believe that human life is sacred: I rest it on the imperative "Thou shalt do no unspeakable cruelty to any human being." And I say to everyone, do not argue about capital punishment until you have tried a little empathy.

Imagine that you are in the death-cell, with three weeks to wait. Everyone is very kind to you, specially kind: particularly the pair of warders who are with you and watching you every hour of the day and night, for fear that you may find a way of taking the thing into your own hands and "cheating the gallows". They chat with you, they offer to play cards with you, in the hope of "keeping your mind off it": but all the time a little door in the side of your cell reminds you of what lies just beyond it. The doctor treats you like a king, for you must be well enough, on the day, to be killed: and the chaplain offers you spiritual consolation. They even give you special food ("hospital diet, with such additions as the Medical Officer considers advisable") and stout or beer. Yes, they are exceedingly kind: and their very kindness—the very kindness of these people with a next year, a next month—their very kindness (and the reason for it) stabs you, every minute and every second, with a realisation of what you *are. For you are a new kind of creation, a creation that no Creator, but only human inhumanity, could ever have created: you are not an animal or a man, but something dead while alive, and something* conscious *during death of its deadness. And trapped there, kept "alive" there, even, in a sort of way, pampered there, you have to wait, a selfconscious automaton, for the ending of that consciousness—day after day, hour after hour, minute after minute: but the moment ahead of you is not the sort of happy release that sick people, and even healthy people, sometimes find themselves welcoming, but a moment, your fear tells you, of unutterable horror. "What is it like, being killed?" you keep asking yourself: maybe you ask the warder: and maybe he replies "A matter of seconds: no worse than having a tooth out." But you don't believe him. Death by hanging is perhaps really instantaneous: but the contemplation of it isn't.*

You go to bed and perhaps to sleep, with what nightmares only God can know. You wake up, and maybe have forgotten: you wake up as a real man wakes up, with the joy or the burden, the ordinary happiness or the ordinary misery, of a new day before him. But if you have forgotten you have forgotten only for a second: and the rushing, stabbing realisation of what you are *is all the more dreadful for that momentary oblivion.*

And then the sickening round starts again: exercise, food, "rest" to keep the dead thing—you—alive.

The hour grows nearer, and your mental agony increases. You cannot get away from it, this horror that is you: *it lives in every breath you draw, in every word you speak, in every movement you make: it eats with you, drinks with you, goes to bed with you, gets up with you. . . . And now the last full day has come, and somehow or other you have got through it: and the last of your nights has come and gone: and they ask you what you would like for breakfast: and footsteps have approached: and the executioner is in your cell. . . .*

The last word was said about capital punishment by Dostoievsky in 'The Idiot':

"'Yes—I saw an execution in France—at Lyons. Schneider took me over with him to see it.'

"'What, did they hang the fellow?'

"'No, they cut off people's heads in France.'

"'What did the fellow do?—yell?'

"'Oh no—it's the work of an instant. They put a man inside a frame and a sort of broad knife falls by machinery—they call the thing a guillotine—it falls with fearful force and weight—the head springs off so quickly that you can't wink your eye in between. But all the preparations

are so dreadful. When they announce the sentence, you know, and prepare the criminal and tie his hands, and cart him off to the scaffold—that's the fearful part of the business. The people all crowd around—even women—though they don't at all approve of women looking on.'

"'*No, it's not a thing for women.*'

"'*Of course not—of course not!—bah! The criminal was a fine intelligent fearless man; Le Gros was his name; and I may tell you—believe it or not, as you like—that when that man stepped upon the scaffold he* cried, *he did indeed,—he was as white as a bit of paper. Isn't it a dreadful idea that he should have cried—cried! Who ever heard of a grown man crying from fear—not a child, but a man who never had cried before—a grown man of forty-five years. Imagine what must have been going on in that man's mind at such a moment; what dreadful convulsions his whole spirit must have endured; it is an outrage on the soul, that's what it is. Because it is said "thou shalt not kill", is he to be killed because he murdered someone else? No—it is not right—it's an impossible theory. I assure you, I saw the sight a month ago and it's dancing before my eyes to this moment. I dream of it, often.*'

"*The prince had grown animated as he spoke, and a tinge of colour suffused his pale face, though his way of talking was as quiet as ever. The servant followed his words with sympathetic interest. Clearly he was not at all anxious to bring the conversation to an end. Who knows? perhaps he too was a man of imagination and with some capacity for thought.*

"'*Well, at all events it is a good thing that there's no pain when the poor fellow's head flies off,*' *he remarked.*

"'*Do you know, though,*' *cried the prince warmly,* '*you made that remark now, and everyone says the same thing, and the machine is designed with the purpose of avoiding pain, this guillotine I mean; but a thought came into my head then: what if it be a bad plan after all? You may laugh at my idea, perhaps—but I could not help its occurring to me all the same. Now with the rack and tortures and so on—you suffer terrible pain of course; but then your torture is bodily pain only (although no doubt you have plenty of that) until you die. But* here *I should imagine the most terrible part of the whole punishment is, not the bodily pain at all—but the certain knowledge that in an hour,—then in ten minutes, then in half a minute, then now—this very* instant*—your* *soul must quit your body and that you will no longer be a man—and that this is certain, certain! That's the point—the certainty of it. Just that instant when you place your head on the block and hear the iron grate over your head—then—that quarter of a second is the most awful of all.*

"'*This is not my own fantastical opinion—many people have thought the same; but I feel it so deeply that I'll tell you what I think. I believe that to execute a man for murder is to punish him immeasurably more dreadfully than is equivalent to his crime. A murder by sentence is far more dreadful than a murder committed by a criminal. The man who is attacked by robbers at night, in a dark wood, or anywhere, undoubtedly hopes and hopes that he may yet escape until the very moment of his death. There are plenty of instances of a man running away, or imploring for mercy—at all events hoping on in some degree—even after his throat was cut. But in the case of an execution, that last hope—having which it is so immeasurably less dreadful to die,—is taken away from the wretch and certainty substituted in its place! There is his sentence, and with it that terrible certainty that he cannot possibly escape death—which, I consider, must be the most dreadful anguish in the world. You may place a soldier before a cannon's mouth in battle, and fire upon him —and he will still hope. But read to the same soldier his death-sentence, and he will either go mad or burst into tears. Who dares to say that any man can suffer this without going mad? No, no! it is an abuse, a shame, —it is unnecessary—why should such a thing exist? Doubtless there may be men who have been sentenced, who have suffered this mental anguish for a while and then have been reprieved; perhaps such men may have been able to relate their feelings afterwards. Our Lord Christ spoke of this anguish and dread. No! no! no! No man should be treated so, no man, no man!*'"

But I must add a few words about justice, for a lot of people genuinely fear that, with the abolition of capital punishment, justice is somehow impaired. Now our trouble about justice is that we tend to think of it as an entity in itself—as a god, a mumbo-jumbo to which we must bow down and sacrifice. But in fact there is no such thing as justice! there are human beings, and justice is a relation between them.

In what does doing justice to a man consist? In giving him his due. You give a fish its due by allowing it to live in water: you give an artist his due by encouraging him to paint his best pictures: and you give a man, any man, his due by fostering his power to realise, as completely as possible, his man-ness, his essential humanity. You cannot do that by killing him.

Or consider, not a single man, but all the members of a community. Justice is something that binds them together in a particular way: in such a way that everyone may develop to the limit of his human potentialities, but in such a way, also, that no one may interfere with the free development of another. At first, in the societies out of which our culture grew, people knew no better than to secure their individual freedom anarchically: if anyone interfered with or offended against them, they just killed him. Then came a first great advance, with the 'lex talionis': an eye, but no more than an eye, for an eye, a tooth, but no more than a tooth, for a tooth, a life for a life, but only for a life. That is the origin of judicial murder, or capital punishment.

But another great advance was to come: Christ came, into the race of the 'lex talionis', and explained what was wrong with that law. You can never get a positive adjustment between a number of individuals all born for freedom—you can never get a just society—by a mechanical squaring of accounts: you can get it only when people learn to give and to love—and once they have learned it they discover that the giving and loving is their own free development itself, as well as that of others. So you must forgive, unto seventy times seven: must love your enemies, including "the enemies of society": and must be perfect as your Father in heaven is perfect, for he maketh his sun to rise on the evil and on the good, and sendeth rain on the just and on the unjust.

And so, in the name of the only true justice, retaliation is abolished, and love takes its place. So—with every possible safeguard for the community by way of restraints on the criminal, but the most merciful that goodwill can devise—you say to him, "Go, and sin no more."

VIII

SALZBURG

THERE WAS A lady at Salzburg who used to model, with delightful freshness, I thought, simple-minded figurines of prancing horses, a slender young woman like a Botticelli Venus, etcetera etcetera. We bought three of them, and they are now on one of the shelves at Bottom House. So are half-a-dozen of those familiar coins, issued by Prince-Archbishops in the seventeenth century, that you could get at the shop called Sportlanz in Bismarck-Strasse, hard by Palmer's lingerie store.

§2

Our first Salzburg year was 1930, and we went every subsequent year till, and including, 1936.

Newest, most freshly delightful to us was the regular conjunction of music with those meals in the open air—or, if the open air has been impossible, by a window overlooking a pleasant expanse—that have been such a happiness to me all my life. I think of the restaurant on top of Danieli's, with tinges of green creeping over the water after the flaming of San Giorgio at sunset; of Valadier on the Pincio, with St Peter's and half Rome in the distance—one Christmas, it was so hot we had to move into the shade; and, better even than these, of lunch in the window of the Savoy on a blazing summer day, with the Festival Hall over in the distance beyond the leafy Embankment. (And yet the happiest of the Savoy ones was on a first day of spring, which happened to be my birthday. Two American friends sat in the sun there with Ruth and Livia and me: we had smoked salmon, asparagus from Lauris and strawberries from California, and drank champagne with the asparagus and Château Yquem with the strawberries and cream.) Then there were lunches at Ledoyen, with the chestnut-trees in blossom, and petrol smelling faintly, and the cars, smooth and muted, on their way to the Etoile or the Place de la Concorde; and a special sort of cheese, capped with cinnamon, that we ate one July afternoon at a window with another sort of prospect, the courtyard of the Hôtel de la Poste at Avallon.

But such occasions have been, and are, unconnected with music: at Salzburg they were all mixed up with it. During our whole seven years there we could not have lunched, dined or supped more than a dozen times or so indoors, and there was always music just before or just after our meals. We would lunch either on the terrace of the Österreichischer Hof or at a little inn near Aigen. In the earlier days, that is before the Toscanini time (when fashion deserted Estoril and irrupted into Salzburg), you could get an admirable *Suppe mit Huhn* at the Österreichischer Hof for an Austrian schilling, or possibly two, that is to say for about sevenpence or double: not *Huhnsuppe*, which is chicken soup, but *Suppe mit Huhn*, which is soup with a great piece of chicken in it, quite enough for an ample meal in itself. But we preferred the inn. This was fifteen minutes or so by car from Salzburg: an unpretentious little place, with an old-fashioned umbrella-stand in the vestibule. But it was not an ordinary inn: across the road it had an orchard, and there, also for a schilling or so, we used to lunch under the apples, or, a little deeper in, under the plums. Bruno Walter was often at a neighbouring table.

And then for dinner, or more usually supper, there was the Mirabell. It was at this end—at the end opposite the Schloss—of the Mirabell Gardens, and to the left of them; and its own garden (no one would have dreamed of dining or supping indoors except on dripping nights, which were rarities) was part of the larger one. Kasznár, the Hungarian proprietor, ran the place much as Mr Abel used to run the Ivy: slowly perambulating round the tables, he would nod to and even take a cup of coffee with the customers he preferred, and raise his eyebrows as he passed those he thought less of. The head waiter, who looked rather like Gobbi in the less sinister moments of *Tosca*, was in the habit of suggesting, with a hopeful inflexion, either paprika chicken or what he called paprika gooze: and he usually carried me with him, for I am ancestrally addicted to the *Salzgurken* that accompanies such dishes. (This is something very hard to get at English restaurants, even at the Savoy, though immediately obtainable in Soho or at any delicatessen; and if you do get it what they bring you, as often as not, is a mingy little affair, with none of the rich liquidity to it that is its whole meaning. The fact is that the English have never understood cucumbers, nor apparently the Italians either: I have been trying for years to make successive Pietros at the Savoy Grill prepare the things properly, but though they promise they never perform. For a good salad the slices have to be sprinkled with salt, left to lie for a couple of hours and then drained: the result is as different from the hard ungracious stuff you usually get as an egg to your tea is from an egg at breakfast.)

The Mirabell is associated for me with one of those magical visitations, as Shelley called them, that occur, if they occur at all, but once or twice in a lifetime. This was in 1932. Sigle Lynd was staying with us, and among others in Salzburg were Robert Nichols the poet and Dr Stella Churchill, our Jungian friend whom I greatly loved and who greatly loved me, until she quarrelled with me years later because she thought me wrong for not hating the Germans. I had arranged a supper party for the five of us one evening in Kasznár's garden after the performance, and had taken special pains with the menu, conferring with Kasznár himself, and inducing him to grant us a very special wine that I knew he possessed, Imperial Tokay he alleged, to sip with our sweet. The weather turned out to be almost tropically breathless, of the kind I had known in Singapore, and everyone had been more than usually happy all day: so that when we arrived at Kasznár's we were in tune with grace. Just as we had taken our places Bruno Walter, who had been conducting, came in, and I got up and went over to greet him. I do not remember for sure what he had been conducting, but it was almost certainly Mahler and probably *Das Lied von der Erde*, for it was this that he began talking about with the quiet homage he always accorded his master, and a look on his face as of a man seeing visions. He went on and on, standing there in his battered old raincoat, and people gradually got up and surrounded him, with Kasznár hovering about the empty tables; and such a paean of praise and devotion came singing from him—from musician to musician, from friend to friend—that time, and what divides human beings, were annihilated. Then we all went back to our places and had supper.

I can best describe what happened as we sat there in the words of Shelley himself:

"We are aware of evanescent visitations of thought and feeling, sometimes associated with place or person, sometimes regarding our own mind alone, and always arising unforeseen and departing unbidden, but elevating and delightful beyond all expression: so that even in the desire and regret they leave, there cannot but be pleasure, participating as it does in the nature of its object. It is as it were the interpenetration of a diviner nature through our own; but its footsteps are like those of a wind over the sea, which the coming calm erases, and whose traces remain only, as on the wrinkled sand which paves it. These and corresponding conditions of being are experienced principally by those of the most delicate sensibility and the most enlarged imagination; and the state of mind produced by them is at war with every base desire. The enthusiasm of virtue, love, patriotism, and friendship is essentially linked with such emotions; and whilst they last, self appears as what it is, an atom to a universe."

And there is a passage in Swedenborg's description of Unity in the dwelling-place of the Beatified:

"Heaven is so full of delight that, viewed in itself, it is nothing but blessedness and delight: for the Divine Good proceeding from the Lord's Divine Love constitutes heaven both in general and in particular with every one there; and Divine Love consists in desiring that all may be saved and made happy from their inmost being and in full perfection. So that it amounts to the same thing whether you say heaven or heavenly joy. . . .

"How great the delight of heaven is, may be seen from this fact alone, that it is delightful to all in heaven to share their delights and blessings with others; and since all in heaven are of this character, it is plain how immense is the delight of heaven; for in the heavens there is a participation of all with each and each with all. Such community of life results from the two heavenly loves which, as was said, are love to the Lord and to the neighbour, and it is the nature of these loves to communicate their delight to others. Love to the Lord is of this character because the Lord's love is the love of communicating all that He has to all mankind, for He desires the happiness of all. There is a similar love in every one who loves Him, because the Lord is in them; and so the angels share their delights with one another. That love to the neighbour is of a similar character will be seen in what follows. It is evident, therefore, that it is the nature of these loves to share their delights with others. . . ."

I ought to add that I think all five of us except my wife and myself were technically atheists.

Next morning we all got presents from Robert Nichols. Each of the girls got a rose: I got a copy of the paper-back of his poems I had published at Benn's. The writing on the front, which has become rather faint, is as follows: "To V.G. remembering his party Aug 16th 1932, Salzburg. 'Hush! hath not the world now become perfect? What hath happened to me?' Zarathustra. Noontide. Book IV (which is for the Initiates)." The passage from Nietzsche runs like this:

"And Zarathustra ran and ran, but he found no one else, and was alone and ever found himself again; he enjoyed and quaffed his solitude and thought of good things—for hours. About the hour of noontide, however, when the sun stood exactly over Zarathustra's head, he passed an old, bent and gnarled tree, which was encircled round by the ardent love of a vine, and hidden from itself; from this there hung yellow grapes in abundance, confronting the wanderer. Then he felt inclined to quench a little thirst, and to break off for himself a cluster of grapes. When, however, he had already his arm outstretched for that purpose, he felt still more inclined for something else—namely, to lie down beside the tree at the hour of perfect noontide and sleep.

"This Zarathustra did; and no sooner had he laid himself on the ground in the stillness and secrecy of the variegated grass, than he had forgotten his little thirst, and fell asleep. For as the proverb of Zarathustra saith: 'One thing is more necessary than the other'. Only that his eyes remained open—for they never grew weary of viewing and admiring the tree and the love of the vine. In falling asleep, however, Zarathustra spake thus to his heart: 'Hush! Hush! Hath not the world now become perfect? What hath happened unto me? . . .

"'O happiness! O happiness! Wilt thou perhaps sing, O my soul! Thou liest in the grass. But this is the secret, solemn hour, when no shepherd playeth his pipe.

"'Take care! Hot noontide sleepeth on the fields. Do not sing! Hush! The world is perfect. . . .

"'What hath befallen me: Hark! Hath time flown away? Do I not fall? Have I not fallen—hark! into the well of eternity?'"

§3

That year of our Salzburg visitation, 1932, is memorable to us for a second happening as full of horror as the first had been of grace. We had hired a car to take us home, and were idling a little at Munich to see a *Figaro* at the Residenz Theatre, a place almost as exquisitely rococo as the music itself. Strolling one afternoon to the *Alte Pinakothek* we passed the Brown House. Guards, with steel helmets and bayoneted rifles, were standing on the pavement; and as we hurried away I had a feeling of naked contact with bestiality such as I had never had before and have rarely had since, except when reading of executions. We left next morning, and stopped first at Rothenburg, loveliest of mediaeval cities; for we had been told that a clock-tower played a series of pretty melodies at midday there, and we wanted to hear them. Anxious to be home as soon as possible, we lunched on the pavement opposite at half-past eleven, so as to be off without a minute's delay when the performance was over; and were so hungry by the time we got to Stuttgart that we had a second lunch at the Hotel Marquardt. Back in England, I found the manuscript of Edgar

Mowrer's *Germany Puts the Clock Back* on my desk: I rejected it, as far-fetched and war-mongering. A few months later Hitler was in power.

§4

The previous year, 1931, had been equally full of adventure, not on our way back from Salzburg but on our way out there. I had heard that at the Villa d'Este on Lake Como you had all your meals by the waterside, dinner (with little candles) as well as lunch, and thought it would be a good idea to stay there for a week or so before going on to the Festival. But I did not like the atmosphere; the puritanism in me overcame my love of luxury. So we took a car to Verona, and again were deceived. It was high summer, there had been a drought for three months, and the heat was intolerable. Sitting at midnight in the amphitheatre at an open-air performance of *William Tell*, with a huge orchestra and a flock, equally huge, of bleating sheep, we sweated horribly; so we asked next morning whether a car might be available to take us to Meran, which we thought would be cooler. A racing motorist, who had broken the record in some contest or other the previous week, was glad to oblige us, and turned up with a very long and very low car that appeared to be made entirely of wood. Parts of the structure flew off half-way to Meran, and the driver had to turn back and recover them; but in spite of this he told us, when we arrived at the Meraner Hof, that he had broken his own record, and I was not at all surprised.

It was the dead season at Meran, and we were alone in the gigantic hotel. But the town was adorable—more beautiful, I thought, than any small place I had ever been in, except perhaps Bibury or Winchelsea. The day we had intended to spend there lengthened into a week and then into a fortnight. In the early morning, before breakfast, I would walk barefoot on the hotel lawn, to feel the dew between my toes. For lunch we would sit alone at a little table on the veranda. In the afternoon we wandered in the cool shade of the pines down the long Tappeiner Weg, or in the cobbled and arcaded streets; and at tea-time we paraded in the square for the town band, in the company of half Meran and (in patent-leather shoes) Sir Thomas Beecham. We would gladly have prolonged our stay there till winter, even at the cost of missing Salzburg. We did in fact miss three or four performances.

Once we had decided to be off I was in a frenzy (characteristic, I am told) of impatience. I kept urging the chauffeur to go faster, but he insisted on slowing down every time he approached a pair of railway lines, pointing, when I protested, to *Halt wenn ein Zug kommt!* We arrived late, rushed to the Festspielhaus without washing, and were allowed to stand at the back. Lotte Lehmann was singing 'ein sonderbar Ding' just as we got in. But the journey had been too much for my wife, who nearly fainted, and was given brandy in the women's cloakroom by one of the Sitzkissen girls.

§5

Music in the open air is even better than meals in the open air preceded or followed by music, and this is another of the pleasures I had been looking forward to when contemplating Salzburg. Parks—'the country' as I called them; for my father had a low opinion of the other kind and rarely took us there: "parks are good enough for me", he used to tell us—parks, and Hyde Park in particular, had initiated me into open-air music when I was six or seven: I would stand and listen to the band 'with the sweet and curious apprehensions of the world I had as a child', while the smell of cigar-smoke hung mingling with the summer heat.

The next thing in open-air music after Hyde Park was the White City; and since then my pleasure in it has never waned. The Embankment Gardens for a few minutes before lunch, with the Blue Danube just catching your ear as you approach the band-stand; *Otello* in the courtyard of the Doge's Palace; Berlioz's *Symphonie Funèbre et Triomphale* in Regent's Park, with the roses afterwards; the town band in the middle of the Piazza San Marco, maybe with a whole act from *Traviata* and an occasional rarity, something from *Le Villi* perhaps; chamber-music in the courtyard of the Pitti about the time of the flower-show; even strolling musicians, like the man who entertains me with a concertina every Sunday at lunch-time—they all please me, irrespective of quality in the music or skill in the performance: I just like the sound of pleasant noises in the open air, especially if it comes from a distance.

Then there are 'German bands' (now unhappily almost extinct); barrel-organs (the same applies); Salvation Army bands; and, as I heard once but once only, musical glasses: as well as casual noises of several kinds, such as the cloppity-clop of horses' hooves (ubiquitous in my boyhood and still to be heard most mornings in Eaton Place, when mounted soldiers ride down to some barracks); the whirring of a Bentley in Hyde Park; Cunard sirens both in harbour and at sea; and the puffing of smoke from the engine at the beginning of a railway journey.

Open-air music at Salzburg was deficient in quantity but superb in quality, for it consisted of Mozart serenades played by candlelight in the courtyard of the Prince-Archbishop's Palace at nine o'clock in the evening. The programmes were delightfully varied: we had quartets with the Mairecker people in 1935, and the Vienna Philharmonic, in such things as the Haffner serenade and the one in D major for two violins, viola, bass, two oboes, a bassoon, two horns and two trumpets in 1930.

I think that of all the concerts at Salzburg these were the ones I enjoyed most, though you could hardly call them concerts, you just sat there and assisted: I may even have enjoyed them more than those resplendent operas with the wonderful casts that were the principal raison d'être for our being there. I was about forty: and the tendency that had begun to develop in early manhood and was to end by making me even happier with the Schubert octet than with his 'great' symphony, and prize Beethoven above all for some of his trios and late quartets, was growing stronger and stronger in me.

Apart from the serenades, the only open-air music at Salzburg was an occasional performance of *Bastien and Bastienne* in the Mirabell Gardens with the Schloss as a background. But open-air talk about music, almost as good as the thing itself, was another matter; for we would often hang about the whole morning in the garden of the Café Bazar, to read the notices of last night's performance or look out for celebrities or gossip with friends.

Stephen Spender might be there, eager and handsome (he was writing or had just written *Forward from Liberalism*); so might Toscanini's brother, at sight of whom my daughter Diana, about twelve at the time and just learning about *café complet*, used to mutter "Maestro brother complete"; or Clemens Krauss, who 'mixed' more than any other of the conductors except perhaps Bruno Walter; or Madame Sukerkandel, who invariably asked us whether we didn't think it had been a wonderful performation; or Madame Homburg, in a pink linen costume and wearing a huge floppy hat, who was in the habit of crying at Mozart's Mass in C minor.

For the rest, there would be St Gilgen to visit, our favourite excursion; or St Wolfgang, with the Michael Pacher altar-piece; or one of the more distant lakes. It was near one of these that we encountered our shepherd. He was sitting by the roadside and put his hand up as we passed, so we stopped and told him to get in. He had never been in a car before, and asked me innumerable questions about how it worked, which I could not have answered even if I had fully understood him; and he giggled all the way, and more than giggled when, to his enquiry as to where we lived, I replied 'London'. You might have judged from his paroxysms of laughter either that he placed it on the other side of the moon or that he thought I was lying.

Another special delight at Salzburg was music at eleven in the morning. Can there be anything more like heaven than this? Your proper business, all at once, is to be a cherub and hear the angels quiring: at the very moment when at ordinary seasons the muddy vesture of decay—working out costs, drafting advertisements, etcetera—doth most grossly close you in. For now 'love's a duty'. I have always felt like this at the Edinburgh festival, to which, I must shamefacedly confess, my general attitude has been rather mixed: the theatre is so inadequate, the weather usually so dreadful (not only by rumour but in fact), the beauty of Prince's Street and its public gardens so wretchedly diminished by all that belching smoke; but on the other hand the hospitality is so warm-hearted and the generosity of the Scots as a people so overwhelming. But for one thing I have always been grateful, even on the wettest and smokiest days: namely for the concerts at Freemason's Hall—the Archduke, the *Geister*!—at that same improper hour of eleven in the morning. Materially improper, I mean: it is indeed its impropriety in the material sense that gives it a supreme propriety in the spiritual one.

§6

For seven years in succession we went to Salzburg, as I have said, but the seventh, 1936 (memorable for the production of Hugo Wolf's exquisite concert-opera *Der Corregidor*), came abruptly to an end. On our first visit we had put up at the Bristol, but had soon moved to the more spacious Österreichischer Hof. We had a magnificent bedroom on the first floor, with great windows looking on to Hohen-Salzburg, and my wife would paint there in the late afternoon while I lay on a sofa in the bay reading a detective story. The general atmosphere had been rather worrying us for some time: Sigle Lynd, for instance, had been invited to a reception by local bigwigs, and had been asked to bring along anyone "except Jews". As Isaiah Berlin was of her party she declined—but of course she would have declined, if given that proviso, anyhow.

But now, in 1936, things seemed tenser, for already, before the Anschluss, Austria had been declared a German State. It was either this year or the previous one that we went to some performance at the little Stadttheater, and felt horrified when Prince Starhemberg arrived with a large body of storm-troopers, who occupied the place till he left.

After a week or so of our 1936 visit my wife began to look tired, and to nod during performances. She shook her head when I asked whether she felt ill, but when I insisted she came out with it. An anti-nazi had just been smuggled out of Prague and murdered: I was by then a prominent anti-nazi: Salzburg was on the German frontier: our bedroom door was never locked (I am slightly claustrophobic): and might not someone break in when I was asleep and kidnap me? So she at least would not be caught unawares: she would keep awake all night and take care of me.

Of course we left three or four days later, and have never been back, for from what I hear we should not greatly care for the Festival nowadays. It turned out afterwards that a prominent employee of a leading Salzburg hotel was one of the top Austrian Nazis, so my wife's fears had not been unjustified.

§7

I often ask myself: what, next to Mozart, does Salzburg above all mean to me thirty years later? And I always reply in the end, after rejecting this or that, the Toscanini *Meistersinger*.

The twenties and thirties had already been, and even apart from Salzburg were still to be, a great *Meistersinger* time for us: I doubt whether, during the period in question, we missed more than half-a-dozen Covent Garden performances, and those we heard were of the quality that makes one reluctant to criticise occasional defects. Bruno Walter conducted mostly till about 1932, and then Beecham. Both were peculiarly fitted by temperament to give exceptional renderings of the score, Walter a beautifully flowing and gracious and Beecham an immensely exciting one.

So we were particularly expectant when *Die Meistersinger* was announced for Salzburg. Would the London performances be surpassed, almost impossible though that might seem? How would Toscanini compare with Walter? With Beecham? We must have been optimistic in the way we answered ourselves, for we booked for the whole series of performances that were to be given during our visit.

I do not recollect what year it was: I do not recollect the cast, even to the extent of a single name, though I suspect that Lotte Lehmann sang Eva: I remember only that the second act was so beautiful in the inevitability of its orchestral flow, so ravishing in its combination of countless felicities with unity of texture, that never, I thought, had I heard anything like it in a symphonic piece of that length. I still think that my judgment was a sober one.

We went to the whole of only the first of the performances we had booked for: in the case of the others we arrived for the second act and left at the end of it. The reason was that we wanted our ears to be absolutely fresh for the beginning of that symphonic marvel, and were equally anxious that the impression should remain undisturbed when it was over. Eccentric, no doubt: but as a result we had a musical experience almost certainly unique.

VIII

ASSISI · PERUGIA · NAPLES

IT WAS ON a comparatively recent visit to Assisi that we bought the Donkey of God, which now lies on one of the shelves at B.H., surrounded by other animals of similar manufacture. These latter we came upon late one June, together with quite a collection of Aesopian tiles, on the burning sea road near Salerno.

I am heretical about Assisi. I 'like' it, of course; but St Francis is not there for me, and without St Francis it is no more than rather commonplacely charming—less charming than for instance Burford, which it somehow reminds me of (I carry about with me the vivid but erroneous impression that both are places you enter through an actual gate, a massive and lofty one). Even the Giottos in the Basilica mean, in recollection, very little to me. I have been to Assisi several times (and shall go again, I am sure), but have always come away disappointed.

My very love for St Francis may be the reason. I love him in the way one loves a living friend one is constantly seeing: and perhaps in a steadier way, because with ordinary daily friends there are apt to be occasional frictions, whereas when the other is materially dead nothing can ever happen to disturb the relationship, even for the briefest of moments. And he is not only the most lovable of men for me, he is also the sanest: saner, that is, among those I have any knowledge of, than anyone except his master, Jesus of Galilee. By this I mean that my image of him, true or false, is of a man for whom nothing made sense, in the context of human relationships, but fellow-feeling, compassion, love.

Why, then, have I always failed to feel his presence in the streets, churches and squares of Assisi, as I once felt Beethoven's in Grinzing? I was strolling about on that occasion while my wife sat painting in the courtyard of Probusgasse 6, where he wrote the Testament; and a peace as of the Elysian Fields arose quietly to welcome me—Beethoven's peace, for inner peace was as surely essential an element in his make-up as inner and outer turbulence, or the agony he reveals in the Testament itself. I felt the same when, a few years later, we were walking by the little stream, now dried up (or it was, on the day we went there), that partly inspired the sixth symphony. I do not mean merely that I was remembering, merely that the *bächlein* was recalling the symphony to me: I mean that Beethoven was walking beside me. This must sound extravagant, but I am to be believed when I say that I am describing, with all the scrupulousness I can master, the exact sensation that came to me—and always will come to me, I am certain, in that part of Vienna.

I have often asked myself why there should be this difference—between St Francis and Assisi on the one hand, and Beethoven and Vienna on the other. It cannot be a question of reminders: there is if anything more in Assisi to remind one of St Francis—the Basilica, Santa Chiara, Santa Maria degli Angeli, and much besides—than there is in Grinzing to remind one of Beethoven. Nor can it be a question of relative dates, of erasure by time, for in the matter of spiritual persistence a few hundred years are as nothing: and if it is true that Grinzing is beautifully deserted in the sunshine of a summer morning, whereas Assisi is always packed with ruthless tourists, I doubt whether I should have felt any differently at the brook if it had been flanked by a grisly cavalcade of quasi-Greenline buses.

The fact, anyhow, is as I have said. St Francis does not walk with me in Assisi: he comes closer to me in Laurence Housman's 'Little Plays', mawkish though some of them are, than even in the Porziuncola or the Cappella del Transito, where his heart is. In his birthplace, in the city of his compassion, he is little more to me than a very famous and very attractive historical figure: and I feel an outsider, bereaved.

By a curious quirk, as a matter of fact, my vividest memory of Assisi derives from a Hebrew, not a Franciscan, consciousness, and has to do with a room in a modern hotel: the dining-room in the Hotel Subasio, hard by the Basilica. This, the dining-room, was a walled-in terrace on the piano mobile: overhead, for roof, strands of creeper had been trailed over a lattice, through the interstices of which you could see the sky: and beyond, as you sat and ate your lunch by a low parapet, lay the vastness of the Umbrian plain. I glanced up as we entered (this was the first of our visits, in the late twenties or early thirties) and suddenly I was a schoolboy again: I was in a succah.

I have described elsewhere how little to my taste were the Jewish practices I was brought up in, and particularly those of Kippur, the Day of Atonement. But Tabernacles was an exception: it always transported me. For a week—actually for a little longer, but that is a refinement I need not go into—we 'dwelt in booths': so obeying the Levitical commandment "Also in the fifteenth day of the seventh month, when ye have gathered in the fruit of the land, ye shall keep a feast unto the Lord seven days: on the first day shall be a sabbath, and on the eighth day shall be a sabbath. And ye shall take you on the first day the fruit of the tree Hadar [a citron, emblem of sweetness and beauty], branches of palm trees [symbol of majesty], a bough of the tree Aboth [myrtle, evergreen and abundant], and willows of the brook [with their cool and refreshing graciousness]; and ye shall rejoice before the Lord your God seven days. And ye shall keep it a feast unto the Lord seven days in the year. It shall be a statute for ever in your generations: ye shall celebrate it in the seventh month. Ye shall dwell in booths seven days; all that are Israelites born shall dwell in booths: that your generation may know that I made the children of Israel to dwell in booths, when I brought them out of the land of Egypt: I am the Lord your God."

Thus what was originally, no doubt, a purely agricultural celebration received an added significance: a festival of Ingathering became also a festival of freedom. And because freedom and ingathering are what, above all, make the natural man happy, it was called, uniquely (in spite even of Passover), the Festival of our Joy.

This is how we 'dwelt in booths'. The moment Kippur was over—this immediacy, the Talmud comments, was to signify that, under the Mercy, bygones were bygones—the work of construction began. Three imperatives governed it: the booth must be designed—a balcony or back yard might be the basis of it—for temporary use only: there must be more shade than light in it: and part of it must be open to the sky. As to its furnishings, for so you might call them, fruits of every kind—I remember cape gooseberries in particular—were hung about with ritual lavishness; the roofing was thick with branches and leaves; and no square inch, if there was any way of covering it, must be left bare. Unaccountably, for my father was orthodox, we never had a succah of our own: but I would drop in as often as possible on friends and relatives in the neighbourhood, and the greenery, the fragrance and the festal profusion were always a happiness to my spirit and senses.

But the succah was only half, so to say, of the festival of Tabernacles: and my father, who forewent it, as I have said, could never have contemplated foregoing the other and equally important half. After all, you could borrow your neighbour's succah, but not his citron and palm branch. Indeed my father was particularly fussy about his citron: he would examine it with meticulous care to make certain that it was 'unblemished', and, above all, that a remnant of the stalk by which it had depended was still intact. (Our lawgivers were fanatical about 'blemishes': I quite recently saw an ultraorthodox rabbi saluting my wife in the Hitler fashion instead of shaking her by the hand, his fear being, I was told later, that like Sarah she might still be suffering her monthly uncleannesses and might be suffering one of them—how could one know?—at that particular moment.)

The palm branch, with myrtle and willow attached to its base, was for waving and shaking at various times during the festival; and the citron was for smelling as you did so. You waved and shook in all directions, and up and down: by way of demonstrating, to yourself and others, that God was everywhere. If I remember aright (and I confess that as I grow older I remember aright far less often than formerly), the festival more or less ended with a procession of elders round the synagogue, waving and shaking their palm branches: as it had begun, a week before, with the following prayer, or meditation, in the succah:

"May it be thy will, O Lord my God and God of my fathers, to let thy divine presence abide among us: spread over us the tabernacle of thy peace. O surround us with the pure and holy radiance of thy glory, that is spread over our heads as the eagle over the nest he stirreth up: and thence bid the stream of life flow in upon thy servant. O wash me thoroughly from mine iniquity, and cleanse me from my sin. Keep me in life, O Lord; vouchsafe unto me the abundance of thy blessings; and to such as are hungry and thirsty give bread and water unfailingly. Make me worthy to dwell trustingly in the covert of thy shadowing wings at the time when I part from the world. O deal graciously with us in the decree to which thou settest thy seal, and make us worthy to dwell many days upon the land, the holy land, ever serving and fearing thee. Blessed be the Lord for ever. Amen and Amen.

"Blessed art thou, O Lord our God, King of the Universe, who hast sanctified us by thy commandments, and hast commanded us to dwell in the Tabernacle.

"Blessed art thou, O Lord our God, King of the universe, who hast kept us in life, and hast preserved us, and enabled us to reach this season."*

It is a long way, in space and time, from desert booths to our Donkey of God, which I must now return to. I had thought, before starting this chapter, that those pottery donkeys you were always coming upon in the souvenir shops of Assisi, mixed up higgledy-piggledy, with other animals but in greater profusion than the rest, were traditionally called Donkeys of God by way of commemorating some local or Franciscan legend. But if I have now got things right, this is not so. They have never been called Donkeys of God: they are quite ordinary donkeys, and if you see them more often in Assisi than anywhere else (itself perhaps an illusion) this may be because the donkey as such is the most Franciscan of creatures, if one may dare to differentiate. There is indeed a legend, but it is only a few decades old, having been invented by the American poet Louis Untermeyer after a visit to Assisi. But whatever its origin I like it immensely and shall

* This is the blessing, prescribed for all specially joyful occasions, which is printed in Hebrew immediately after the title page of this book.

reprint it here with Mr Untermeyer's kind permission: well aware that many will call it sentimental, for this, with 'unrealistic', 'unpractical', 'hard-headed' and the like, is one of the worst-treated adjectives in the language. If, for instance, you abjure tit-for-tat, and try to succour your enemy, you are called sentimental, while you are really behaving with the starkest realism: and if you decide to hang a man by the neck until he be dead, after keeping him in an agony of expectation till twenty-one days have elapsed, you are called hard-headed, while you are really behaving like a criminal lunatic. To be sentimental, in the proper meaning of the word, is to be facile and shallow in your emotional responses: but what is commonly called sentimental in a piece of writing is as often as not a basic simplicity of feeling, invention or expression, which comes, not from the shallows, but from the depths. Anyhow, here is Untermeyer's story: react to it as you will.

One day as he [St Francis] was walking among the ruins of monuments as old as the stone-age, he noticed he had gone farther than usual and was straying in a circle of queer structures that the natives called "Fairy Houses." He smiled as he thought of the fear the peasants had of these stone-chambers and the superstition that anyone resting within the circle would "dream true". He noticed a donkey standing in the shade of a stunted tree, but it did not appear in the least astonished to see him. Now that he observed it closer, he could not remember ever having seen a donkey so small. It was no larger than a large dog, a sheep-dog with unusually long ears. Its ankles were more delicate than a deer's and the eyes had a speaking softness. But the most peculiar feature was revealed to Francis only when he stood close. The colour was a soft pigeon-grey without a spot except for one distinguishing mark: a pattern made by two intersecting lines of black, one line running down the back from head to tail, the other line running across the shoulders. Presently, Francis noticed that the animal was speaking to him and he was aware that he understood it.

"Tell me, my good man," it was saying, "for I can see you are good, is there no justice in creation? Isn't it bad enough that we donkeys have to carry every sort of burden—twice as much as the much larger horse—without also being a joke among men and animals? Is that just?

And if that were not enough, why should we be made still more foolish by having to wear such a disfiguring pattern on our back? Can you answer that?"

To his surprise, Francis heard himself replying to the little donkey as if he were a priest and it were one of his flock.

"Yes, my daughter, I think I can. There is a justice in all things, though we cannot see it at once. We must wait until the pattern is completed before we judge any of its parts. In your case the answer is easier than most, for you are the donkey of God."

"The donkey of God?" asked the little animal.

"Surely," replied Francis, amazed at the way he was talking, but keeping on in an even voice. "If you do not know your own story, I will tell it to you."

And Francis, who had never seen the creature before, and who certainly had never thought of its origin, heard himself telling this strange legend:

It was the morning of the Sixth Day. God had spent the First Day inventing Light. Then, seeing that continual light would be too cruel on the eyes, He made Darkness for relief. On the Second Day God had designed the seas and had put a clear border of sky about them to prevent the waters from overflowing. On the Third Day, being dissatisfied with the emptiness of a world of water, He had gathered the waters in one place and had put dry land carefully among the seas. He called the dry land Earth and liked it much better, especially after He had caused green things to grow and had planned fruit to come after the flower. He had told Himself it was good. On the Fourth Day God had looked at the widespread Heaven and realised it needed something. So He had put lights in it: a great gold light to rule the day, and a soft silver one to rule the night, and a lot of lesser lights to decorate the evening. And once more He had been pleased. On the Fifth Day He decided He wanted more motion and sound in the universe. So He had filled the waters with whales and minnows and the air with insects and eagles. He had smiled when the first whale, that island afloat, had blown his first spout, and His great heart had tightened when the lark, hoping to reach heaven, sang his first song.

And now it was the Sixth Day. The earth, God saw, needed life no less than the sea and sky. So early in the morning He began making animals. First He made small simple ones: the snake and the snail, the mouse and the mole, rat and rabbit, cat and dog, lamb and wolf, goat, mink, fox, hedge-hog, beaver, woodchuck and a hundred others, each after his kind. Then, watching them leap or crawl or dig or prowl, He tried the same design on an ever-growing scale. It was then He made donkey and deer, horse and cattle, lion and tiger, bear, buffalo, elk, the great apes, the giant lizards, the mammoths like mountains on the move. Then God, out of the humour of His heart, indulged himself in a few experiments. He made the giraffe with his feet in the mud, his long neck lost in the leaves, and his silly head trying to scrape the stars. He tied a bird and a snake together and made the ostrich. He took a lump of clay, shaped it, unshaped it, dug His thumb twice into it and threw it away—and that was the camel. He thought of a hill-side with a tiny tail and nose-arm-fingers in one long trunk—and thus the elephant was made. He took some river-mud, breathed on it, changed His mind, saying, "No animal that looked like that would want to live"—and it was the hippopotamus. When He saw these absurd shapes strut about, He laughed so long that the stars began to fall from their places—some of them are still so loose that they tremble in the sky—and, for a while, He did nothing at all.

But since He was God, He could not stop creating. So in the afternoon He looked at everything and said, "It is good." After a little while He added, "But it could be better. It lacks something."

All afternoon He sat pondering among the clouds. At last, toward evening, He said, "It is not enough like Me. I will take the very best soil from the earth, for this will be an earth-creature. I will mix it with water so he need not be afraid of the sea. I will knead it with air so he can trust himself in any element and even fly if he wishes. I will then put a spark of Myself deep in him so he may be God-like. And it will be Man."

When the animals heard this they began arguing with God. "Consider, O Lord," said the lion in his gentlest, most persuasive roar. He was already known as the king of beasts, so he spoke first. "Consider, O Lord, before You breathe life into the creature. If You make him of the elements, he will be master not only of them, but of us all."

"Yes," said the elephant with a gruff simplicity, "such an animal as Man will do no labour at all. He'll say he's not made for it, and we'll have to do his work for him."

"Not that we mind, Lord," hissed the serpent with false meekness. "But if You put Your spark in him, he'll think he's divine. And after he's mastered us—not that *we* mind—he'll try to master what created him. And then—"

"And then," said God in the still small voice which was more terrible than thunder, "he will be part of Me again. Meanwhile, I have no need of advice from My own creations."

And so He made Man.

You are wondering, I see, what had become of the donkey. Up to now he had done nothing but listen and mind his own affairs. While the others were arguing with God or grumbling among themselves, the donkey calmly went on eating rose-leaves and lettuces and growing lovelier every minute. Perhaps I should have told you that he had been born the most perfect of four-footed creatures. He was very much like the donkeys of today except that his colour was softer, his eyes more tender, his ankles even more graceful—and, at that time, the long ears of his great-great-grandchildren did not disfigure his head. Instead of the grotesque flapping sails of the donkey of today, the original donkey had two of the finest, most perfectly shaped ears you can imagine. They were like those of a dainty fox, only smaller, and so wax-like that you could half see through them. Everything satisfied him; he feared nothing; the world was good. So he continued to munch lettuces and rose-leaves.

The donkey was so busy eating—it was at the beautiful beginning of things when there were no worms in the lettuces nor thorns on the roses—that he did not see God make the first man. Nor did he see Him, late in the night, creating the first woman. The next morning—it was Sunday—the other animals told him about it and said the man-animal was called Adam and the woman-animal was called Eve. A little tired of doing nothing but eating, the donkey joined the other beasts and peered into the garden where the two newest-born creatures were sitting. When he saw them he burst into the loudest and most ridiculous laugh on earth. It was like no sound that had ever been made; it was the first wild, weird, astonishing bray. Today only the smallest echoes are in the throat of all the donkeys, but then it rang so fiercely against the skies that it almost threw the fixed stars out of their courses.

"Ho-hee-haw!" screamed the donkey. "It is *too* funny! *Such* animals! They're made all wrong! No hide! No hoofs! Not even a tail! And so pink—so *naked*! God must have meant to put a coat of fleece on them and forgot it! Ho-hee-*haw*!"

Eve, frightened by the screaming and screeching, ran into the woods. Adam sprang to his feet.

"And look!" the donkey brayed in a still ruder laugh, while the other beasts roared and cackled and barked. "Look! The she-man runs on her hind legs! She doesn't even know how to walk! Ho-ho—hee—haw hee—HAW!"

This was too much for Adam. He ran over to the donkey and grasped him by the ears. The donkey tried to pull himself free, but Adam held fast. As he tugged and Adam tightened, his ears began to stretch, grow long, longer. . . . And while they were pulling God suddenly appeared.

Said the Lord, "Because you have spoiled My day of rest and because you have made fun of My creation you shall be punished. Because you saw fit to laugh at your betters, you shall never cease from laughing. But no one will listen with joy; your voice will be a mockery by day and a horror by night. The louder you laugh, the longer will you be despised. You shall serve man and be subject to him all the days of your life. Other animals shall serve him also: the horse, the cow, the elephant and the dog. But, unlike them, you shall work for man without winning his love. Unlike them, you shall resist him foolishly, and he shall beat you for it. You who are the most comely of My creatures shall be the most comic. Instead of roses you shall feed on thorns and thistles. You shall have a rope for a tail. And your ears shall remain long."

So it was decreed. And so it turned out. When Adam and Eve were forced to leave the Garden and go to work, the donkey went with them. Adam rode on the horse, the dog trotted at Eve's side, but it was the donkey who carried the tools, the spinning-wheel and all the household machinery. Throughout Adam's life the donkey was reminded of the saying about laughing last instead of first. Sometimes he was ashamed and dropped his long ears like a lop-eared rabbit; sometimes his pride came back and he refused to take another step. At such times Adam beat him and the donkey remembered the Lord's prophecy. He wondered how long the burdens would be piled upon him.

After Adam died the donkey thought things would go easier, but he soon realised his hardships were only beginning. He belonged, he discovered, not to one man but to all men. Cain, the brutal son of

Adam, broke him to harness and made him drag a heavy plough. When Noah built the ark the donkey carried more timber than the elephant, but no one praised him for it. Forty days and forty nights the floating menagerie breasted the flood, and every day and most of the nights the other animals jeered and mocked him. He knew now what it was to be laughed at. And when the windows of heaven were closed and the fountains of the flood went back into the heart of the sea, the donkey walked the earth again with meek eyes and bowed head. From that time on he swore to serve man faithfully and ask no reward.

At the building of Babel, the donkey was there, working willingly although he knew no tower built by hands would ever reach Heaven. After the city was deserted, the donkey helped Abraham with his flocks, and carried for Isaac, and wandered with Jacob. So, through Bible times, the donkey remained loyal to his masters. He brought Joseph and his twelve brothers together; he dragged bricks for the Hebrews during their long slavery in Egypt; he crossed the Red Sea with Moses; he was beaten for trying to save the wizard Balaam; he entered Canaan with Joshua.

He worked; he wandered; he did not die.

Years passed; centuries vanished. The donkey was in Palestine. His master was a carpenter in the little town of Nazareth, a good master by the name of Joseph, though far different from the Joseph who had become a ruler in the land of Egypt. He had worked for him a long time, and he had served his owner well. A few years ago, when Joseph and his wife Mary were on their wanderings, the little donkey carried them everywhere without complaining. They were terribly poor and innkeepers had no room for them. The donkey trudged on, carrying his load that seemed to grow heavier with each step. For a long day and a longer night, he plodded toward the distant haven, never stopping or stumbling till he brought them to the little town of Bethlehem. That night, in a cattle-stall, Mary's child had been born.

The donkey obeyed his master, but he worshipped his master's small son. The child was not only beautiful, but even as perfect as he seemed to his mother. Goodness shone from his eyes; miracles, they said, flowed from his hands. The donkey believed it, for he had seen one performed.

Once, when playing with some other children in the streets of Nazareth, the carpenter's son picked up some clay from the gutter and kneaded it into a shape. His companions gathered around to watch him.

"Good," said Simon, "let's all do it. What shall we model?"

"Let's make horses," cried Zadoc, the son of the priest. "When I grow up I'm going to have six horses of my own—two white ones, two black ones and two horses with many-coloured coats."

"Stupid!" said Azor, the broom-maker's child. "There are no horses with many-coloured coats. Besides, horses are too hard to model. Let's make pigeons."

So they started to make pigeons of clay. After a while Zadoc called out, "I've made seven. How many have the rest of you?"

"Five," said Zithri, the beggar's boy.

"Four," said Simon.

"Three," said Azor.

"Two," said Jesus, who was the carpenter's son.

"Only two!" sneered Zadoc. "And not even good ones. Mine look much more like pigeons than yours!"

"You are right," said Jesus and he tossed his aside. But though the clay pigeons were thrown, they did not fall to the ground. Instead, they hung in the air, spread wings and flew away.

The other children stared for a moment and then grew angry. "He's playing tricks on us!" cried Zadoc, son of the priest. "Let's play a trick on him!" The others joined Zadoc and soon they had tied the little Jesus tightly. The cord bit deep into his wrists but he did not cry.

"He's just making believe he's brave," said Zadoc. "He acts as if he were a king."

"All right," jeered Azor. "Let him be king."

"I'll get him a crown," shouted Zithri.

They pulled down part of a withered rose-tree and twisted two small branches into a crown. They pressed this upon his forehead and cried, "King Jesus! Hail to King Jesus!" Then they ran away laughing, while tears stood in the eyes of the carpenter's son.

The donkey had seen it all, had seen that the hands of Jesus were still tied and that the child could not remove the crown of thorns. Then he nuzzled his soft nose along the child's shoulder, raised his head and, though the thorns stabbed his lips, lifted the piercing weight from Jesus' forehead. He tugged at the cords till he freed the child's hands; then he carried him home.

More years passed. Jesus had gone away. Though the donkey did not know it, the carpenter's son had grown from childhood to manhood, had travelled and studied, had healed the sick, restored eyesight to the

Mansell-Alinari

LA MADONNA DEL PARTO

Mansell-Anderso

SANTA MARIA DELLA CONSOLAZIONE

blind, cast out devils, had suffered untold hardships. But now the moment had come; Jesus was to enter Jerusalem in triumph.

It was a tremendous moment; one that must be celebrated in the proper manner. Naturally, Jesus could not enter the queen-city of Palestine on foot; he must ride, they said, on a charger worthy of the event. So the Archangel Michael called all the animals before Jesus that they might plead their case.

"Choose me," said the lion. "I am king of the beasts; you are a king among men. Men respect royalty—but only when they recognise it! When the people of Jerusalem see you riding on my back, they will know you are of noble blood and they will bow down and fear you. With me as your mascot, they will never dare oppose, but follow you in terror."

"Choose me," said the eagle. "I am lord of the upper air. Choose me and you will have power to leave the earth and fly on the very back of the wind. I will take you to the borders of the sky; there, from heights unknown to man, you shall see everything that happens below. When you enter Jerusalem flying between my strong wings, the people will believe you are a god and they will worship."

"Choose me," said the mole. "I go where the eagle is helpless and the lion cannot follow. Choose me and I will give you the keys of earth. I will guide you to the roots of power, to secrets buried beneath the stones. I know where every vein of gold is hidden; my home is among caves of rubies, hills of emerald, ledges of pure diamond. Choose me and you will be greater than the greatest; you will be able to buy empires; you will not only be a king, but King of kings."

"The great ones laugh at treasures," whispered the fox. "Who but a fool desires gold and glittering pebbles that turn men against each other with greed and jealousy? Choose me and I will give you cunning. I will show you how to outwit all men and overcome your enemies with shrewdness. Choose me and I will teach you cleverness that is better than wealth and craft that is stronger than strength."

"Craft!" trumpeted the elephant. "Craft and cunning are for knaves who will never be wise. Choose me and I will give you true wisdom. I am the oldest of living creatures; my years span a century and I have watched the comings and goings of all the races. Choose me and you will rule the changing mind of the unchanging world."

"Choose me," lowed the cow. "I am sacred. India and Egypt worship me. I feed the world."

"Choose me," bellowed the dragon. "I will spread fire before you and magic wherever you go."

"Choose me!" neighed the horse. "I am swift as rage. The glory of my nostrils is terrible to the enemy. I swallow the ground; I laugh at fear."

"Choose me!" screamed the camel. "Choose me! Choose me!' cried all the animals separately and in chorus. Only the donkey was silent.

"And what can you give?" asked Jesus, speaking for the first time and turning to the dusty little fellow. "What have you to promise?"

"Nothing," murmured the donkey. "Nothing. I am the lowest of all God's creatures and the least."

But Jesus remembered. "The lowest shall be lifted up," he said, "and the last shall be first."

And so the meekest of men chose the meekest of animals. And they entered Jerusalem together.

But the great moment passed. Proud Jerusalem sneered at the carpenter's son even as it had stoned the prophets before him, and only a handful of poor folk listened to his words. He was despised and rejected. The people turned against him. He was imprisoned on a false charge and condemned to death. They put a crown of thorns upon his head, mocked him and made him carry his own cross.

It was while Jesus was struggling up the hill that the donkey saw him for the last time. Their sad eyes met.

"No," said Jesus. "You cannot help me now. Yet, since you have done more for me than have most men, you shall be rewarded. I cannot undo what God has done; what He has ordained must be carried out. But I can soften His decree. True, you will have to fetch and carry and feed on thorns. Yet these things will never again be hard for you. Because you carried me three times, so shall you be able to carry three times as much as animals thrice your size—and your load will seem lighter than theirs. You suffered thorns for my sake; so shall you be nourished when others can find nothing to feed on. You shall eat the thorns and nettles of the field—and they shall taste like sweet salads. You bore me when I grew to manhood, when I was a child, and even my mother before I was born. So shall you bear my cross—but you shall bear it without pain. Here—!" And as Jesus touched the shoulders of the donkey, a velvet-black cross appeared on the back of the kneeling animal.

And Jesus, shouldering his burden, climbed up Calvary . . .

Francis heard the last syllable leave his lips in a kind of wonder. His tiredness had gone: everything in him was full of strength. He was surprised to see that the sun had set and that a little horned moon had come into the sky, one horn pointing to Assisi. He thought he understood the sign. When he turned back, the donkey had disappeared. The field was dark. But a light greater than the moon's was on Francis' face.

§2

To Assisi, for all that it meant to me historically if not personally, I far prefer neighbouring Perugia: I like it, indeed, or did, more than any other Italian city except Venice, though in the twenties and early thirties I should have put Florence first. After a couple of exploratory days we have been there twice, the second time, about six years ago, with John and Diana Collins; and on both occasions we stayed more than a fortnight. Our hotel *patron* thought us a bit eccentric or even m'shuggah, or that is the impression he gave me: "A fortnight?" he exclaimed, when on the earlier occasion we told him what we intended. "No one ever stays more than a week: a couple of days is more usual." As he saw us off a fortnight later he murmured something about Lord Bristol, which, in view of his comparative youth, I did not fully comprehend. The waiters at dinner began treating us as one of themselves. "Hyenas!" cried our own *chef de rang* one evening at dinner as a party of English-speaking tourists erupted from a transcontinental bus. "They are ruining us." And indeed a peace you felt natural to the place was already, on certain days and at certain hours, beginning to vanish.

The fact is that, even in our heyday, we were never great sight-seers. We have seen most of the sights in most of the obvious places, of course: but what we have really liked most, from the very beginning, is just living in a foreign city as if we were living at home, but carelessly and with infinite leisure. Now Perugia is as good as anywhere in the world for this purpose. Unless you are a devoted student of art, and not merely a lover of it, you soon exhaust the picture gallery even if you have a special liking for Perugino and his school (but Bonfigli is wonderful): and though there are several buildings of beauty and interest, you can 'do' them in the *patron*'s couple of days. But you could walk about the place, and not get tired of it, for far more than a fortnight, for months. The variety of levels, which is for ever giving you sudden glimpses of the unexpected, never fails to send you home with a feeling of satisfied excitement, quiet though your strolling has been: and you are constantly happening on some new vista of the vast Umbrian plain.

It was partly the plain that made us put up at Brufani's, the other reason being that I fancied I had heard my Aunt Minna, the travelled one, make some mention of it in my grandmother's drawing-room in Elm Tree Road. Its atmosphere was Victorian (and this we both like), and it was exceedingly comfortable in its old-fashioned way: but above all our bedroom, on both occasions, looked out over the Umbrian plain. Little lights with great distances between them—monastery lights, I remember thinking—came out for us by night as we watched from our window before getting into bed.

We always dined at Brufani's, but preferred to lunch in the open-air courtyard of the Rosetta, with coloured umbrellas to protect us from the sun. There must have been many other restaurants scattered about; but with the innate conservatism that has always characterised me, we stuck to, and were happy with, the Rosetta and Brufani's day after day.

Best of all for us was the afternoon parade in the Corso Vannucci. This, the main thoroughfare, was always closed to vehicular traffic from tea-time onwards: whereupon the young people would start strolling up and down in the road, while their elders took tea on the pavements. Ourselves, on most afternoons, we strolled with the young, and felt very close to them: much as, when a couple of years ago I stood night after night in the arena at the proms, I felt a boy again. (There was a ceremonial courtesy about this parading that I find it impossible to convey: perhaps the Japanese tea ceremony—but I know nothing about it but its name, never having been in Japan—has the same sort of flavour.) Moreover the whole atmosphere of the place was friendly: we liked the Perugians.

We found Perugia, too, a happy centre for occasional motor-trips. It was during one of our visits there that we spent a day in the Piero della Francesca country. We went to Borgo San Sepolcro, where they had just uncovered, on the wall of an old bathroom away from the centre, the head of an angel, which they showed us *in situ*: Arezzo, where the frescoes were already so damaged that you could hardly have made them out anyhow—even, that is, if there had been no mass of hideous scaffolding still further to obscure them: and the little town of Monterchi, where, in a small, bare chapel close to where one enters it, we saw the Madonna del Parto. This is a supreme masterpiece, and I cannot refrain from reproducing it. (It faces page 196.)

We started out, one day, for Orvieto, but never got there. (We knew it, however, fairly well: we still occasionally bring out for tea the small table-cloth, with tassels and golden embroidery, that we bought in the vestibule of the Duomo.) We were held up a full hour on the way—after leaving the great pottery works at Deruta, where we bought a few pieces including a flower-pot —for the following reason.

At the time when my wife was a student, training at the Architectural Association, one of the lecturers there was E. R. Rickards, who built the Central Hall, Westminster. He was a great enthusiast for the Renaissance, and often spoke of a church near Todi, which, he insisted, was one of the best in Europe. This was in 1917. My wife was eager to see it, and indeed had looked for it in the Todi near Florence, to which she thought he referred, never having heard of any other. But it was not there, and she gave up the search, though the memory of what Rickards had said hung about her mind. From time to time she would mention it to me.

And now, as we went on our way after leaving Deruta, wondering what we should do with our flower-pot, we rounded a bend in the twisting road: and there, suddenly standing by itself on the wayside, was a building she immediately recognised from so many years ago. It was Santa Maria della Consolazione—the very name makes one happy: the Umbrian Todi was the Todi to which Rickards had referred.

And Rickards had not exaggerated. It is quite small, far smaller, for instance, than St Paul's: but its isolation gives it stature, so that it looks a great deal larger than it actually is. It hugs the ground, with neither steps nor forecourt to break the continuity: it might almost be said to *grow out of* the ground: all the weight is below. It is very simple and very grand: I have asked my wife whether "essentially architectural" might describe it—this is the impression it immediately made on me—and she has said yes, that puts it exactly. Or you could speak of its strong grace, its elegant plainness. (Its photograph faces page 197.)

We asked a passer-by how we could get in: he pointed to a neighbouring farmhouse, and someone eventually brought the keys. The inside matched the outside. There was no church furniture, nothing in the way of pictures, statues, altars, or crucifixes: such things had either never existed or had been removed. And yet it did not look stark: it was simply alone with its bare and monumental nobility.

Santa Maria della Consolazione is abandoned and deserted. The people of Todi up above do not use it, and visitors are extremely rare. And I cannot help being glad about this. It is itself, and not any worship that might be celebrated in it, that praises God.

We went back to Perugia: the great black and white Cathedral at Orvieto would for the moment have looked wrong.

B.H., August 19th, at 8.30

I have just had an outstanding experience. For some time now a number of my musical friends have been talking to me about Janet Baker, and among them Frank Hollins, whose judgment one can invariably rely on (a pity he is wasting his time as Chairman of the Covent Garden Authority, when he ought to be doing something musical):* and now I have heard her for unaccountably the first time, and everything they have told me turns out to be true. She has been singing the *Kindertotenlieder* at a Promenade concert, and I have been listening on the wireless.

What a voice, and what musicianship! You rarely hear anything of the kind nowadays. She has all the volume, the fullness and the strength that anyone could want: perfect phrasing: a moving delicacy when the music calls for it: a wide range: top notes that are nearly always secure, with no screaming on the one hand and no wavering on the other: deep but controlled emotion: above all the sense of authority that is the *sine qua non* of great singing—and this is only a brief catalogue of her virtues, with much left unsaid.

How, too, her performance (and that of the Moscow Radio Orchestra, under the baton of Gennadi Rozhdestvensky) has confirmed me in my old view of Mahler's supremacy, which I have sometimes, of recent years, been inclined to question! As I heard that music tonight there was nothing mawkish about it, nothing overemotional or effusively self-conscious: what had gone into it, apart from musical genius, was the profound compassion of a greatly sensitive human being.

* He died, very sadly, of a heart attack, a few weeks after V.G. died.

§3

Yesterday, September 29th, the garden here (I am writing at Bottom House) looked wretched: grey with mist and wet with rain, it reminded me of Naples. This afternoon, after a bad morning, the sun has come out, and the garden is aglow with colour and light. It reminds me of Naples.

For Naples is of dual aspect. On fine summer days it could put up a case, in spite of Venice, for being the loveliest city in the world, so ravishing are sea and sky from wherever you may look at them. You stroll down the Via Partenope, and beyond those clustering rocks, where a child or two may be scrambling, the open sea—a blazing expanse, or a softer ground, in breezy weather, for little points of sparkling light—lies before you. You turn to your left, and Vesuvius looms misty and aloof across the bay; or to your right, and Posillipo, an almost theatrical fringe of (from that distance) trim little climbing houses, meets your eye. Nor does it matter when you look. Daybreak, with Posillipo slowly changing as the haze clears and the light grows stronger; noontide, a motionless intensity; night, with its conjuncture of moonlit waters and twinkling lights in the distance—all give a raptly lingering quality to human existence. At such times you know the meaning of 'See Naples and die'.

But in really bad weather you are more likely to say "I shall die if I stay here much longer". For in Naples itself (as distinct from its neighbourhood) there is remarkably little, apart from two or three museums and the Aquarium, that could please or interest anyone except a devoted student of art, however minor; and, in that weather, the place itself looks so wretched and sordid as now to make you feel queasy and now almost to break your heart. For then the poverty, otherwise overlaid by the sun, obtrudes, every here and every there, appallingly.

About five years ago we were walking along one of the main streets in the greyness of a sun-forsaken morning, on our way to buy tickets at the San Carlo (I do not remember its name, and am hopeless at map-reading), when we saw on the other side of the road a series of long but narrow alleys, all hung about with washing, opening out of it; and we were so sickened by their wretchedness that we had not the heart to go on, but, forgetting the opera, went back home to sit and read. Things, I suppose, have improved in the meantime, but how much? This summer (we stayed for a fortnight, most of it drizzly or grey) Father Borelli took us to a shanty-town away on the other side of some railway lines. Useless to attempt a description of how people were living there: the worst of the underground hovels that I saw in Jülich just after the war were better than this. Not that one felt anything like despair: there seemed such comradeship among the people, and even, in spite of everything, a kind of sober *joie de vivre*. But what heartened us most of all was the primitive dispensary that Dr Rutherford, a Catholic lady from the North of England, had opened for those down-and-outs: her natural goodness seemed to lighten the gloom.

We spent the evening with Father Borelli, Dr Rutherford and two or three others. I had met Father Borelli twice before, once in Oxford and once in Leeds: on both occasions he had come to raise money for his *Casa dello Scugnizzo*, his House of Urchins. Morris West has told the story as well as anyone could tell it, and I shall not repeat him; but I shall say a word or two about the man himself, whom I love.

He is a deeply religious priest of the unstuffiest kind possible, totally devoid of solemnity. When we were talking to him at the Casa I mentioned a book I was trying to write called 'The Sanity of Christ'—a book he could write perfectly himself, but has no need to, for he lives it instead—and told him that I was being put off by all the theology, particularly German theology, I was reading. "Theology!" he exclaimed. "What has that got to do with it? Drop it, and get on with your book." (His English is almost perfect.) The key to his nature, I should have said, is his feeling for a coincidentally spiritual and physical freedom, a feeling that implies love of God. Before starting the Casa dello Scugnizzo he lived for two or three years as a scugnizzo himself, in order to win their confidence; and I shall never forget how vividly he described the sense of freedom he felt when he was resting, 'with nowhere to lay his head', on the paving-stones of

Naples. And I shall not forget, either, the retort he made (and yet not a retort, for there could be no question of 'scoring off' or 'answering back', he is at once too kind and too spontaneously honest for that) at the Oxford Town Hall. He had been recommending, so to say, his scugnizzi, and begging for money to help him in getting them jobs. There were many sympathetic questions; and then a fellow at the back of the hall got up and asked with a sneer, "But isn't it the real fact, padre, that these boys are plumb lazy?" "Oh very very lazy," Borelli replied, with what one can only call a boyish grin, and convulsed the house. I took the collection half-an-hour later, and got more than five hundred pounds: and I should not be surprised if a good quarter of it can be credited to that exchange.

The ecclesiastical authorities, I suspect, do not much care for him, any more than, in the United States, they care for Dorothy Day. But things might have been different if Pope John had lived. He was clearly sympathetic, as would have been expected; for a few months before his death he agreed to receive a deputation, with representatives from several countries, charged with the duty of obtaining official support for the Casa. Father Borelli sweetly asked me to be the British representative, but the Pope's death intervened. I had been in a bit of a dilemma. My *tenue de soirée* was unsightly: the shirt bulged, the waistcoat would not lie flat, and the silk hat, forty years old, looked ridiculous, my head having grown in the meantime. But what should I do? To buy a whole new lot would be very expensive: on the other hand to hire the equipment from Moss Bros—would not this, somehow, argue lack of respect for His Holiness? Whether anyone but myself would know was irrelevant; and could I, anyhow, be sure that no one would? I was once at the Royal Garden Party, and I amused myself by spotting friends, judging, in each case, whether their tails were real or Moss Bros, and then asking them. My estimate, over all, was 88·9 per cent accurate.

Our dinner after that visit to shanty-town was in one respect full of delight, in another a nightmare. Anyone who has read the bit about Edmond Fleg (and I hope everyone has: that at least, if little else) will be aware that my wife and I detest shellfish: detest its taste (though we have never tasted it but that once), detest its look (dead octopodes with bulging eyes!), detest its smell (particularly its smell: we abandoned the Hotel Vesuvio because the stench from all those restaurants opposite, Auntie Teresa, Bersagliera and the rest, was intolerable). Well, Borelli, in his kindness, had chosen a 'characteristic', a genuinely Neapolitan bistro: and everywhere you looked and everywhere you smelled there was shellfish, shellfix, shellfix. I had had no idea that there were so many repulsive shapes in this world: I thought of inventing a negative b'rōcha, so to speak, to intone over them.

And everyone ate great platefuls of them, the women, except Dr Rutherford, I either think or should like to think, included. My wife and I, on the other hand, ordered cups of consommé and deliciously clean pastas. Father Borelli was greatly surprised and begged me at least to taste this or that. He understood my objection: namely that apart altogether from the smell of them and my ancestral stomach, they were so *suggestive* of living things (being complete) in a way an adequately cooked slice of mutton or beef isn't, that to eat them would make me feel like a cannibal. He understood, but was carnally unaffected; and such a paean of affection for these dead creatures issued from his lips that I began to wonder whether he might not be mixing them up with his living scugnizzi. However, neither of us has allowed our gastronomic differences to come between us.

But after the horror, the delight. There was a 'characteristic' orchestra there; and Father Borelli, who was dressed very queerly, and looked half-way between a priest and a clown (forgive me, Father, forgive me, especially if that is the garb of your order), led the singing. This was 'characteristic' indeed: highly rhythmical *canzonette* (or they may have been up-to-date jazz affairs—if so I have missed something) sung with terrific brio. Borelli got a great reception: everyone there—guests, waiters and musicians—clearly knew and loved him. I emerged with (I imagine) shining eyes, the nightmare forgotten.

Otherwise, we did little in Naples itself this grudging May (the worst, our concierge assured us, with misplaced cordiality, on record), apart from idling up and down the streets if the sun had ventured to come out, and even if it hadn't, or sitting at our ease in a snail-like clippity-clop (the adjective refers only to its pace) whenever we could find one. The man would always ask me "Where?" as we got in, and I would always answer "The bay, and then anywhere"; for, with that single exception, what mattered was the clippity-clop itself, not where you went in it. They are said to be grasping, these clippity-clop men; but we were only swindled once, and that was when, driving up to the hotel for lunch, we were so hungry as to have no time for the usual exchanges of abuse. The man seemed very grateful, and hung about the hotel entrance the next few mornings until we appeared, when he smiled ingratiatingly.

I adore clippity-clops: they are almost the first thing I look for when I go anywhere new, either in England or abroad. The tap of the horse's hooves on the tarmac or whatever it may be is as grateful as the click of croquet-balls in summertime. Whenever I go to the Plaza in New York, as I am often forced to do, I long to get into one of those easeful antiques that hang about the place and will take you for a drive round Central Park; but business—what a world! what a New York!—always prevents me.

But we did spend a morning in each of two museums: the Capodimonte (for the first time) and the Nazionale (for the fifth—we had always taken it in when staying at Naples).

IX

ROME

BASING MYSELF ON the six hotels we have stayed at, in some cases more than once, I find that we have visited Rome (and visited, not lived in, is now the word) nine or ten times in all; and yet neither of us has ever liked it to excess, though there are things in and about it that we have not merely liked but loved. The reason I think is that it is too vast, that there is too much in it, that it is crowded, even, with too many masterpieces or near-masterpieces. When you can hardly stir from your hotel for more than a minute without seeing a great building of sorts or, say, simply a great building or the remains of one; and when you can stroll into any one of a couple of dozen galleries or churches and pick and choose among works of art that have made aesthetic history, then the appetite for such things tends to vanish and to be replaced by a feeling of indifference or positive surfeit. Moreover, beautiful though certain of its aspects undeniably are, I could never describe Rome, *sans phrase*, as a city of beautiful aspect, like London or Paris: thereby differing, I suppose, from the generality of travellers in all periods of history. For my wife and me, in a word, this is not a place to live in; and a place to live in, as I have said more than once, is what we look for when going abroad. Active participation in social life would, I suspect, make all the difference; but this is not what we like on our holidays—we like ourselves and a friend or two.

There is something else, and here I can speak only for myself. Contemporary Rome always, sooner or later, suggests iron Rome to me: contemporary Rome in nearly all its aspects, the Christian or Church ones included. I do not of course mean that anything actually happening in Rome today has this effect on me, nor would I deny for a moment that many liberal, humane and Galilean influences have been at work in the place on a hundred occasions for more than a millennium: what I mean is that as often as not, as I sit or stroll, I feel the atmosphere of that iron civilisation, as repulsive in its republican as in its Imperial phase, persisting in my consciousness. I feel it most of all when enjoying the sun on the Palatine: and the clash between one's inevitable enjoyment—who could resist the shining vistas of grass between the ruins?—and grief at all that evil can be heart-breaking. Nor am I any less troubled when sitting in Santa Maria Maggiore or approaching St Peter's: their vastness suggests, not the Via Dolorosa, but the power and organisational efficiency of Rome.

It is our dislike, I suppose, of all the gigantism that makes us seek out, visit after visit, Peruzzi's little Palazzo Massimo alle Colonne, so unpretentiously hidden away in the Corso Vittorio Emanuele that it can easily be missed. We might have missed it ourselves if my wife, when a student of architecture, had not noted what W. J. Anderson had to say about it in his *The Architecture of the Renaissance in Italy*. "This by itself," he wrote, "is a library of the architecture of the period, a perfect mine of wealth, while, under a simple and severe aspect, it buries its treasures from eyes that do not bring with them the power of seeing." Its refinement and grace, Greek in feeling, are indeed irresistible. Only four other buildings, so far as I can remember at the moment, give me the same sort of peace and pleasure: the Miracoli at Venice; Brunelleschi's radiant Cappella dei Pazzi in Florence; the pure and simple Badia on the way to Fiesole; and our own St Paul's Covent Garden (the interior) across the road from my office. This is a place to sit in when the world is too much with us: thereafter one may walk in the garden, spruced up a bit lately but not enough.

Perhaps I ought to add to this list the Casa di Livia on the Palatine, after which we had anticipatively (I mean before we had seen it) named the first of our daughters in May 1920. When we did see it on our belated honeymoon seven months later we fell in love with what, by way of a pathetic fallacy transferred from nature to builders, we saw as an expression of marital peace: as well as with the beauty of its mural paintings, especially those of foliage, fruit, little landscape and trees. This summer we found, after several intermediate visits, that our affection was intact.

Domestic architecture and its decorations, in point of fact, is the best thing—apart from stories of the Marcus and Epictetus type and some literature, Vergil and Catullus, for my taste, in particular—about the civilisation of ancient Rome.

That first visit, the honeymoon one, started off inauspiciously. My father-in-law had taken charge, at his own insistence, of our financial arrangements, such as they anyhow could be, and this ended in disaster. Naïve and lovable, he was very much of a 'plain man', in contrast to his wife, who was a woman of great spiritual power and intellectual eagerness, uneducated though she was, like most of the women of her time (except in music—one of her ancestor-cousins was Beethoven's Moscheles): what he really liked was tinkering with his car, one of the first in England, collecting model engines, and constantly adding touches to the railway he had built round his garden at Addison Road for the amusement of the children. But he was a stock-jobber by profession, if that is the word for it, and was always making and losing large fortunes (he had just lost one when I married his daughter); and was modestly convinced—for he was genuinely modest, if rather pig-headed—that if he understood nothing else he really did understand money. So he would look after things for us: he would arrange for a draft on the Bank of Rome. I didn't like the idea at all, for I am always imagining that things will go wrong, and wanted to feel secure: suppose the draft didn't arrive? Please, I begged, let me take the money with me. Nonsense, he said, it might get stolen: take only a pound or two, enough for anything you may require before you get to the bank. Well then, I replied, at least cable the bank: a letter can always go astray. He scoffed at this: if I began thinking of cables when letters would do I should never 'make good'.

So we set off, though I still felt a bit uneasy (my wife, who is a woman of unexampled serenity, never worries about anything): and we arrived at the Quirinale—a second-rate, rather dingy hotel in those days, though now, I believe, one of at any rate medium *luxe*—with a few pounds in hand. We booked in, changed our money and hurried off to the bank, nerving ourselves (or myself, rather) to spend a few of our exceedingly precious lire on a taxi. Arrived, I tipped the man extravagantly (I have always tipped taxi-men, and everyone else, extravagantly, being guiltily aware that I am far better off than they are, and the compulsion, even in present circumstances, prevailed), presented myself at one of the desks and stated my business. "A moment," the attendant said, strolled off, and was away a good quarter of an hour, while my worry became something like panic. At last he returned, smiled, and pronounced sentence of death: "Nothing," he said. I got, I am ashamed to say, into a rage. "Nonsense," I said, far too loudly, "there must be something. Look again." "No point in doing that," he replied—I remember him vividly to this day; he was hardly more than a boy, had charming manners, and was clearly English; "there really is nothing. Where are you staying? I will let you know as soon as anything arrives." I thanked him, and we walked back to the hotel. I was now utterly calm. This is one of my idiosyncrasies, the explanation for which I have often tried to fathom (being interested in myself) but with a total lack of success: I worry myself sick about trifles, but lose no jot of my habitual happiness when disaster has come upon me. I remember a case from the early days of the war. I had made an unseemly row in the office about a comparatively trivial error in a book we had just published: the author was a knight, and what I read on the title page was such and such by "Sir" somebody so-and-so. After dismissing the delinquent (to his desk, I mean, not permanently) I paced up and down my room in terrible anxiety: what would people think of me, could I ever survive such a solecism? At this point the production manager came in, and told me, in a low and literally trembling voice, that the whole of our stock, more than a million volumes, had been destroyed at our binder's by a fire-bomb. I was wholly and genuinely unperturbed: "Oh, well," I remember saying, with a tap on the girl's shoulder (or more probably a smack on her bottom), "you'll have to work devilish hard to build it up again." I offer this odd psychological conundrum to my friend George Stroh, who will solve it if anyone can: at any rate he will refrain from maddening me with some string of pseudo-Freudian absurdity, as another of my psychoanalytical friends did by owlishly assuring me that Moses was nothing but the insubstantial symbol of a castration complex. I had trouble with Moses, who was furious, for weeks after.

Back at the hotel, we soberly discussed things. No point in calling my father-in-law, for calls were expensive, and our remaining store of lire, after the taxi, was meagre enough already. No point, either, in lunching and dining at the Quirinale on tick, though this was what it might come to: we should find, when the money arrived, as it eventually must ("it must, it must, mustn't it?"—I was momentarily getting nervous again), that we had run up a huge bill we should never be able to pay. So we would buy a little stock of bread, olives and cheese, the cheapest we could find, and eat them, by way of lunch or dinner, *al fresco*. After all we both enjoyed picnics, and I had inherited a passion for olives from my Jewish home in Elgin Avenue. To this day Basil sees to it that there is a dish of them on my table—rich green ones, intact, with nothing alien stuffed into an unseemly hole—when I lunch at the Savoy Grill.

For two days we took our precious aliments up to the Pincio—it was a long walk there, but the Christmas weather was beautifully fine—and ate them on a seat by the lake (ate our lunch, rather: the evening weather turned out to be extremely cold, and we dined at the hotel, but still on our olives and cheese): and afterwards we wandered about in that pleasance, specially enjoying the Viale dei Bambini, if I remember what they call it aright, with its Punch and Judy show and its foregathering of babies and children. Then on the third morning, as we were drinking our breakfast coffee and I was wondering whether I could possibly afford an egg, our telephone rang: it was our Englishman at the bank, to tell us, bless him, in a voice that reflected an obvious happiness, that our money had arrived. I immediately ordered three eggs, and later on we had enormous steaks at Marinese's, a restaurant we had noticed in the Via Nazionale on our way to the Pincio. We lunched there three days running, and mentioned on the third occasion to Marinese or the head waiter, whichever it was (a man with a sugar-loaf head and a single lock of hair plastered over a bald dome, who used to stand the whole time in total immobility, staring into space), that we would come in that evening for dinner. He at once became agitated, shook his head, pointed to my wife, and, taking me aside, muttered something about *sposa, Inglesi, ver' bute ver' yoonga, onorabile niente lika*, and words to similar effect. I eventually gathered that just behind the restaurant was a not very decorous brothel, and that the two tended to get all mixed up. So we dropped the place, with less regret than might otherwise have been the case because I had just made a fool of myself. My eye had caught *Zuppe Inglesi* when I was given the menu, and "Look at this!", I said to my wife, "Scotch broth, not a doubt of it [thereby infuriating any Scotsman who might have been telepathising with me]. Don't you think it's a good idea?" So I ordered, first, *zuppe inglesi;* second, veal; and third, a sweet. The waiter looked puzzled. "*Due dolci*?" he enquired. "Certainly," I replied. "One for each." The waiter shrugged ("mad Englishman!") and brought us the *zuppe inglesi*, which turned out to be trifle. I smiled brightly when I saw what I had done, and said to my wife "For God's sake don't give me away": so we ate the horribly sweet decadent stuff, and I murmured "Excellent!" to the waiter when he came to remove our plates and the dish. The veal, malgré tout, tasted excellent (perhaps sweet first and meat second is really a better order of dishes than the usual one?—or does the order matter? the French, after all, eat their cheese penultimately); but now came the problem of sweet number two. Could we manage it? Of course we could, and we got up from our places with an air of triumphant Englishness. I have nothing of the chauvinist in me, quite the contrary, as anyone who has ever heard of me (and there are not so few of them, I am assured) must be aware: but I sympathised at that moment, I am ashamed to say, with a Major-General, now dead but formerly notorious as a gigantically high Tory, of whom the following story is authentically told. He had gone out to India as a subaltern at the age of seventeen, and had never been west again until, now sixty, he had returned to contest at the Parliamentary elections. Towards the end of his first session his party friends, who found him—yes, even they—a bit excessive, suggested that he should join a group of them who were to visit Europe during the recess—he ought to know something about the countries they were always talking about. "What!" he replied. "Go and see a lot of dagos? Englishmen are good enough for me." "At least then," they urged, "go and see Paris." Yes, he thought he might do this: he had heard Paris well spoken of. So they ushered him on board the cross-channel steamer, and he successfully alighted at Calais, and was directed to the douane. There a short, aged and feeble douanier awaited him, who courteously enquired "Avez-vous quelque chose à déclarer, monsieur?" He drew himself up, screwed an eyeglass into his eye (I am assured that he really had one—an eyeglass, not an eye—though it sounds too good to be true), and said in his best parade manner "Speak English, my man, or not at all!"

The Quirinale, as I have said, was not all that it might have been, but we would have stayed at a flea-pit if it could have given us, morning after morning, such experiences as were ours at the Quirinale: for our room looked on to the Costanzi, the Christmas season had just started there, and we could hear the rehearsals quite clearly, those for *Tristano e Isolta* included. Nowadays, as I have explained elsewhere, I am ambivalent about Wagner; but I wasn't ambivalent about him then, and least of all about *Tristan*. For this, after all, was not so long after 1914, when *Tristan* was a swooning ecstasy: we used to say in the gallery that if the moment had come to commit suicide (though why on earth, in those golden days, should anyone have wanted to?) one should throw oneself down from gallery to stalls during 'Mild und leise'. I have never really got over *Tristan*: the other evening, here at Bottom House, I suddenly ran into a bar of it when fiddling with the wireless, and my heart was in my throat.

But these performances were better for us, in one way, than vis-à-vis ones inside the Costanzi itself would have been: just as something precious was added when we heard Verdi's Requiem this July at St Paul's, not from the front, as would have been usual, but from behind, in the muffling remoteness of the Dean's Closet. For this was no longer the divinest of things, music on earth: this was something even diviner, music in heaven, ideal or

Platonic music, the music, one might say (if the meaning of that expression were not altogether different) of the spheres. And in addition to everything else there was still a bonus: there was a garden between the Quirinale and the Costanzi, and the moment the rehearsal got going the air would come alive with a chorus of chirruping birds.

We could rarely manage tickets, even after our money had arrived, for the performances themselves. Weingartner conducted: with a single finger of his right hand, as always, and with the other arm down the seam of his trousers in correct military fashion. His prelude to *Carmen* was the most incisive I had ever heard, or have ever heard since. As you waited for the curtain to go up the ushers shouted at you 'Programma dell' opera! Programma de' grandiosi balli Russi!' At Salzburg, later, it was to be 'Sitzkissen bitte! Einen Schilling!' and in the Verona amphitheatre 'Cioccolata! Caramelle!'

Weingartner was the greatest conductor of his time, at any rate in Beethoven, and has had only one rival since, Otto Klemperer: both of them being men, at the podium, of an almost superhuman undemonstrativeness, with Weingartner winning, perhaps by the shortest of heads. We would sometimes meet him in London, after one of his concerts, at Rose Morley's: she was an amateur of warm hospitality, and many of her friends would forgather round about eleven on musical evenings, at her house in Sussex Place. Weingartner liked changing on such occasions from tails into a flowered waistcoat. He was as plain and simple as his conducting, with an air of quiet authority, however, that he sought to conceal behind a singularly gentle smile. He spoke fairly good English, but his inability to choose the appropriate rendering of a German word with several meanings often produced a charmingly comical result. Casals was once playing the Haydn concerto at a concert he was conducting, and half-way through the first movement suddenly stopped. There was a conference on the platform, then Weingartner turned to the audience and said: "Mr Casals has the cramp. We shall play the symphony now, and Mr Casals shall play the concerto at the end from the evening."

We have heard little music in Rome since those Weingartner

days: the opera, whenever we have been there, with two exceptions, has been as poor as it has been pretentious, and notable concerts have been virtually non-existent, almost as a matter of course. But the two exceptions are worth recording, and are particularly memorable for us as Edmond and Madeleine Fleg were our guests at the Excelsior, or we were theirs, or we were doing it Dutch, I cannot remember.* This was Christmas and New Year 1933/1934. Edmond would afterwards refer to our New Year's Eve dinner at the hotel as '*la soirée des bretelles*', because Bertrand de Jouvenel, whom I had no more than heard of, rang me up at a quarter to nine and asked me to lend him a pair of braces: and when we saw him in Paris shortly before his death he called the Excelsior Monsalvat, because I had described the head doorman, who wore ruffles of lace and looked unusually stupid but also unusually gentle, as a kind of Parsifal. He moved over, the moment we left, to the Hotel de la Ville. He couldn't abide the Excelsior: nor, for the matter of that, could we.

The first of our two performances was *Otello*, conducted, I am almost sure, by de Sabata, and all I remember about it is that the crash with which it opened was more glorious than any I had heard before or have heard since. The other was then a rarity of rarities (though it is better known now), Monteverdi's *Orfeo*, which Tullio Serafin conducted. I recall it in considerable detail, having eked out old memories by the frequent playing of a gramophone record: and I shall indulge myself, if my readers will forgive, by repeating the description I gave of it in *Journey Towards Music*. For I love it exceedingly, so manifold is its loveliness:

Orfeo's invocation to the woodland groves, with the quiet but growingly insistent enthusiasm of love in it; the setting of the messenger's 'La tua diletta sposa è morta' and his reply 'Ohimè', exact, the latter, for all its simplicity, as a musical expression of grief; Orfeo's song of gratitude to Hope, and her reply; the sinfonia that describes Charon's slumber; and above all Orfeo's appeal to Charon, 'Possente spirto, e formidabil nume'. The last, with the increasing urgency of its ever more elaborate coloratura,

* A photograph, taken on the occasion is reproduced facing page 105.

and the variety of aspiration in its exquisite accompaniment, is a miraculous expression of a singer devoting resource after resource of his musical art, and then another and another, to the desperate achievement of a supreme object. "I cannot force my way in," voice and orchestra are saying. "I cannot take the kingdom of heaven by violence: but listen to spirit and beauty, and relent." . . . I felt throughout at that performance in Rome the same hush, the same careless sense of being engulfed in an eternity of peace, as I had experienced at the other *Orfeo* in London a few years before the war.

One more musical experience, and I have done with that topic. Quite recently we dined one Christmas Eve with the Robertses—a charming host, a charming hostess—at the American Academy; and afterwards a number of journalists had the kindness to take us for a run through the moonlit streets. We ended up at midnight Mass in the Aracœli, one of those indecorous affairs, with people strolling in and strolling out, that express with such immediacy the essence of Catholicism as all mixed up, in a taken-for-granted sort of way, with daily life. The crib was in the vilest of taste, and quite beautiful. . . . My ear was suddenly caught by familiar tones in the distance: familiar but unfamiliar too, for I was certain that this was nothing I knew. So we went out to investigate, and there at the porch were a couple of musicians with odd instruments that looked like bagpipes and oboes. I asked a bystander who they might be, and he told me that they were up from the Abruzzi, as was their custom at this time of year. Then it flashed on me that there was a resemblance between these rhythms and those of *Harold in Italy*, and that the scene of *Harold in Italy* was the Abruzzi; so when we got home I looked up Berlioz' 'Life' and this is what I found:

"In the miserable oblivion and dishonour into which music has sunk in Rome I found but one small sign of honest life. It was among the pifferari, players of a little popular instrument, a surviving relic of antiquity. They were strolling musicians who, at Christmastide, came down from the mountains in groups of four or five armed with bagpipes and piffere, a kind of oboe, to play before the image of the Virgin.

"I used to spend hours in watching them, there was something so quaintly mysterious in their wild aspect as they stood —head slightly turned over one shoulder, their bright dark eyes fixed devoutly on the holy figure, almost as still as the image itself.

"At a distance the effect is indescribable and few escape its spell. When I heard it in its native haunts, among the volcanic rocks and dark pine forest of the Abruzzi, I could almost believe myself transported back through the ages to the days of Evander the Arcadian."

For the rest, we have enjoyed, on various visits, the cloisters of San Paolo fuori le Mura and the Lateran; an occasional few minutes in the Pantheon; the Piazza del Popolo, with the ragged greenery beyond, where Carlo Levi lives, or used to; all the fountains, the Tritone perhaps even more, for me but not for my wife, than the Trevi; the steps from the Piazza di Spagna, and particularly the glory of its flowers (but these had vanished this summer); San Pietro in Vincoli, with its Moses; a glimpse of the Castel San' Angelo (but mainly because it makes me feel operatic); buying the brightest, grandest stuffs we could find at the Campo dei Fiori; and, always, strolling on the Pincio. But there were three great climaxes this summer, and I shall deal with them in their climacteric order.

First, however, there is something I want to get off my chest. One must be chary of bandying about accusations: people in glass houses, etcetera. Or, to put it in another way, one must be chary of self-righteousness. I am going to talk about corruption: and the corruption in contemporary Soho, as I recently discovered, is as vile as anything you could imagine, even if you were one of the choicest of modern American novelists. (But they have a wit, these Soho people. I was walking down one of their streets on my way to a dinner-party, limping a lot worse than usual, for I was exceedingly tired; and a tout at the door of a stew-cum-strip-tease boutique called out to me as I passed "Hallo, Colonel! Come in and have a rest." I turned on him as hideous a leer as I could manage: "Not good enough for me," I shouted in a cracking voice.

"Try someone older, m'boy.") There is nothing new, of course, about this: we are simply returning to a hallowed London tradition. Nor am I in the least prudish, as some of my British colleagues imagine, about sex. When I talk of corruption, I mean that the photographs outside these crowding strip-tease places are a beastly offence to the human body.

Well, Soho is a backwater (and the surreptitiousness of all that filth might perhaps, on one view, make it worse): but the Via Veneto is the Mayfair of Rome. Not that sexual corruption is in question on the Via Veneto: the corruption you feel in the air as you sip your coffee is a financial one. You watch the parade: you turn round to have a look at the touts hanging round the Excelsior: and money power, money intrigue, money at any price hangs about you and stinks in your nostrils. And what made you hurry over lunch and get away as quickly as possible comes back to you: the matter-of-course jauntiness of a young waiter as he flirted at the top of his voice with two American women he was serving, both fiftyish and rather ill-favoured, and both, as anyone could see, adequately rich.

I may be doing Rome an injustice: how can any real judgment be founded on a chance episode in one fashionable restaurant, or on the physiognomical peculiarities and gesticulatory technique of a few individuals taking the air on a pathway between café tables, or forgathering at the entrance to a particular hotel? What, for instance, about Hamburg?—from all accounts, one might see far worse there. So take it that I have merely been giving a quick, subjective impression, based on ludicrously insufficient evidence; but take it also that I did have the feeling this summer in Rome, more than in any great city, New York not excluded, and more devastatingly than ever before, that modern society is becoming increasingly a money, a corrupt money, one.

§ 2

The first of our three climaxes was a visit to Hadrian's Villa. This was not new to us: we had been to it three times already, and had always enjoyed it: but our enjoyment, or mine at least, was now in a different dimension. Formerly it had depended on

Mansell-Anderson

ETRUSCAN WINGED HORSES

CERVETERI:
SARCOPHAGUS
OF THE MARRIED
COUPLE

historical interest: you really could get an idea, in that isolation, of how Emperors might have spent their leisure, as you can learn little that is clear-cut and vivid about anyone when successive buildings, in a jumbled mass, compete for your attention. But now my enjoyment was spiritual.

Nothing is beautiful in Hadrian's Villa except the grass, and even the vista beyond is 'ordinary', unpicturesque. Nor could any of those buildings, I think, have at any time been beautiful, except perhaps the Canopus (and it would then have been the water that was beautiful): though to stroll in fine weather at sunrise down the incredible Philosopher's Wall must have been to experience alike gratitude, wonder and peace. No: what moved me this summer was not the vast scale of those buildings but the vaster greenness between them and beyond: the very vastness of the buildings, now ruined, served to confirm, as I looked over to the horizon, the immortality, or if you like the comparative immortality, of nature. And if nature too went at the last, some development of creative divinity—I was sure of it—would ensue. Suddenly, for the first time in my seventy-three years, I felt careless about my own death: yet loved life more than ever. As we strolled about on our way to the Canopus I picked a piece of flowering privet from a hedge by the water and kept smelling it till we got back to Rome: it was the fairest thing in Hadrian's Villa.

That same day we had another adventure, but of a more mundane kind. My wife, though coolish in the main about Roman architectural aesthetics, had nevertheless been fascinated, ever since her time at the A.A., by Roman methods of construction, and had communicated this interest to me. Now people have fads and fancies about practically everything: quite irrationally, they prefer one kind of cat, dog, mineral water, pyge or whole human being to all other kinds: and my wife, who shared this propensity, strongly favoured, in the sub-department of Roman wall-building, the device classified, I imagine by the Romans themselves, as opus reticulatum, namely a mess of concrete with a facing of pyramidal stones, or say teeth, set diagonally.

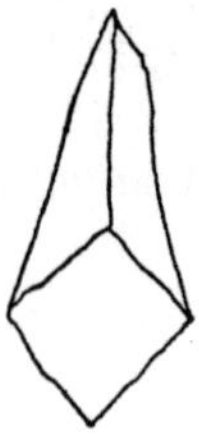

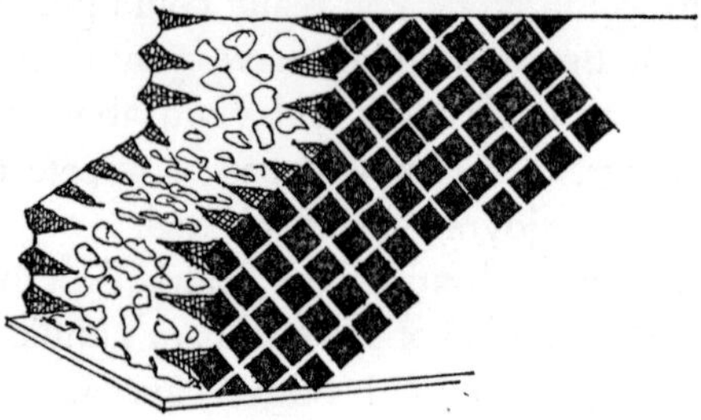

But there is no finer example of opus reticulatum than the Philosopher's Wall at Hadrian's Villa, and my wife took a careful look at it here and there, in the hope of finding a loose tooth she might steal. She was unsuccessful, and we went on our way, a few yards apart from one another; and suddenly I heard "Look, look!", and there was my wife, holding aloft, for everyone to see (including the custodian—I felt rather nervous), a tooth fit for the jaw of Polyphemus. We got it home at considerable expense (excess luggage); and now it lives, a peculiar treasure, on one of the shelves at B.H. And no force had been required: it was lying about, quite casually, on a low wall near the Canopus.

We had a slight *déception* on our way back to Rome. I told the driver, whom our concierge had kindly provided (a good driver, though his looks rather displeased us), to stop at Tivoli: we wanted to lunch, I explained, at a little restaurant I knew there. He shook his head, and gave me something between a knowing wink and an affectionate smile: "I'm going to take you," he said, "to a place, high up in the mountains, that was opened only last year. Marvellous food. Marvellous view." (His English was perfect: his profession, whatever it may have been apart from chauffeuring, perhaps required a command of languages.) Thinking of all the eminences I had so delightedly lunched on top of—Valadier, Asolo—I happily agreed; and we drove up and up, and again up and up, till we arrived at a long wooden shanty. We went to the window. All places are good to look down on, but this was almost an exception; and as for the food, it was what, if it had been a conductor, I should have described as useful. We met our man two or three times subsequently, in the neighbourhood of the Via Veneto, but never employed him again: for we had happened in the meantime on a taximan who would take us anywhere we wanted at half the hotel price. He was an excellent driver and a conspicuously decent human being: Massimino Toti, whom we now recommend to all our friends. It was he who took us both to Tarquinia and to Paradise.

§3

We had wanted to visit Tarquinia ever since we had seen it, high up on our right, as we approached Rome and looked out from our wagon-lit in 1920; and we had failed to do so either then or on any subsequent holiday right down to our last one this Spring. The reasons were various. It would be too expensive: it would take too much time: it would be awfully tiring: wouldn't it be better, on so lovely a day, to wander about on the Pincio or in the Forum? But meanwhile the picture I was painting in my mind was becoming ever more irresistible. A sleepy hill-town in which you felt in another century as you walked down narrow streets with shutters, green or subfusc, fastened together, but not quite, to keep the sun off little houses and shops: and, somewhere at the end of it, a dozen steps leading down into a vast Hall of the Dead, where, in a cool, subdued light, you might see funerary marvels all about you—this is what, with the assistance of a couple of guide books, my imagination had conjured up. But the propensity to exaggerate of which my wife justly complains, as I confessed on the very first page of this memoir, had led me astray or, to put it more candidly, I had imagined the opposite of the truth. Tarquinia is a dull, featureless little town, sleepy only in the unromantic sense, tricked out with a few buildings of the sort guide books describe as 'likewise of interest'; and as for the 'vast necropolis', it consists (as I should have known, if I had studied the literature with greater care) of an array of knolls, scattered over the country beyond, into which you descend at your peril.

After a poorish lunch we first had a look at the museum, where we saw a masterpiece or two, including the winged horses, but somehow, I do not really know why, felt rather depressed, and then joined a glossolalic but predominantly German party that was driving out with a guide to see the tombs.

When we came to the first of them I took a step or two down the black and slippery incline, supporting my damaged thigh with that wonderful stick of mine that is supposed to give me a firm purchase, not merely on wet pavements, but on glass, ice, and sopping leaves; but in spite of the nicht besonderers (with an occasional achtung) that did their best to encourage me I desisted, and waited on the surface. This happened a few dozen times (or perhaps only a dozen) and then we drove back to Rome. My wife told me I had not missed very much: she may or may not have been lying.

But the winged horses kept recurring to my mind. Now as I suppose everyone knows, or everyone, at any rate, with more than a minimal interest in cultural phenomena, there is a museum in Rome, the Villa Giulia, devouted to Etruscan art: and we decided to have a look at it. Why we had never been there before is a mystery, which I shall make no tortuous effort to explain: we had never been there before, that is the shameful fact. We had indeed some difficulty in getting there now: the taximan took us in the first instance to the Galleria d'Arte Moderna, from which, however, we escaped easily enough, a few minutes later. Our man (whom we had fortunately retained) then held a couple of conferences with people passing by, both of which ended with a joint shaking of heads. But his third attempt was successful. Twice he shouted "Villa Giulia": twice the other looked as blank as that great panel, with its all-over wash of uniform magenta, at the Guggenheim Museum in New York. Then "Ah" he said, or the Italian equivalent, and pointed a decisive finger. We arrived.

The relative strength of two impressions, one earlier and one later, as they linger in the memory, may or may not depend on the amount of time that, in each case, has meanwhile elapsed. A year ago I heard the Amadeus ensemble play the whole series of Beethoven quartets, as I had heard the Busch people in the twenties and the Lener before them; and if I have the idea that the latest of these three experiences moved me more than either of the

NUREMBERG 1949

FRANKFURT 1960

earlier ones this may be, and almost certainly is, merely because I am still under the relatively immediate spell of it. So when I say that I enjoyed myself more at the Villa Giulia than at any museum previously this is a statement, I am well aware, that I might have to revise in a longer perspective. But at the moment it seems true to me.

I had seen nothing, even in reproduction, before except the Cerveteri sarcophagus and the Apollo of Veio, and the whole experience was quietly overwhelming. What is so beautiful in these things in their candour: a certain plainness, straightforwardness, even austerity, issuing, however, not from any studied intention to achieve these qualities, but from an honest, unselfconscious fidelity to basic realities as the artist or craftsman naïvely sees them. (This is particularly true where Greek influence is absent.) And what a dignity of stance and movement! What a speaking directness in facial expression! The gestures, too, formal, hierarchical almost, in their simplicity, nevertheless convey their intention with an eloquent exactitude. Withal, you are aware, as you pass from room to room, of eager activity all around you, coupled with a serene love of life and sometimes with great tenderness, as in the case of the headless woman carrying a child; and the comradeship of husband and wife, rarely the subject of artistic expression, is with a total lack of the romantic insistence that would have falsified it. All in all this must have been, in many ways, an unusually attractive civilisation. But it should not be idealized: there was room in it for human sacrifice.

This survey of Etruscan life is astonishingly wide, ranging from temples and tombs to jewellery and implements for the care of the body: the profusion of objects in every one of the varied departments is likewise extraordinary: yet you make your way through the succession of rooms without a trace of fatigue. This is partly due to an interest and excitement that never leave you, and partly to the airy freshness of the gallery itself and the excellent arrangement of its contents. You feel as you go home after a couple of hours as fresh as the Pastoral Symphony.

A footnote. Some of the pieces, particularly the sculptural ones, are surprisingly and delightfully 'modern', in the manner of sane and beautiful modernity, not of a deliberate or *faute de mieux* freakishness, that is often cacodorous into the bargain.

§ 4

Hubert Howard and his wife Lelia, inheritor of the Caetani estates, kindly invited us to lunch at the Palazzo Caetani (on the Via dei Botteghe Oscure, eponym of the magazine founded and edited by Lelia's mother), when they heard we were in Rome; and Howard asked us as we were leaving whether we would care to spend a few hours with them at Ninfa.

Now we had heard about Ninfa from a lady who lives just above us in Eaton Place, Lela Maxwell-Arnot: a relative of the Caetanis, and, even more enticingly, the granddaughter of Olympia Baronat, a radiant soprano of the late nineteenth century, known to few, with any phonographic intimacy, except Desmond Shawe-Taylor and myself. We had been excited by what Lela told us, so we eagerly accepted the Howards' invitation, got in touch with Massimino Toti, and started out a few mornings later.

The town or garden of Ninfa lies on the edge of the Pontine marshes, with Norma and the cyclopean Norba towering above; and these we decided to visit first, as the Howards had advised. Norma is a featureless little hill town, poised, as if precariously, on a precipice of the Volscian mountains; but we found to our delight, as we arrived at the piazzetta, that the weekly market was in progress, and this, anywhere in Italy, is a separate holiday by itself. (Besides, the view was magnificent.) Indeed we spent so much time at the stalls that we had to cut out the reputedly far more interesting Norba altogether. There were a lot of things I wanted to buy: shirts, but they were all too narrow for me; ties, but these were somewhat in the American taste; hats, but my wife said I looked ludicrous in them. She was luckier herself, for she found a strainer with the finest mesh, so she told me, that she had ever seen, and a glorious red handle. I wanted to put it on our shelf, but she said its proper place was the kitchen; or at least to reproduce it in colour 'as if' it were on the shelf, but she thought this a silly as well as a dishonest idea. I regret her ukase: the red handle really is quite gorgeous. A reproduction, it is true, would cost more than a thousand times what the original did, but to calculate like that is in my view wrong-headed.

It was now time to descend. We knew exactly where Ninfa was: Hubert Howard had given us exact instructions, and there was even a signpost: but we could find no trace of it. We did come upon a ruined tower down a nondescript lane, but that looked like an isolated phenomenon, unconnected with Ninfa: so we turned and cross-examined a woman who was sitting by a well a few yards away. She was dumb, but finely gesticulative; and with her aid we found a blind concrete blockhouse we had previously overlooked. Toti went in, and emerged with the information that we must return to the tower and ring a bell there. We did so, and peal after peal clanged around us like the fanfare in Verdi's Requiem. Next, a man came up from the bowels of the earth, like Erda (to similize from music again), but unlike Erda in every other respect: for he was the man who had driven us home after that lunch at the Palazzo Caetani, and was smiling in a way that the solemn ur-goddess could never have managed. He took us through abounding grass to a place where it grew high against two metal plates, almost concealing them, opened them with a key; and shut them behind us with another Verdian clang. We were in Ninfa. A cherub at the gate, recently a chauffeur in Rome, had reversed the role of his predecessors: he had shut us up in, instead of shutting us out of, the Garden of Paradise. For that is what Ninfa is.

The bare facts about Ninfa are simple and well attested, in spite of the mystery that at least one of its previous chroniclers has seen fit to make play with. These include Gregorovius, a proposterously romantic historian of the eighteenth century who was born in Munich, studied in Königsberg and lived for more than twenty years in Italy; the amiable Augustus Hare, whose *Walks Near Rome* was published in 1875 by Dalbay, Isbister and Co., a name that will delight any amateur of publishing; and our own Rose Macaulay, author of *Pleasure of Ruins*, which George Weidenfeld, happily still among us, brought out for her in 1953.

They have failed, all three of them, to give any accurate and living impression of the place: and I shall no doubt fail as disastrously.

Ninfa is a mediaeval town of moderate size, owned by the Frangipani in the twelfth century and thereafter by the Caetani, who retain it to this day; for Pietro Caetani, nephew of Boniface VIII, gradually bought up its houses and possessions towards the end of the twelve-hundreds. Pope Alexander III was consecrated at Ninfa in 1159, and fifty years later a church was built there by Gregory I, and dedicated to S. Maria del Mirteto—Saint Mary of the Myrtlegrove. But it has been deserted, and a total ruin, for centuries: malaria from the Pontine marshes had put an end to it as a town to be lived in. Then Lelia's grandfather, father of Rodolfo Caetani, the musician, drained the marshes and made it habitable; and now she and her husband spend most of their time there in a small and moderately restored palazzo, she painting, he administering the Caetani estates (which include neighbouring Sermoneta). He has been building a yearly festival there, with the assistance, among others, of Yehudi Menuhin: who when staying with the Howards, Hubert told me, used to worry the outside staff by doing his yoga exercises, standing on his head included, in the open air at dawn.

But Ninfa is no longer a town: with its ruined houses, etcetera, 'all overgrown with azure moss [grass and ivy] and flowers, so sweet the sense faints picturing it', it is now—I hesitate to say a vast garden, for vastness is by no means the mark of it, but a broad demesne of almost uninterrupted nature, incomparable for its tranquillity. Even Rose, whose description is far the best I have read, suggests, though with qualifications, a lushness and air of romanticism wholly foreign to it, at any rate in 1966. And I should call it careless rather than wild, as all three of the writers I have cited either imply or insist: this may be due to the skill of the present incumbents, whose staff of gardeners has brought a certain orderliness into it without spoiling its informality. I think that this mixture of freedom and order must have characterised the original Garden, seeing that God designed and supervised it.

Nor did I get the impression, as again even, apparently, Rose did, that we were really in a town. Perhaps the grass and ivy have rapidly and extensively grown during the last fifteen years, and perhaps the ruins have still further crumbled. However that may be, I was hardly aware of more than a construction or two as we walked round after lunch (served by the cherub in an open summer-house, as the weather was threatening, and beginning with a salad of crude vegetables, so refreshing to spirit as well as to body, such as I had eaten only once before, in Provence—I asked for and was given a large second helping): the walls, the tower, the modest palazzo, a biggish church, a damaged bridge over the Nynphaeus (the eponymous rivulet, unless you care to believe that the place is really named after 'la bella Ninfa', an allegedly love-lorn young woman who threw herself from the tower in defiance of her match-making parents), these are all that I noticed. The houses of Rose Macaulay's day may have become ivy-covered tumuli, the streets may have become grassy lanes.

What I experienced above all in Ninfa, as I have already suggested, was spiritual peace—the sort that passeth all understanding. I felt what I had felt at Hadrian's Villa, but even more, contradictory though the word is, intensely: and hardly knew I had done so till we were on our way back to Rome. Nature was immortal, and the death of God was a myth.

It was getting late. We returned to the entrance: the cherub emerged, with a happy-looking Massimino: and we gave my friend Hubert, as he had already become, the latter's card, in case he might one day have a use for it. We also carried away an oversize lemon, with an unusually thick and heavily pitted skin, as I wanted it for one of our shelves. But I failed to embalm it, and it got nasty, as my wife said it would; I am sad to be without a reminder of what travellers of universal experience might well consider the most beautiful place in the world.

X

GERMANY

THIS CHAPTER, ON Germany, will be the shortest in the book, partly because we have never spent a holiday there, though we have frequently passed through, and partly because I have dealt with everything I think memorable, particularly with my 'remote contacts' with Beethoven and my experiences just after the war, in other writings. But I must make an exception at the very least in favour of Nuremberg, for my memories of it are of the happiest: nor would I have wished Germanophiles, Jewish or gentile, to assume that the silence they would otherwise have found about Germany and its people, apart from a passing word or two, was unregenerately deliberate. Sooner than this (and I really mean it, for there is nothing viler than hostility to a whole people), I would have suppressed the manuscript altogether.

The University of Frankfurt—the Goethe University—had been so kind, back in 1947, to award me an honorary Doctorate of Laws, in gratitude (a quality no one could ever say the Germans lack) for what I had tried to do for them, by way of relief and advocacy, when they were starving in 1946 and 1947. Such an award implies an informal obligation on the recipient to deliver a lecture or oration in the aula of the University: but circumstances prevented me from fulfilling it for the time being. Then, in 1950, the German authorities, in conjunction with a German publisher, Karl Anders, who had been a good friend of mine when he was in London during the war, suggested that I should do a short tour, beginning at Nuremberg, ending at Bonn and Hamburg (particularly dear to me, for I remembered the self-sacrifice I had seen there in 1946, as well as the kindness, specially to children, of English journalists and our occupying forces), and lecturing at the University on my way. The idea appealed to me, and I consented.

Our reception at Nuremberg station was very moving: I shall not attempt to describe it, but shall try to convey the spirit of it by means of a photograph. But even more moving was the meal they took us to at the Carlton Hotel. Here is the menu:

Feine gemischte Vorspeise
Toast u. Butter

—

Echte Schildkrötensuppe

—

Frühmastente gebraten
feine Erbsen—Nusskartoffeln
Schmorapfel

—

Kalifornische Pfirsiche "Melba"
Kleines Gebäck

It must be remembered that food conditions were still very bad, and that you saw ruins everywhere; and it requires no great effort of the imagination to understand how "Feine gemischte Vorspeise: Toast and Butter" affected me. Afterwards we signed the Golden Book, with the Burgermeister looking on.

But most moving of all was the ceremony in the opera house. We found, when we got our programmes, that they were to play chamber music before and after the addresses, and that alone would have been sufficient to make me feel warm and grateful. But there was something that meant even more. Despite my ambivalence about Wagner, I had never ceased to cherish Die Meistersinger—Die Meistersinger von Nürnberg: and when I found myself on the stage to start my address, and looked at the audience that crammed every corner, I could not speak for several minutes. Standing there, a Jew and but recently an enemy, I somehow felt myself all mixed up with, even a participant in, one of the greatest works of art that the world had ever known, and a very German one at that; and I felt that there was nothing, at that moment, to divide me from the people I was looking at. The barriers, that even a year before I had occasionally remembered but tried to forget (after all, any one of these people might personally have murdered Renée Bernheim), were now wholly down.

When I did get going on my address (which I had called 'Religion and Humanity') a good deal of comedy ensued. They wanted a sentence-by-sentence translation, and a distinguished-looking man in our box (I never found out who he was) volunteered for the job. Now my stuff was no doubt a bit difficult: it was all about the coincidence in *Fidelio* of Leonore's pistol with God's trumpet-call, which, as anyone who has read any of my books will remember, is one of my favourite themes. Anyhow, the translator was flummoxed, and Karl Anders came down to assist him. But Anders was flummoxed too. I would say something, and they would confer: but when they gave voice to what they imagined I had said, I had to interrupt them, for I knew just enough German to realise that they were putting their own words into my mouth. Chaos threatened, so I took it upon myself to announce that further translation would be dispensed with: anyone who didn't understand English should leave. No one did: to judge from the murmur of applause, everyone seemed not only satisfied but relieved: and there was such a storm of clapping and stamping when I finished that I felt, perhaps erroneously, that they really had understood me and sympathised with what I had said.

I shall pass over Frankfurt, with its crowds that swamped not only the aula itself but the vestibule outside (it was 'Religion and Humanity' again, but untranslated this time from the beginning, for they made it clear that there was no one in Frankfurt who did not understand English). Next, to Bonn. I told Jewish, or Armenian, stories to President Heuss, as I have already related, and he told Jewish, or Armenian, stories to me; and then, just as we were leaving, I asked him would he do me a favour? Could he get hold of a couple of late eighteenth-century gouaches, one of

Bonn and one of Hamburg? Two mornings later they were at our hotel. How do they do these things in Germany? In England you have to wait a fortnight at least for a recently published book that happens to be out of stock at your booksellers': not to mention a rare print.

XI

LAST CHAPTER

FEW OF THE museum pieces I have so far mentioned come from England. There is a good reason for this: you do not commonly pick up souvenirs in your own country, nor is it of your own country that your friends commonly give you souvenirs. In the matter of serious collecting the position has, in our case, been reversed: we collect English pottery, and only three examples in the collection come from abroad. But our pottery is now housed at Eaton Place, and can therefore find no place in this memoir: though an occasional piece has descended to Bottom House, either because it is too late for our collection—we stop soon after eighteen hundred—or because it is at B.H. illegitimately (I like looking at the circumcision mug over week-ends), or even because it is only fictitiously there at all, the Madonna and Child, for instance, as I shall explain later. Then, English pottery apart, there are the few odds and ends that have, exceptionally, been picked up in England and have gone naturally into the museum; and so I find myself, after all, with enough material for this, which is also unhappily for me my final, chapter.

Half-way down on the left outside shelf of the museum is an amusing collection of figures. A pottery Queen Victoria is flanked on one side by a doctor staring at her inquisitively, and on the other by a little Dutch girl, arms akimbo, who seems to be saying, apropos of Her Majesty, "*Je m'en fiche*". [In the frontispiece both figures appear to the left of the Queen.]

The Queen, who has inscribed on her base the words 'Published in Lambeth 1837', is in grey stoneware, and is very similar in type to the brown 'Reform' flasks, made at the time of the Reform Bill and with the head and shoulders of the Duke of Wellington, Cobden, etcetera, forming their tops, that you could see lying about in junk-shops when I was a boy and could buy for a shilling. The Queen must have been made in enormous quantities at the time of her accession, and probably cost a few farthings: you still come across her fairly often. I bought a second one a couple of years ago, and gave it to Elizabeth Longford in celebration of her book on Queen Victoria: it was better than the first, which was poorer in colour and had had its head slashed off and stuck on again, while the second was intact. I am glad I gave Elizabeth the better, for she is worthy of the best.

In learning excellent, in wisdom rare,
In style and wit beyond compare,
In form and face exceeding fair:
This is Elizabeth.

I apologise for this. To say that Elizabeth is as clever as she is beautiful would have sounded banal, so I searched for a poem about any Elizabeth that would say the same thing for me: but I failed to find one: so I made up that doggerel myself.

While I am pleasurably talking about Elizabeth I may as well add a line or two about her husband, who however deserves a book to himself. I rate him as one of the best and most compassionate of men, as well as the untidiest: and as I dress rather carelessly myself I am always happy to run across him at a crush, for he puts me in countenance.

I forgot to say that both Victorias have holes in their heads, and were used as candlesticks.

No spiritual distance could be greater than that between Victoria and Lambeth stoneware on the one hand and the Commedia dell'Arte and Capo di Monte on the other. We were at Cheltenham one day either during or shortly after the war, and for a Left Book Club or a Save Europe Now meeting: and on our way back to the hotel passed a large and particularly shaggy junk shop, and of course went in. My eyesight was a good deal better then than it is now, and looking up to a high shelf crammed with everything from art vases to chamber pots I saw a diminutive white beard sticking out. When a grumpy little fellow, who happened to be very short, had at last got it down for us it was easy to recognise: the doctor from the Commedia dell'Arte in Capo di Monte of a late period, with nothing but his left hand missing. It was valueless, of course, as a collector's item, but even so it was worth more than the fifteen shillings we gave for it.

We bought the Dutch girl from old Pease of Nottingham, who had been a famous dealer in pots since the eighteen-nineties, and at the time, about 1942, was getting on for eighty. Everyone called him old Pease, just as everyone called another famous dealer, Fred Elson of Christmas Steps, old Fred Elson. I hope, as one may infer from these cases, that antique dealers as a class enjoy unusual longevity, for I like the better sort exceedingly and love hanging about in their shops: I put them with florists and fruiterers rather than with butchers and fishmongers. Perhaps their delightful calling explains the length of their lives.

The figure of a Dutch girl is of Dutch not English manufacture, and would therefore (literally) be thought less than nothing of by the average English collector of English wares. That is why we dare not have it in London, but have put it with the Queen and the doctor on the Bottom House shelves. I am going to say, nevertheless, that I find it far more attractive than anything of the kind I have ever seen in English delftware, which does not greatly attract me anyhow.

Old Pease was a great gossip and had a wonderful repertoire of stories, which he used to bring out after showing us round and when we were just on the point of leaving. The one I liked best was this. He was sitting in his shop one morning in the middle nineteen-hundreds when a carpenter who did odd jobs for him came in, and, noting a slipware dish propped up on a shelf, asked, "Is that worth anything?" Now seventeenth-century slipware is the most desirable, as well as the most expensive, of all varieties of English pottery (with the possible exception of pew-groups) and has always been hard to come by: the which being explained to the carpenter, the carpenter told old Pease "I know another one like that; I've been making a frame for it to hang on the wall by." The owner, it turned out, worked in a neighbouring coal-mine,

MEDIAEVAL EARTHENWARE EWER, *c.* 1200

EIGHTEENTH-CENTURY STAFFORDSHIRE MUG · LORD GEORGE RIOT MADE A JEW

and old Pease, getting a quantity of gold sovereigns from the bank, went down to see him. He presently came in thick with pit-dirt, and asked old Pease (the lady of the house having told him to wait) what he wanted. "Will you sell me that dish?" asked old Pease, pointing to it. "Is it worth anything?" rejoined the miner. Old Pease poured out his pile of gold sovereigns and said "It's worth that": they amounted, Pease told us, to a sum two or three times larger than the man's yearly income. The man looked at them for a moment, and said "I've eaten my Christmas dinner off that dish since my pa died, and my pa before me, and my grandpa before him, and right back. I shan't sell it."

One good story deserves another, so here is something Dick Acland told me as we were walking one night through Westminster Hall, lit only by a *phare* on the floor in one of the corners, after a late committee-meeting in the House. The hammer-beam roof of the Hall, constructed in the twelfth century, was destroyed by a fire-bomb during the war; and an Act of Parliament was quickly passed, as the law requires whenever anything has to be done to the Palace of Westminster, providing that the roof should be reconstructed on exactly the old model. A group of timber experts visited several estates for the purpose of getting suitable timbers; and on the last day of their tour they were in a place somewhere, I think, south, the name and precise geography of which I have forgotten. As they were leaving after lunch they noticed, in a distant part of the estate they had omitted to visit, an oak that looked specially fine, and they hurried to it. It was indeed specially fine, and they asked their host whether they could have it. "Ah no," he replied. "We refused you that one the first time."

I do not know which of these stories I like best: they are both quintessentially English.

Old Pease's greatest service was to introduce us to Mr C. T. Campion, a pottery restorer nearby. He, Campion, gave us a piece of fascinating information that I shall put on record here, remote though it may be from the subject of this memoir; for I have seen no mention of the matter in any book on English pottery and believe it to be entirely unknown, except perhaps by a few experts in Nottingham ware, if any such still exist.

Now Nottingham ware, a few examples of which we bought from old Pease, is particularly notable for the excellence of the salt-glaze with which it is covered, and slightly pitted: but for a very short period, a few months at most, Campion told us, it was not only salt-glazed but glass-glazed as well. This came about as follows. During the months in question, and I do not remember whether by accident or design, the pottery works were open to the neighbouring glass works, by means either of a sort of serving-hatch or of a door; and fumes issuing therefrom formed a precipitate (this is science, with which I am unacquainted, and I may have got the word wrong) on or with the salt-glaze. The resulting effect was of extreme brilliance. Mr Campion was good enough to give us a fragment of glass-glaze, and we have it on one of the shelves at B.H.

But this was the lesser of Mr Campion's kindnesses. At the turn of the century there were considerable excavations at Nottingham in connection with work for the railway, and Dr Campion, our friend's father, got permission to make a search in them. He had found, our friend told us, a number of mediaeval pots, one of which was still in the family: it was at his home, which was quite near, and he wondered whether we would care to see it. We walked home with him, and there it was, as noble a pot as ever we saw in forty years of collecting. He let us have it at a gentleman's price.

I am ambivalent about the whole Jewish business, as this memoir will already have made clear; and as to circumcision, I really do not know what to think about it—sometimes I consider it salutary, as removing an itch in the penis and so lessening the chance of excessive masturbation, and sometimes I become Freudian, and fear that it may inflict an irreparable wound on the baby's psyche. But when we saw the circumcision mug in Sellick's of Exeter we knew immediately that it must be ours. Apart from anything else, it was in my experience unique: at any rate I had seen nothing like it before, and it occurred to me that it might be a christening mug, made, to his own order, by Lord George Gordon himself.

It is a piece of late-eighteenth-century cream-ware, or rather pearl-ware, bearing the legend 'Lord George Riot made a Jew'. Lord George lies on a table in the centre, with a couple of assessors on his left, and a nurse, brandishing a pair of what look like secateurs, on his right: the woman (who is hopelessly out of order anyhow, for a *mohel*, or *circumcisor*, must emphatically be a man—whoever heard of a woman doing anything as ritualistic as that?) being supported by a rabbi with a Jewish nose, who is reading the appropriate blessings from a *machsor* or prayer-book. A boy squats on the floor in front of Lord George with a large open box, ready for the pruned fragment: which, we may hope, it was better for Lord George to discard than the rest of his body, unlike a famous Jewish statesman about whom, I have been told, Sir Winston Churchill suggested the opposite. One is reminded of *Rosenkavalier*: not only of the Marschallin's little black boy, but of a certain decorative charm to be found in the better, more soigné productions. The piece was at one time in the hands of Louis Gautier of Glebe House, Chelsea, famous as having provided a considerable part of the fabulous Baring collection. This is attested by a small label affixed to its base: not however that this proves very much, for rumour has it that antique dealers equip themselves with whole stocks of such labels—Gautier, Wallace Elliot, Baring (later Revelstoke), Lensif—by way of 'establishing' doubtful pieces. 'Establishing' is a great thing in the trade. I once saw, in the shop of a notorious swindler, a pair of *famille noire* vases, which are rare and extremely expensive. "What are they worth?" I asked him. "I don't know yet," he replied. "I have to establish them first." This man once swindled even me in my less experienced days: he sold me as English salt-glaze, and even averred that they had been verified as such by the V. and A., a pair of cocks, in plain white, that were being turned out at a few shillings apiece in the China of that day. He sold them to me for forty pounds the pair—"very cheap," he said, "and only because one of them is a bit damaged": I have kept them in a dark cupboard ever since as interesting souvenirs, having shown them to a friendly dealer whom I have always felt I could trust.

Apropos of Lord George himself, he has long been one of my

heroes, and I should have thought this, apart from any question of uniqueness, a good enough reason for buying the piece. The usual view of course is that he was a vintage *m'shugganah*, what with his fanatical protestantism and hatred of Catholics; his instigation of the murderous riots, when they opened the prisons and set fire to the Bank; his apparently crackbrained schemes in politics and finance; his dinners and dances at Newgate; and, oddest of all, his unheard-of decision to have the tip of his penis dealt with as God, via Moses, had instructed.

The late Lord Oxford and Asquith, a man of more moderate temperament than Lord George's, called him "eccentric to the verge of madness, ignorant and uncultured, but a sincere fanatic"; and even his latest biographer, the sympathetic Percy Colson, remarks that "it is among the bigoted, intolerant and emotionally unstable, not the innately religious, that conversion from one creed to another tends to occur." He adds, however, that "Sane or insane, Lord George was the first aristocratic Socialist in England, the first pacifist in the modern sense, and one of the first to make a protest against the extreme brutality of the criminal laws." That, for my money, is good enough: for it connotes, not bigotry, intolerance or emotional instability, but those rarest of qualities, uncompromising humanity and a rebelliousness that is frightened of nothing and no one. If however you would get the true feel of the man you must go back to his friend and first biographer, Robert Watson, M.D., the only other Dr Watson known to history.

Consider his wit, his courage and his integrity. When the jury were called at his trial in February 1781, he objected to no less than nineteen of the names, including that of a rope maker: "He is too interested by profession," he exclaimed. When he was fighting the innumerable taxes that the Government had imposed on the wretched and already over-taxed people, and particularly the hated shop tax, he persuaded shopkeepers from Bond Street downwards to shut their shops and put up long poles decorated with black crepe and bearing the inscription 'This shop to let', instead of confining himself, in the ordinary politician's manner, to respectable speeches. And when he was solemnly excommunicated, by order of the Archbishop of Canterbury, by bell, book and candle, "To expell me from a society to which I never belonged," he retorted, "is an absurdity worthy of an archbishop."

His greatest act of courage was the way he worded "The Prisoners' Petition to the Right Honourable Lord George Gordon, to preserve their Lives and Liberties and prevent their Banishment to Botany Bay", to which, for the most trivial offences, young boys and old offenders alike could be iniquitously transported: for he referred to 'the Statutes of the Almighty' as 'falsified and erased by lawyers and judges'. He had spoken the truth, as it should be spoken, but as only a man of exceptional courage could speak it in such a connection; and by doing so he had libelled the judicature and the administrative authorities, and so, indirectly, the King. No defence was possible. Equally cavalier was his reference to Marie Antoinette, the other issue at his second trial: "Everyone knew that the Queen of France was a very *convenient* lady, and that the Ambassador's reputation in Paris was of the worst," he repeated.

He was sentenced, but escaped: and on his return four months later was committed to Newgate for five years, when he would have to give security for fourteen years' good behaviour as the price of his release. When the time came Israel Ben Abraham Gordon, as he now was, appeared before the Court in a gaberdine and with a bird's-nest beard: all really orthodox Jews wore bird's-nest beards (if they were virile enough, as most Jews are) in obedience to the biblical command 'Thou shalt not mar the corners of thy beard'. For a similar reason he tried to keep on his hat: as he was living, now that he had been circumcised, in the Jewish Palestine of two millennia ago he would have thought it disrespectful to appear uncovered—disrespectful, that is, not to the Court, for which he did not give a damn, but to the Almighty. When his hat had been forcibly removed he replaced it by a nightcap, which he had specially brought with him, knowing it would serve as well: just as, at official Jewish banquets, you may see numerous gentlemen, who do not wish to appear unfashionably orthodox, nor apostates either, using inconspicuous handkerchiefs instead of the black paper caps that are always provided.

Israel Ben Abraham's behaviour on that occasion was a lesson in sane ways of thinking. He was asked if he had the necessary sureties in court to the amount of two thousand five hundred pounds each. He said he had, and pointed to two Polish Jews of the poorest class. Upon the judge refusing to accept them he asked leave to address the Court. His two sureties, he said, were men whose characters were beyond reproach and—unless the Court judged them from the lower standards of pounds, shillings and pence—would be found completely satisfactory. "As it was a mere fiction," he continued, "which the Court themselves chose to adopt, by supposing me worth ten thousand pounds, the same fiction ought, in justice, to be held good in proportion to the sureties—unless the Court really intended imprisonment for life when they demanded such excessive and unprecedented bail."

Equally admirable was Lord George's conduct in prison. A lot has been said about his dinners and parties: less about his continued political activity. Among his constant companions were the famous radical Horne Tooke; Charles Piggot, an ardent champion of the French Revolution; Daniel Isaac Eaton, who had been indicted for publishing *The Rights of Man*; John Frost, who had attended the trial of Louis XVI as representative of the Corresponding Society; and 'Peter Pindar' (John Wolcot), whose satires on George III had delighted London. A roll-call, truly, of the elect.

Not that the more personal side of his life was neglected in prison. It is a pleasure to record that, according to rumour, he kept two Jewish maidservants, who stayed with him night and day—though Watson says that they left every evening at nine: and there is a portrait by Ozias Humphry, the miniaturist, of a very pretty Jewess carrying a tray and decanter, described as "Polly Levy, a Jewess in attendance on Lord George Gordon during his confinement in Newgate." And whatever his personal relations may have been with these women, he treated them, and his fellow-prisoners too, with exemplary kindness.

Why did he become a Jew? Because, in my opinion, he had a passion for righteousness of the Old Testament sort, the merits of which, I do not doubt, he exaggerated. In other words, he had always been a Jew of the best kind rather than a Christian of any kind (and the odd thing is that he looked like a Jew, with that aquiline nose of his to which Dickens referred). He must have been rather like a young and exceptionally vigorous version of today's Bertie Russell, with a touch of Moses and Kirkegaard thrown in. As for fanaticism, there is a lot, almost everything, to be said for it: I incline, for my part, to the words of John the Divine, "I know thy works, that thou art neither cold nor hot: I would thou wert cold or hot. So then because thou art lukewarm, and neither cold nor hot, I will spue thee out of my mouth."

I have a link with Israel Ben Abraham Gordon that pleases me. More than half a century after his death my grandfather, "the greatest tenor of the nineteenth century", as my father used to call him, became *chazan* (cantor) of the Hambro' synagogue, which had been central to Israel's life and would have been central to his death too if he had had his way: for he was circumcised under its auspices after another synagogue had turned him down, and is rumoured to have expressed a desire to be buried there when *in extremis*. But the Jews did not want him after death; nor, passionately, did those noble goyim, his kinsfolk, for though they buried him in St James's Cemetery at Hampstead they cared so little to keep him in remembrance that the very site of his grave was soon forgotten.

August 27th

While I am in this kind of mood I shall comment on some news that has just come through on the wireless. The Americans in Vietnam, by one of those military blunders that are by no means uncommon, have sprayed their own troops with napalm.

The effects of napalm, which people talk about quite casually, were described by an eye-witness in the Korean war as follows: "In front of us a curious figure was standing, a little crouched, legs straddled, arms held out from his sides. He had no eyes, and the whole of his body, nearly all of which was visible through tatters of burnt rags, was covered with a hard black crust speckled with yellow pus. A Korean woman by his side began to speak, and the interpreter said: 'He has to stand, Sir, he cannot sit or lie'. He had to stand because he was no longer covered with skin, but with a crust like crackling that broke easily."

The first reaction of most Americans will be, "How terrible that they should have sprayed our own men and not the enemy", and the vast majority of people outside America will take no notice at all. But in a relatively decent world the universal reaction would have been, "How terrible that anyone should inflict suffering so ghastly on anyone else".

I do not need to be told the argument in favour of napalm. Among other things: that war is war, and worse even than war are the horrors that would threaten us all if communism were not 'contained'. I reject the argument utterly. I say that nothing, nothing whatever, can justify the perpetration of such obscenities: come what may in the Devil's good time (and I do not believe in him), let us behave on God's side in the interim. Can good, in the long run, ever come of such evil?

I am horrified by the decay of pacifism in the world: I am horrified that so few Americans should have said before being drafted "I will not do it". How different it was in 1914. A respectable minority, of Englishmen at any rate, preferred prison or ambulance work to military service, and several were killed when succouring the wounded, whether 'their own' men or not, including one of my best friends (Ralph Rooper, quem honoris causa memoro). And what has come of 1914, anyhow?

From the Daily Mail, September 8th, 1966:

"The sergeant explained that some of the casualties happened when one of their own planes accidentally dropped napalm on their own positions.

"'I saw one GI—he was cooked. Done to a rare turn. He was screaming, twitching, moaning. When a man's been hit by napalm you have to take a knife and scrape it off. You scrape meat.'

"But he did not blame the pilot for bombing close to the U.S. positions.

"'Charlie (the Vietcong) was right up close to us. That's where the bombing should be. When you get a few people being wounded by your own bombs and artillery, you know you're in the right place.'

EIGHTEENTH-CENTURY STAFFORDSHIRE FIGURE · VIRGIN AND CHILD

THE WILBERFORCE TONDO

"*The sergeant was sorry but not sentimental about the men who had died.*"

Over against our circumcision mug is my Virgin and Child (I call it 'my' because though my wife is not against Christianity she is not particularly for it, either). Again, it is at Eaton Place: not as part of the pottery collection, but, standing on my writing table, as part of my life. For the fact is that when I first read the Gospels, at the age of about eleven, a love of the man Jesus swept over me and informed my whole being. Nor was it any passing emotion: it became deeper and deeper as the years went by, until, early in my time at Oxford, love could no longer describe it.

That beautiful spirit Father Yelchaninov wrote something peculiarly relevant to my feeling about Jesus in my early teens. "It is impossible not to love Christ," he said. "If we saw Him now, we should not be able to take our eyes off Him, we should 'listen to Him in rapture'; we should flock around Him as did the multitudes in the Gospels. All that is required of us is not to resist. We must yield to Him, to the contemplation of His image, and He will capture our hearts." If only, I often thought at that time, I could have been with Him at the lakeside at the beginning of our era! Or if only it could all be happening now! To stand near Him on the Mount; to hear Him say "Neither do I condemn thee"; to be challenged by His enemies and not to deny Him—this is what I passionately longed for as I brooded about Him—and I did so increasingly—in twentieth-century London.

I thought of Him as the greatest of the Hebrew prophets: I thought of Him as another but far more lovable Socrates: I did not think of Him as what He Himself, knowing God as the Father of all, could ever have described as sinless. Within that ocean of goodness and truth there were currents and eddies that gave me pause. There was the cursing of the fig tree; there was His hatred of the Pharisees (for this was no case, as I saw it, of hating the sin but loving the sinner): above all, there was the Last Judgment. I should have been ashamed, out of very reverence, to explain such enigmas away: I might have said what Simone Weil was to say later, "If you have to choose between Christ and truth choose truth, and you will immediately find yourself in His arms." I was particularly exercised about the bearing of all this on the doctrine of the Incarnation, which was fascinating me more and more. Jesus taught a God of pure love: His life was overwhelmingly a life of pure love: but He was capable of hating, by way of exception, people who he felt outraged God: and He could envisage eternal damnation. How then could He be the unique and absolute Incarnation of the God of love He so marvellously revealed? *An* incarnation, yes: *the* Incarnation, no. Good beyond ordinary human limits, yes: sinless, no.

That was my situation when I went to Oxford. I had continued, in the meantime, to ponder the Incarnation: and my love of Christ, which had been totally unaffected by my criticisms of Him, had continued to increase. Nor has it diminished to this moment; but I still call myself, not a Christian in any orthodox sense, but a heretical Jew.

There are many childish sing-songs in the old Jewish lore that run something like this: "Holy are the seven so-and-so's; holier than the seven so-and-so's are the six so-and-so's; holier than the six so-and-so's are the five so-and-so's"—and so up stage by stage, until you arrive at the unity of God. And I would now say "Holy is our circumcision mug; holier than our circumcision mug is my Virgin and Child; and holier than either is our Wilberforce tondo, for the essence of religion is its materialisation in the everyday world."

Our tondo, in enamel, is about an inch and a half across, and is framed in satinwood. Dominating it is a negro at prayer, his arms, uplifted, fettered by manacles in gold: two ships are coming to release him: and the eye of God is observing from the sky. There is an inscription: "AM I NOT A MAN AND A BROTHER?" We found it in a junk shop near the Abbey, one day in the thirties when we were visiting our daughter Julia at Badminton: we had come over to Bath, which we have always dearly loved, and were strolling about in the sun.

The medallion was wrapped up in a piece of yellowing paper,

an article from the Bath and Wilts *Chronicle and Herald* dated May 5th, 1930. This eulogised Wilberforce, the occasion being a "commemorative bronze" that had just been unveiled by Lady Simon on the façade of number thirty-six Pulteney Street, one of the several houses in Bath that had been the home of "the great philanthropist and leader of the movement for the abolition of slavery, for which splendid cause he laboured unceasingly from 1787 until twenty years later his ambition was accomplished when Parliament passed the Act which set the seal of success upon his rigorous campaign". Lady Simon and her family were also eulogised. The medallion had quite recently been found, the people in the shop told us, in the attic of one of these Wilberforce houses that was being cleared of accumulated rubbish.

I have left to the end the most intimate, and some may think a rather crazy, part of our little collection on the shelves of B.H. It consists of a couple of dozen small stones—mica-schist, etcetera—that we have picked up at various times all over England and Europe: backed by a few flints, one looking like an owl and another like a bird lying asleep, but for the most part merely knobby and holed. There is nothing in any way special about the bits of stone, nothing quaint or rare or in the usual sense beautiful: I have just looked down and felt impelled to pick them up.

My love of geology, which was the beginning of the matter, took its rise from the discovery when I was still quite small of a tiny duodecimo textbook, with only a hundred or so pages of letterpress but a few quite entrancing illustrations. My mother had a bookcase which she normally kept locked; and one day, when she had forgotten to do so, I came upon my little treasure there, and begged to be allowed to keep it. My request was granted; and immediately I was caught by an enchantment that was to hold me for at least ten years and came very near to rivalling my passion for music itself. Soon I was progressing to more and more difficult textbooks: I was given, when *Barmitsvah* at thirteen, the great standard work by Sir Archibald Geikie in two volumes:

and meanwhile I was venturing into palaeobotany and palaeozoology and the other indispensable subsidiaries, all however without the slightest knowledge of botany or zoology themselves, for mere contemporaneities seemed tedious and flat to me—the Switzerlands or Canadas of life, with nothing romantic or "extra" about them. It was the world's magic past that so compellingly called to me: nostalgic with a nostalgia far surpassing mere homesickness or longing for one's own petty past, I lived starry-eyed in the strange vast aeons that had preceded my arrival on earth. Pleistocene and Recent made little appeal to me: neoliths, palaeoliths, mammoths—contemptible proto-modernities, not more than some millions of years old! I wanted the reptiles of the Mesozoic, winged for the air and armoured for the land and webbed for the coraline seas; I wanted the forests of the coal-measures, darkling and steamy with eternal rain; but far more than these I wanted the real earlinesses—Devonian and Silurian and Cambrian: trilobites: the immemorial worm-tracks; and so down at last to the bottommost gneisses, alone before the birth of life. What a glory, this journey through time, for a schoolboy not yet in his teens!

Incapable of mastering even the rudiments of those sciences with which geology is inextricably linked—chemistry and physics and astronomy as well as botany and zoology—I nevertheless developed an odd expertise within the range of my own capabilities. My appetite for detail was immense. I not only knew, as a matter of course, what genera of fossils were to be found in the various strata: I might also know, and always wanted to know, the name and appearance of a particular species characteristic, say, of some band, perhaps only an inch or so thick, in the chalk of Dover or the limestone of Bath. To unravel the whole story of the earth's past: to find that seas had been here, land-masses there, mountains somewhere else, at this or that moment in mundane history: to visualise the appearance of the changing populations—the echinoderms and ammonites and belemnites and lepidodendrons and ichthyosauri and deinosaurs and palaeotheres and mastodons, down, in types that teemed, to the smallest variation in the latest sub-species—it was this that so fascinated me, so compelled me to go ever and ever forward and learn ever and ever more until at last I should have won, as I passionately desired, the last guarded secret of the stony record. I haunted the airy galleries, aromatic with bees-wax, of the South Kensington Museum; I pored over show-cases with pencil and notebook, and made feeble sketches, now of some tiny bivalve, and now, moving on, of the vast megalosaur that bestraddled the length of a neighbouring room. Breaking off, I would eat my sandwiches in the grounds, on a seat by the stump of a fossilised tree, and then go hurrying back to my sketching. South Kensington Station, when nowadays I happen to pass through it, brings back to me, always, these holiday expeditions: airiness, and bees-wax, and summer afternoons.

I was found at my work one day by a man called Sherborne Smith, a kindly and bearded man, almost as big as the megalosaur, who was in some way connected with the Department of Geology. He made me free of the exceptionally fine geological library, and I spent many happy hours there in the months and years that followed, taking down notes, drawing up comparative tables, and copying illustrations of specimens unrepresented in the galleries. When I got home and told my mother how kind this man had been to me, she smiled with a sort of wistful gravity that I often remarked in her. "A world-famous naturalist and writer like that!" she said. "Really great men find time for anything—even for unimportant small boys. It's a sign of their greatness." There had been some confusion, I realised, between Sherborne Smith and White of Selborne; but I did not say so, preferring to trade on a spurious glory. I was equally lacking in forthrightness about my membership of the Geologists' Association, which I joined at the age of ten or eleven, at the prompting of the same Sherborne Smith, who wanted to make me a professional geologist. This was a delightful Association. It staged a weekly expedition for fossil-hunting to such heavenly places as Swanage or the Island of Sheppey; and though I could never go, partly because the event was always on Saturday and partly because I couldn't have afforded to anyhow, I looked forward eagerly to the monthly bulletin, which contained full accounts of the members' "finds". There was another feature of this little booklet that made it as precious to me, on occasion, as the libretto of a Meyerbeer opera. From time to time a member would investigate, band by band, the flora or fauna of some particular stratum; and the results would be published in the bulletin, under some such title as "Notes on the distribution of ammonites in the Lower Lias at Brackenmouth". There might even be illustrations! Here was something really expert, something a serious geologist must immediately take note of, something, above all, that filled in the picture. When a bulletin arrived with an article like this, I would have given up everything, save only the opera, to read it without a moment's delay.

Anybody could join the Association upon payment of a trivial fee. But when my membership of this body was confused at Elgin Avenue with a Fellowship of the Royal Geological Society, to which, it appeared, I had been elected at the age of ten, I was silent. The difference, after all, I may have thought, was not so great. And I was the youngest member of the Association, anyhow. I occasionally signed myself M.G.A.—"Member of the Geologists' Association." Once or twice I may have made it F.G.A. But I am sure I never went so far as F.R.Geol.S.

My own collection of fossils, which was the centre of my geological life, was necessarily a very poor one. To buy any would have seemed indecent, indeed the possibility of doing so would never have entered my mind; and even to accept one as a gift, apart perhaps from some special rarity I couldn't hope to find for myself, would have been a little dubious. For the search, the discovery and the careful extraction—cutting round and prising out so that nothing might be damaged or lost—this was the heart of the matter: the third term in a relation between me as a person and rocks, the holy spirit, which purchase, or previous possession by alien hands, would somehow have robbed of its purity. But my opportunities for fossilising were extremely limited, being confined to the occasional summer holiday or a quarry I might hear of on the outskirts of London. Any opportunity that did occur I eagerly seized, "tapping the strata", as I grandly described it, with my geological chisel, which was an ordinary chisel, and my genuinely geological hammer. Margate was my best treasure-ground; I got some very nice echinoderms in the chalk at the far end of Cliftonville, and a quantity of those small jointed stalks, like miniature bamboo shoots, of which I never discovered the origin. I had excellent ammonites, too, many of them with beautiful convolutions, and one that I loved above all, for it shone with a patina of bright green like Roman glass or peacocks' feathers. But my largest collection was of fossils from the flint. Roads were constantly being made in our neighbourhood, and I became quite an expert at carefully weighing up, from the appearance of a flint, the probability of there being something inside. If I thought there might be, I would smash it along the proper line, and was often rewarded by beautiful sponges, and once or twice by the cast of a shell. I always tried to discover where the flints had come from. My specimens were carefully arranged, each with its own Latin label, in some cardboard nests of drawers that I had bought at a draper's.

Was my love of geology somehow connected with my love of earth? I think so. For I loved earth exceedingly, and anything that suggested it: the smell of violets, and the taste of medlars, and leaves lying sodden on autumn mould.

My love of geology in general, and of fossils, is at most quiescent, but my love of rocks and stones has increased with the years. That is why I feel such fellowship with Pierre Teilhard de Chardin. Like him, I feel in rocks and stones something not indeed better, but perhaps even more exciting, than life itself, namely life potential. And I especially love flints, not for their aesthetic qualities, though they are often amazingly beautiful, but for the assurance they give, with their magnificent exuberance, that life is already there.

I have done: and because most of my days have been happy, with only a small minority of them dull or grim or even agonised; because, though I have done many bad things, I have occasionally done a good one too; and because, if many have disliked me, quite a number have given me their friendship or love, I shall end with the blessing prescribed for joyful occasions—on one's birthday, on eating a first fruit, on hearing a birthcry, on wearing a new suit of clothes or entering a new house or garden or concluding a difficult enterprise: a blessing alike of initiation and fulfilment: Blessed art thou, O Lord our God, King of the Universe, who hast preserved us, and kept us in life, and allowed us to reach this season. Amen and Amen.

But because I do not wish to end, after all, on so solemn a note, I shall put down here the b'rōcha to be said every morning on going to stool.

Blessed art thou, O Lord our God, King of the universe, who hast formed man in wisdom, and created in him many orifices and vessels. It is revealed and known before the throne of thy glory that if one of these be opened, or one of these be closed, it would be impossible to exist and to stand before thee. Blessed art thou, O Lord, who healest all flesh and doest wondrously.

Blessed art thou, O Lord, creator of man.

EPILOGUE

WRITTEN WITH THE LEFT HAND

[This diary has been printed with spelling, punctuation, paragraphing and asterisks as written.]

To see ourselves as others see us.

I can't for the life of me make out why I'm such an ass.

It's extraordinary how often the long chance comes off. Life, in fact, is a series of gambles that come off.

I've got all sorts of things stored up inside me, but cannot express them.

A man can sometimes secretly know in his inner life what he cannot express.

But one day he will be able to express it.

Or that, at least, is what I hope.

I am living behind a veil.

It is lifting fast

I'm looking forward to Mary's* visit tonight

Writing is coming back to me

I love Poo coming in to confer with me

I look forward to seeing the garden and the flowers again this

* Mary Brash, production manager at V.G. Ltd.

spring, when everything is again flowering. I look back to the days when I used to doze in the garden, with eyes half shut. Those were *the* days! I'm merely putting down what comes into my head, even if it makes nonsense! But I wish it made sense.

I do not feel at all well this morning: there is an intolerable ache in my tummy. I feel awfully sick. This is the sort of thing that makes me think I have got one of the dread diseases. Pray God I haven't. I already feel a little better. Perhaps it is going to be all right after all. There is an intolerable "either" "or" about this business.

There is an intolerable uncertainty about this business. The only thing is to be philosophic about it. Its probably a matter of 50/50: 50% life, 50% death. Ruth thinks this absurd! But she was always an optimist.

Anyhow, cheer up! One will know, or the world will know, one way or another, in a year's time! And in a year a hell of a lot can happen.

I think I feel better this morning than I have so far done. My mind is clearer, and I don't make so many mistakes in this writing. Altogether, the whole set-up seems sounder. Is it perhaps possible that I am going to get well? That would be marvellous! One would have to invent a special blessing! "Blessed art Thou, O Lord, who healest the sick" If I get well, I must be very careful in the future.

It's absurd, in life, to rely on certainties. They always let you down. Better to trust in the unexpected, which, time after time, comes up trumps.

I have felt worse this morning than on any morning since this trouble began: and yet somehow not quite so bad as I had expected. I feel wretched: but I have the idea that I shall feel better

V.G. IN
1950

M. Hurliman

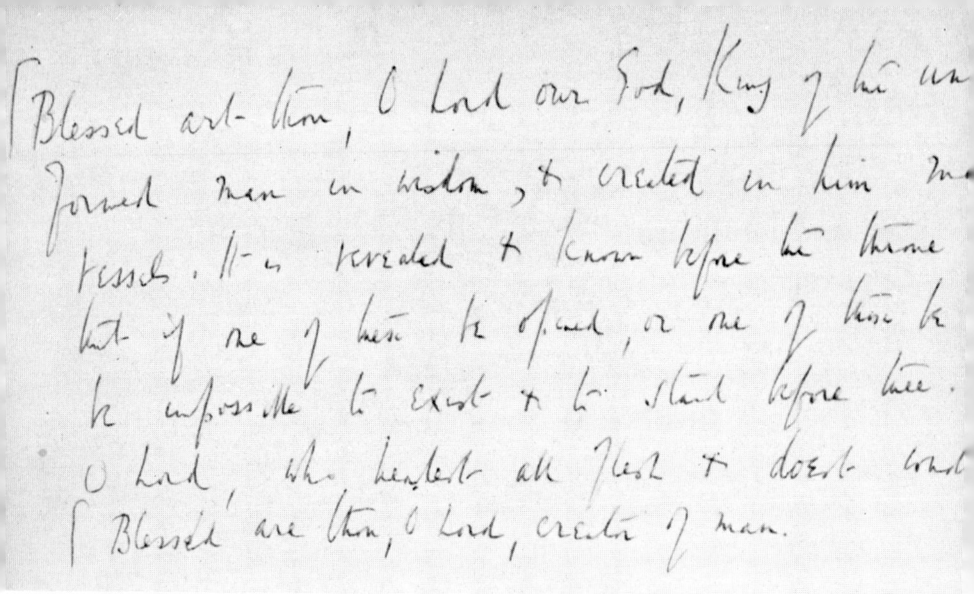
[Blessed art thou, O Lord our God, King of the un
formed man in wisdom, & created in him ma
vessels. It is revealed & known before the throne
that if one of them be opened, or one of those be
be impossible to exist & to stand before thee.
O Lord, who healest all flesh & doest wond
[Blessed are thou, O Lord, creator of man.

NORMAL HANDWRITING · ACTUAL SIZE
(part of page 252)

LEFT-HAND WRITING · ACTUAL SIZE
(part of pages 274–5)

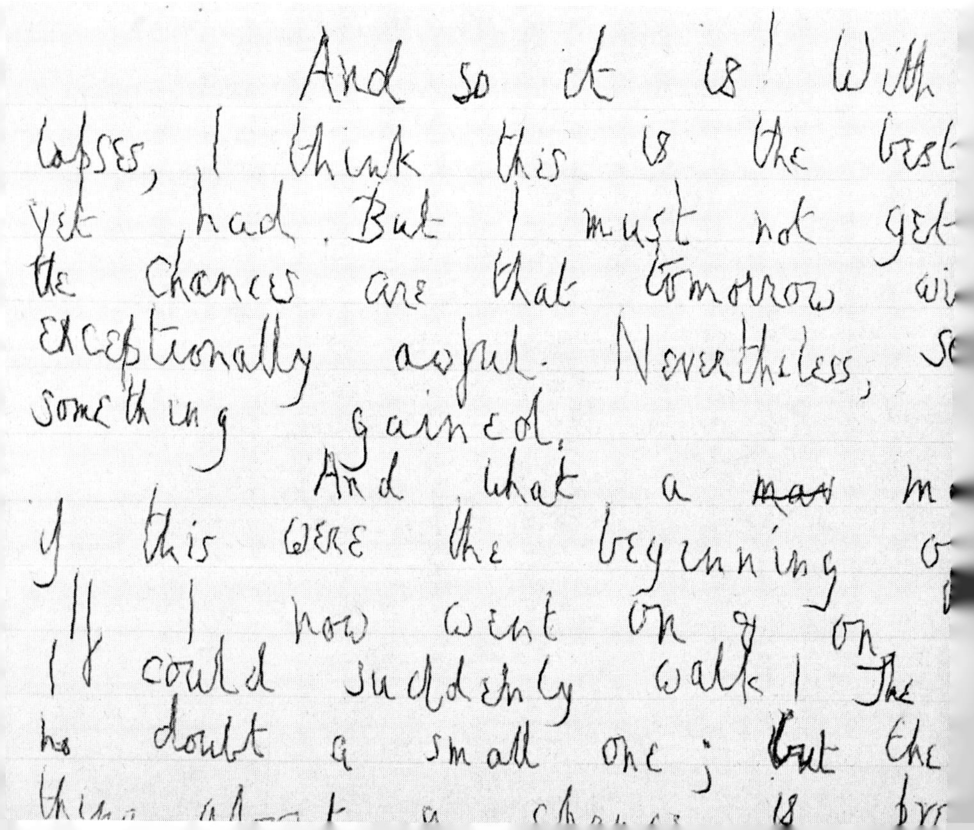
And so it is! With
lapses, I think this is the best
yet had. But I must not get
the chances are that tomorrow wi
exceptionally awful. Nevertheless, so
something gained.
And what a ~~man~~ m
if this WERE the beginning o
If I now went on & on
I could suddenly walk! The
no doubt a small one; but the
thing about a chance is

presently. I simply don't know what to think. One fluctuates so. If one always felt at one's worst, one would have been dead long ago. So perhaps it is better to be optimistic. It is better to be better than one thinks.

In any case, you do no good by brooding on the worst side of things.

But all the same, I wish I knew!

The last few days I think I have been a little better. Somehow the mists seem to be clearing. Perhaps I shall get right again after all. This is too good to be true, and if it's true I thank God Almighty for it. After all, one can be optimistic as well as pessimistic.

If I don't feel so well again, I mustn't go pessimistic. There are bound to be ups and downs.

What shall I write? A poem to Mother Ruth!

For the first thing in the morning, I don't really feel at all bad. Of course there is a suspicion of pain: but really not much more than that. It looks as if things were going to go pretty well. If I felt no worse than this all day, there would be nothing much to complain about. But that's too much to hope for! Ruth, after looking rather grumpy, now looks very bright! All the signs are for a reasonably happy day. I shall do my share: for after all my love for Ruth knows no bounds.

This will make a very interesting diary: for after all I'm not going to die at once, and meanwhile there will be all interesting manner of things to record. I only wish I could write without so much scratching out, which is unsightly. But that will come in time, no doubt.

(This page* has taken three quarters of an hour)

It's a matter of nuances! I felt rather better than usual, and accordingly very optimistic: now rather worse than usual, and

* The above two paragraphs.

accordingly very pessimistic. It seems impossible to keep an even keel. A little better, a little worse—why make such a fuss? But that is the nature of the illness. The only thing is to remember this when things are bad.

Weathercock! When things are slightly worse, they are the very devil; when slightly better, they are paradise. Why not one, two, three instead of one, two, zed?

But some people really are philosophic.—for instance, J. B. S. Haldane. He wrote a wonderful paper on cancer when dying of cancer. But Ruth says I musn't talk about cancer, which she says is all nonsense. Nonsense or no nonsense, I am in the sort of mood in which I fear it. I shall probably come to my senses presently. . . . Now I have come to my senses! So I think I shall play some music.

Music is the only thing that has not suffered: it is the only thing that remains fresh and spiritual. It is the core and centre of my life—a thing that no stroke can affect.

★ ★ ★

Things are really atrocious this morning. I have never had so bad a beginning. And yet even now things are beginning to ease off. This is hardly worse than the opening of a bad day. In one respect I am an incurable optimist, in another an incurable pessimist.

★ ★ ★

I've been reading a Year of Grace. Very odd. In one way it's quite simple and easygoing: but then, in another way, it's all in a sort of fog. My brain is like a baby's. Will the time come when everything is crystal-clear? Or shall I always live in a half-haze?

★ ★ ★

The second is, alas! the more probable: but not certain.

★ ★ ★

Still, it is better than *nothing*—which comes quite fast enough!

★ ★ ★

If I could look at everything with a completely sane eye, I should say that this is almost the best morning yet. A little pain is the worst I can say: and while I'm writing I hardly notice it. I darsay I shall feel worse later on: indeed, it's coming on now; but no one could say that there is anything to make a serious fuss about. The important thing is to keep a sense of proportion.

That is all very well when I've got something to do; but when there's nothing to do the situation is very different. Then the pain reaches proportions that sometimes seem positively gargantuan. I feel certain that I'm going to die!

I'm a bit nervous about the scheme Poo has got going for a conference here every Thursday, to talk about forthcoming books. I shall probably forget everything! The great thing is to be absolutely honest—not to pretend! Then we shall see what I'm really worth—whether there are serious limitations in me, but still I'm worth something. I'm conceited enough to think that I still am worth *something* to the firm. What is worth more—a quarter per cent the brilliant or a hundred per cent the mediocre? Anyhow, that will be my aim.

Poo is an angel!

* * *

Joana* is coming in at four this afternoon. That will be most agreeable! I shall soon fall in love with her!

* * *

What an ass I am! A girl has only to be kind to me, and I at once imagine that she is in love with me! The real fact is that these girls are a bit sorry for the old man, who at once mistakes pity for love. Still, love is agreeable, even when it's only the most obvious make-believe.

* * *

I shall make it my aim to write to Poo a few lines every day in America. One letter in every half-dozen may even be useful.

* * *

*Joanna Goodwin, his secretary.

I have had an awful night again. I woke up feeling worse than ever before. It's true that already I feel perhaps a trifle better again, but that's only because the concentration of my mind prevents any other acute sensation. The moment my attention slackens off again, the pain will come back. And so it will go on till one day the end will come. What an appalling waste! Still, one day its *got* to end. Even if one lives to be a hundred, some day the end has *got* to come. I don't know whether to be thankful or not.

* * *

It's one of those examples of absolutely inexorable fate. From today I'm going to make a completely new plan for this diary. I'm going to give up completely all talk about the state of my health, and concentrate entirely on other matters. There are far more important things than how I am.

I was dissapointed when I read the first part of this diary as a whole. To my dismay, what I had thought perceptive seemed naïve. Well, never mind. The second instalment is going to be a lot better than the first. I shall concentrate entirely on matters of interest to the world as a whole.

For instance, music.

Music is divided for me into two wholly distinct parts. There is that minority which I know from A to Z. I could almost hum most of it without an error. Examples are the fifth and seventh symphonies of Beethoven. On the other hand, other things, though as familiar, are a blank until they start—e.g. the opus 109 of Beethoven. On the other hand, they *go on* as familiarly in the one case as in the other. Start me on the ninth symphony of Schubert, and I'll go on with very few mistakes until the end.

But this has to be said—the familiar is all the time getting bigger and the unfamiliar smaller.

Soon, I hope, I shall be in my old familiar position! That is to say, when everything is familiar! But though I say 'I hope' I don't really believe it. I shall be quite content if my musical knowledge reaches 50% of the original. The curious thing is that I like certain things far better than I used to. I used to find the Brahms No. 1 pretty-pretty: I now find it absolutely glorious. Whether this is an improvement or the opposite in musical taste I cannot say. Its not a question of the simpler or more complicated: the C sharp minor means as much to me as it ever did, and heaven knows that it is complicated enough.

It is the same thing (I think I will now play a little music).

* * *

This is the next morning. It was a mixed sort of night: it started off very badly, and then from three to six I slept very well. I now feel no worse than on a average morning. But I promised not to talk about my health.

I spent most of the time playing music. Among other things I played the Schubert Ninth and Unfinished: the latter extremely slowly. It is strange how slow the latter sounds. Then I played the hierarchical Consecration of the House, among some other Beethoven overtures.

Apart from music, the other thing I read was A Year of Grace. I had exactly the same experience as before. Or rather: the experience was just a trifle better: I understood a trifle more, and rather less seemed foggy. Generally speaking, however, the general effect was one of haziness. Will it always be like this? Or shall I more and more find myself rapidly improving? On the answer depends the question: shall I be a moron, or say a 50% man?

Mummy says there is nothing to worry about; but I say there is everything. The difference between a sort of life and a sort of death. Half a life is one thing, one can do something with it: one can do nothing with no life. Well, the only thing is to wait and see.

I'd better listen to a little more music. I shall begin with Brahams.

* * *

Last night was, I take it, far the best I have had. It is not so much a question of positive aches and pains: there are plenty of those: it is rather a question of general 'feel'. I feel altogether better.

I had a very good time with music yesterday. The second

Brahams thrilled me very much; and after that I played first the Consecration of the House again, and then the Eigth Symphony of Beethoven. All very familiar and very magnificent.

The rest of yesterday was spent entirely with the Witkins and talking. The Witkins* were of course extraordinarily nice and well meaning; and the talk was as good as one could want. But I had forgotten Poo; she unexpectedly came in from nine to ten, and that made all the difference. Vits† also came in for supper. Alogether, it ended up as a most agreable‡ day. It's extraordinary how a few people can turn a tedious day into a very attractive one. Afterwards we spent half an hour gossiping, before turning in for what turned out to be an unusually good night. But the promise of the morning was not wholly fulfilled: I promised, however, not to talk about that. Sufficient unto the day is the goodnes‡ therof.

This writing is improving in speed but going off in acuracy.‡ I am always putting two letters instead of one. I don't know whether this is the inevitable result of speed, or a general deterioration. This is another example of my eternal fear of losing what I have acquired. But when I come to look it up, I nearly always discover that my original idea was correct! So I don't think I shall do any more correcting. After all, it's a question of spelling: and my spelling is as good as most people's. I must acquire more confidence. The absence of confidence is really a form of conceit. An occasional mistake doesn't matter. What matters is a steady deterioration: but that is unlikely.

I suppose I ought to say that I am well aware that this is an unbelievably naïve piece of writing. But that does not matter; what matters is that anything I write should be at least full of common sense. Accuracy is the most important thing at this stage: anything more ambitious can come later.

I don't think I shall do any more today: I'm tired.

* * *

The fluctuations of these mornings is appalling. I am writing

* Friends from New York. † His daughter Vita.

‡ In the m.s. the correctly doubled letter in these words was struck through.

at 8 forty-five, and I feel absolutely appalling. I am really worse this morning than I have felt for ages. I feel it worth using the word 'appalling' twice.

Still, it's no good, just because I feel ill, giving up what I suppose I ought to call my plans—which were to cease talking about my health. So I think I will now turn to consider that—or rather the opposite!

I still find the same thing about descriptions of music. There is the same vagueness, the same haziness, that I found formerly. Maybe the vagueness, the haziness is not quite so great as before, but the difference is only minimal—by and large, the vagueness and haziness that *was* is very similar to the vagueness and haziness that *is*. I find it impossible to say "Yesterday it was hazy, today it is clear." The difference I should put at about 5%. When progress is as slow as that, you cannot talk about progress at all. And yet, just behind the haziness, I do sense the full meaning. What eludes me is something quite definite—something that is almost 100% the real thing. Get a *trifle* extra, and you, instead of nothing, get everything. The missing meaning is just round the corner. But what if that missing meaning should never come? That would mean a whole lost world. And I feel I could not bear *just* to lose *everything*.

Let me be more precise. The full meaning of a great piece of prose is a wonderful thing: a world of wonder is in it. But if you get no *precise* meaning from it, but only a sort of jumble, you lose almost everything.

Still, you've got to take the best you can get. I suppose that if you apprehend 25% of the author's full meaning, you ought to be very greatful. I'm nowhere near 25% yet: nearer, as I have said, 5%.

I suppose I ought to be less ambitious: read only pappy things. Well, that is not my way. I'd sooner understand 25% of stuff that means something than 100% of stuff that means nothing. So I'll continue on my path: trusting that enlightenment will come to me. If it does not—well, so be it. At any rate I shall have tried.

I think I shall break off there. I've got infernally tired. I shall have my usual recourse to music: music will always be my solace.

If I only understand 25% of music, it is sufficient: Music, Heine said, is halfway between spirit and matter: spirit that requires manifestation in time and matter that can do without space. "We do not know what music is."

* * *

I find that music means more to me than it did. A thing I would pass over without a thought now affords me the utmost delight. The Unfinished Symphony, for instance, I used to listen to as something at best pleasant and rather stale: now it comes to me as a heaven-sent thing. And there's very little indeed that nowadays I don't like. It is as if everything nowadays had taken on a new and delightful meaning.

Take, for instance, the Siegfried Idyll. I was awfully tired of it: now, whatever one might think of the man Wagner, as music one would listen to it with supreme pleasure. The only things I didn't care for were light operatic things like Don Pasquale: my taste for those, I found, had gone. Apart from that, "character" pieces were less to my liking than pieces of strong emotional content: for instance, I preferred Brahms to Ravel. But though my taste varied, there was little that I positively rejected. Generally speaking, a thing only had to answer to the name 'music' to find in me an immediate response.

By and large, then, I was first and last a musician.

What, then, is a musician? I take it that a musician is a man who feels his whole being transformed when music is played. The great musician feels this transformation: whether he really understands what is happening to him is a different matter. He may not understand what is happening: for all that, it *is* happening.

* * *

How silly atheism is! As silly as definite theism! I believe in God: but what type or manner of God I haven't the smallest idea. The definite atheists are as stupid as the stupid theists. How on earth can a man comprehend a millionth part of his own Godhead? I am content to say "I do not know what I believe, but I believe" A man who goes further than that is an utter fool; but so is a man who goes less far. For my own part, I prefer the utter sceptic to the utter believer: I find him less irritating. But the true aristocrat is the man who says "I do not know what I believe" but still, in his heart of hearts, does believe *something*. The man who resolutely believes *nothing*—who is certain that Death is the end—is amusing enough, but not to be taken very seriously.

That was not worth saying, no doubt; but I like the idea that a sort of agnostic is more serious than an out and out atheist.

* * *

It's astounding how comparatively well I feel this morning. I don't mean that I feel positively well or anything like that: I've got pains in my stomach, as usual; but at the same time there's a general feel of comparative well-being. When I'm writing I forget the pain. This is a lovely privelege.

There's no topic I particularly want to write about. I feel more inclined simply to sit and enjoy the weather. I don't of course know for certain whether I'm going to live; but this morning I feel inclined to take it for granted.

* * *

I'm just back from my walk—it's half past ten. As I've been doing nothing for an hour the pain is of course worse than before; but for all that I cling to my optimism. It is impossible to feel really pessimistic on such a morning.

* * *

I do hope that things won't be too bad in the hour or so after lunch; then I shall be able to call it a record day.

* * *

12.15. I find myself very much looking forward to lunch. Lunch is almost painless: I sometimes fail to enjoy it because I feel miserable, but never because I positively lack appetite. My appetite is always excellent. But sometimes the weight of misery is too great. That, however, does not happen very often. More usually, lunch is one of the things I enjoy. The trouble is, lunch is followed by the hideous period of afternoon rest—the worst time of the day. Things get better about four o'clock. Best of all is the period from four to eleven. If agreable people are coming in, that is often most enjoyable.

* * *

It is now three o'clock. I feel as usual pretty bad: muddled in my head, and confused in my reactions. The last half hour I read the Year of Grace: but it was very vague, and not at all lucid. I feel the best I can hope for is a sort of twilight existence. This is what things have come to. There is only one thing worse that can be imagined—death. I persist in thinking that that *is* worse. But poor Mummy!

* * *

I finished yesterday pretty badly, as I've hinted. I had an excellent night, but felt awful this morning. It's now eight-thirty, and I feel a little less awful. But I know it's only temporary: sooner or later the pain will come back. Still, I must stick to my bargain.

I wonder whether one can enjoy a thing purely temporally, knowing that the cessation of pain will only be brief? I suppose that one can, if only one is philosophic enough. There is no need to be wretched because something is *going* to happen: death, after all, lurks inevitably in the background. And when it comes to it, what is the difference between a second and an hour? The only thing to do is to be happy, if only for a minute! I may die tonight: I may die in ten years: what difference will it make in a thousand years time?

So I shall try—knowing very well I may fail—to be happy when it is possible to be happy. Of course, I may fail; but I can try to achieve happiness when the objective conditions render that possible—at the present moment, for instance, when I've just drunk a little hot soup. There are some people—rare souls—who can even be happy in the very middle of a violent stomach ache, but I am not one of those. My ambitions are more modest. But I see no reason at all why one should not be happy for say half an hour, if during that half hour one is devoid of pain. And what if it's three quarters of an hour, or even, maybe, two hours? That's the value I find in this writing: you write for say two hours, and you find that, during that two hours, you haven't been aware of feeling pain at all. The question is, have you in fact felt pain at all during those two hours? I think the answer is, a little, but not much. If that's true, it's rather wonderful; for it means that one is feeling no more than the discomfort an ordinary unathletic person feels most of the time. After all, half the time everyone of seventy feels a bit lousy. (I must beware of too much repetition in this writing). So this piece, which started off so pessimistically, ends on a note of qualified optimism.

* * *

It seems rather boring to keep harping on my health, but to say nothing about it this morning seems rather churlish. For I think I feel better this morning than ever before. There is pain if for a moment I stop to think about it; but if I don't, I feel nothing at all. So I think I am right in calling this the best morning I have had. The question is, will I be able to keep up this insensibility all the time I'm out? Or, the moment I stop concentrating, will the pain come rushing back? We shall see; but in the meantime I feel reasonably optimistic.

In another sense this is a red-letter day; Poo goes to America tomorrow for a month.

I have grown extremely fond of Poo this last couple of months. She is so sensible; at the same time she is so affectionate. And she shows me an extraordinary courtesy: she really appears to believe that I know more about the business than anyone. So, in a sense, I do; but that isn't saying very much. She is an extraordinarily able person, who is willing to try her hand at anything. I count myself extremely lucky in having her as my—dare I say?—chief of staff.

Poo is going to spend her last Saturday with us. It will be a real red-letter day. I shan't let her go till she's really tired. Perhaps Mummy will let us have a little champagne, and we'll make a real celebration of it.

But first I've got to get through that awful hour after lunch. It's a horrible time, obscene and confused. Still, even that passes.

Gradually, one comes back to sanity again. That there should be such an hour in a day is dreadful, but it has to be endured.

* * *

That hour was better than I expected, owing to an accident: as Ruth had forgotten to wind it the previous evening, the watch was half an hour wrong. I thought I had half an hour to wait, and suddenly it was three.

But it wasn't such a good day after all. I had niggling pains all day: and Poo, having arrived at five o'clock, left at about a quarter past nine. It was very good of her to stay so long; but even so it was very disappointing. Then I had the worst night I have ever had. I don't know how Mummy managed to put up with it. I began to be disturbed at half-past twelve, and so it went on and so.

It wasn't altogether bad, but, as I have said, it wasn't very good either—I mean, apart from the horrible climax. It's always a bit disappointing when an evening guest leaves before ten. What I love is saying to an evening guest "What's the time?" and getting the reply "Twenty to eleven". Then you really feel you're well on the road to the next day. Still, it could have been worse.

* * *

I have sent off my first letter to Poo.

* * *

My first letter to Poo consisted simply of a page of greeting, sent off on the day of her departure and timed to arrive three days later. I had no news, of course; but I just wanted to take the earliest opportunity of reminding her of my existence.

An excitement is in the meanwhile looming: Ruth and my visit to Nancy's* this Wednesday. I confess, I am rather nervous about it. The idea is that I should go up in the lift (tiny) as far as the first floor, supported by Nancy and should then transfer: whereupon I would dress on a separate chair, having dinner in my smoking jacket. It will be delightful if it comes off; but I can't help fearing

* Nancy Raphael.

that there will be some horrible fiasco. If it comes off, Voss Bark* will bring us back by road about ten. Well, there it is; either a catastrophe, or a triumphant success. We shall know by Wednesday night. Everything, of course, will depend on my wretched nerve. Anyhow, it will be fun to tell Poo all about it.

One thing is important: to think as little as possible about it between now and Wednesday evening. The really important thing is to be as unselfconcious as possible. Once get selfconcious, and you get jittery; and the next you know, you have collapsed. So I shall simply try to ignore the whole busines between now and the moment when, on Wednesday evening, I find myself in the lift. Then, if you simply can't go through with it, you can't. But I shall feel rather ashamed of myself if I collapse: for, after all, nothing can in actual fact happen to me. Nothing but a little screaming and clutching!

If, then, I succeed after all, I shall feel rather proud of myself.

* * *

The usual business this morning. I woke up feeling awful; but after writing a few minutes I don't feel so bad. It is as if the very thought of writing removed the pain.

The prospects of today are fairly good. The afternoon and evening are pretty attractive: John, followed by Tiny,† this afternoon, and then the Nibs‡ in the evening. I am greatly looking forward to the evening: the Nibs are entirely delightful. I shall encourage them to do most of the talking. Of course, the night is bound to come: but in the meantime there will be many incidental attractions. If only the nights could be miraculously expunged! But it's no good crying for the moon. The thing is, as far as possible to forget about the unpleasant parts, like the couple of hours after lunch: then the whole day will be fairly attractive.

I really don't know what I shall actually do, apart from what I've already described; but I shall certainly finish off the chapter

* Conrad Voss Bark, B.B.C. Parliamentary Correspondent and one of the firm's authors, had offered to call, on his way home from the House of Commons, to push the wheel-chair.

† John and Sheila Bush. ‡ Rosemary and Jennifer Nibbs.

on Beethoven,* and probably start the one on Schubert. There is this advantage, that I read them after lunch; and this makes the awful after-lunch hour just a trifle less tedious.

Or just set your teeth, and regard the awful after-lunch hour as non-existant. If, to be honest, one has to sum up the day, call it—moderate!

Tomorrow my first letter to Poo will be acknowledged.

There's not much point in my writing to Poo till I actually get a letter from her to answer. She won't write till late Monday at the very earliest so that I can't hope to hear from her till Thursday. And then she can merely tell me that she has had my letter.

So the only thing to think about at the moment is tonight's affair. I've said everything that there is to be said about that: either all will be well, or I shall funk it. I simply don't know what will happen: clearly everything will depend upon the state of my nerves. But what I do know is that if I funk it I shall feel most bitterly ashamed of myself. I shall be giving up a delightful treat because of a silly fear, which means absolutely nothing.

Fear is an idiotic thing. I know perfectly well that I shall be doing nothing in the least risky; and yet, when it comes to it, I may betray myself. I must cling firmly to this thought: Mummy wont conceivably let me harm myself. Whomever else I may mistrust, I am safe with Mummy.

So don't be silly, but go through with it!

* * *

It's now approaching the lunch hour. One, one thirty—then zero! But somehow I don't feel quite so alarmed today. Somehow I think I shall take it more calmy. When the time comes to read, and there is still say three quarters of an hour to go, I shall steadily press on—looking at my watch at most twice! Who knows—I may even enjoy it!

And before one-thirty, there will be a delightful lunch!

After all, it is all a matter of nerves. Why should one not *enjoy* three quarters of an hour's reading? And if I succeed, I shall

* He was reading *Lives of the Great Composers.*

consider it a positive triumph. It must be at least a month that the hour after lunch has haunted me!

* * *

I woke up at two fifteen, and then read quite calmly till three thirty when Ruth came down. Quite a triumph!

* * *

Well, it's all over: and it's ended in a triumphal success! I felt frightened during that last few minutes in the lift, but didn't show anything: and I got home without an apparent qualm! In addition, I enormously enjoyed much the greater part of the evening.

I really looked quite smart! We went into the dining room, and Nancy gave us an excellent Martini; it was the first Martini I had had since I had been ill. Edmund Tracey arrived and we chatted for half an hour before dinner, which was really excellent. First there was a sort of tomato soup; then a sole; and finally a meringue gateau. I enjoyed every minute of it. It was the perfect dinner: rich and light. Nancy had clearly taken great pains over it. When we had finished, we settled down for an hour's talk: it was most agreable. So far as I know, I made no howlers; though every now and again there may been a little light skating over difficulties. Generally speaking, however, no one would have known there was anything odd about the affair.

When I finally got away and was back again in Eaton Place, I felt that the evening bore the same reaction to a real evening as fifty per cent to a hundred per cent.

On top of all the rest, I had an extraordinary good night. So I suppose I ought to be content.

Last night came the first letter from Poo. I must answer it. (*Later*. Answered.) Tonight Diana* comes to dine with us. That is always for us the chief event of the week. I suppose she'll come about seven, and stay till about ten thirty. I only hope I'm feeling at the top of my form. I have grown to love Diana more than any human being except Ruth. She's like an utterly steadfast rock.

* * *

* Diana Collins.

Yesterday I had a ghastly night. I turned out the light at eleven; and at eleven thirty I was absolutely wide awake, without, I felt sure, the smallest possibility of my going to sleep. Fortunately Ruth had not yet gone to sleep; and was able in a few minutes to calm me. I eventually got to sleep about one-thirty. It sounds good enough—about five and a half hours sleep; but in reality it was appalling.

I feel rather melancholy this morning. Everything seems drab and dull. I wish I could feel brighter, but it isn't within my will. Life absolutely lacks savour. It is about a quarter what the real thing ought to be. I don't think that this sort of life can ever be really worth living: it recalls too vividly just what one is missing. One lives in a sort of twilight world. And it's really awful to have to endure what one knows one is going to endure after lunch. In spite of that, the thought of suicide never enters one's head for a moment. I suppose the feeling for life is too indestructible.

* * *

Another very bad beginning of the day. Not only do I feel awful, but the pencil threatens to run out at any moment. I don't know why I feel so rotten, but I do.

The only thing to do is to think of something else. . . . And, all at once, I don't, somehow, feel so bad: there were moments of the walk (just ended) when I didn't really feel at all wretched. These fluctuations of feeling are really very extraordinary. I am convinced they have very little to do with objective feeling: it's a matter, primarily, of the particular emotion that happens to thrill you at the particular moment. At one time this emotion may seem enormous; at another time tiny. There are occasions on which the pain, apparently colossal, has been trivial.

It all boils down to this: try to remember that the whole question is largely a relatively unimportant one. What really matters is the particular *mood* in which you meet a particular crisis. According to this, a thing may be of vast moment, or of almost no moment at all.

* * *

Last night was Sunday night and we had the Miller Jones* in after dinner. This is one of the best evenings we have had. The talk was very frank; there was no pretence of any kind. We discussed how long the thing† was likely to last; I thought that a year was a reasonable period, and there was general concurrence. It was generally agreed, also, that there would be some lapses. Altogether, there was no gloom; nothing but good cheer and frankness.

It follows that today has started pretty well. I don't think there is a single mistake so far! I don't think that, whatever other lapses there may be, there's very much wrong with this writing! It pleases me that, in one thing, at any rate, I'm pretty expert—after three weeks. The pain, it is true, is quite bad, when I stop for a moment to think about it: but, for the most part, it doesn't bother me at all. "After lunch," it is true, is another matter; but—well, let us wait and see.

Music gives me more and more pleasure. I have an idea for this afternoon—the whole of Monteverdi's 'Orfeo'. I look forward enormously to that third act—the attempt to entice Charon, and the ultimate success. I think that, in many ways, that is the finest single act in the whole repertoire of opera. The climax of that act is superb.

It's now time for lunch—and after! Well, we shall see. It wasn't so bad yesterday.

* * *

This is the worst morning I have yet had. I feel absolutely dreadful—muzzy and confused. I do not understand how anyone could possibly consider himslf clear-headed on a morning like this. I can only pray that it will pass.

It is difficult to know how to spend the time after lunch. To follow the pattern of previous afternoons is impossible; the fretful dozing in the armchair, and waking up in the dreadful heat. I think the best thing to do will be to doze sitting upright.

* * *

* Keith and the Hon. Betty Miller Jones. † V.G.'s illness.

Well, I went into the armchair business after all. And, odd though it must seem, it wasn't so bad. Most of the time, I read quite happily: the whole of Glück's Exposé. Gluck was not in the least the sort of man I imagined: he was a business man, and, for all that, a very great musician. One quite wrongly imagines him a supreme idealist: he was only that by accident.

Mummy came down at three. It was one of the best afternoons I have had.

* * *

And it was the best evening I've had, too. I feel altogether different this morning. Its difficult to explain exactly why, but my sensations are quite fresh. I've a sort of springtime feeling about me which is different from anything I've experienced before. I feel almost normal.

I don't particularly want to write a great deal this morning. There's an alert 'newness' in the air that makes everything come alive. Of course, I don't expect it to last; but while it does I'm determined to enjoy it. I only wish this was a perpetual sensation: perhaps it is. Anyhow, let's have it while we can. After all we've had enough miseries! It's time for a little joy.

It's time to go out, but it has just started to rain. We shall go out all the same. It does'nt look as if it's going to be very much. Even if it comes on quite bad, there's no harm in having a little fresh air. But we'll probably cut it short.

* * *

Everything now depends on "after lunch". If I can only manage to do as well as yesterday—fairly good, steady reading—things should turn out as well as yesterday. I have a sort of idea that all will be well. I'd very much like this to be a record day.

* * *

And so it is! With a few trifling lapses, I think this is the best day I have yet had. But I must not get over-excited: the chances are that tomorrow will be exceptionally awful. Nevertheless, something gained is something gained.

And what a marvellous thing if this were the beginning of the end! If I now went on and on until, one day, I could suddenly walk! The chance is no doubt a small one; but the wonderful thing about a chance is precisely that it is small! The wonderful success is the almost inconceivable one.

* * *

The afternoon has proved a most pleasant one. We had Mary for a couple of hours, which were altogether delightful; and when she had gone we settled down to music. We did not go to bed till eleven.

* * *

The early hours of this morning have not been so good. I wrote a tiny note to Rupert,* after which I felt a bit better: I am returning to normal. It is now just on nine, and I shall feel quite well soon. The thing that worries me most is the total silence from Poo. Her last letter was Saturday: it is now Friday.† There will probably be a letter from her by the next post.

* * *

We are just back from our walk, which is early this morning, in view of the doctor's fortnightly visit. I really don't know how I feel—neither very good nor very bad. It's just a general level of wretchedness. A very different state of affairs to yesterday's, when everything seemed so (relatively) happy. Today all is flat and dull. But still, I'm familiar with it—it's just the state of things I know only too well. It's simply no good grizzling: the thing is to grin and bear it. Someday, it may suddenly go.

I've just got up from my rest. I've had an hour and a half's reading—mostly an hour of Rollo Myers on Tchaikowski. It's of course of fascinating interest; but I'm in the sort of mood in which everything can barely be got through. All that can be said is that I *did* manage not to wake Mummy up. I only hope that I shall feel better soon, and be able to enjoy an hour or two with

* Sir Rupert Hart-Davis. † It was in fact a Thursday.

Diana and John.* I just could not bear an evening with them to be a flop. I would sooner put them off.

* Diana and John Collins.

[The next morning, February 3rd, 1967, my father had a second stroke. He and my mother had eaten breakfast, and my mother had gone upstairs to have her bath and to dress. She had left him in his wheel-chair, sitting in the window of their living room, with pencil and pad, as he wished to write a line to an author who had won an award. When my mother came downstairs again she found the letter started, the pencil on the floor, and my father peacefully in a coma. He never recovered consciousness.—*L.G.*]

ACKNOWLEDGEMENTS

The letters from Rose Macaulay, and the extract from *Personal Pleasures* (published by Victor Gollancz Ltd), are used by kind permission of Miss Constance Babington Smith and Messrs A. D. Peters Ltd. The letter from J. L. Garvin is used by kind permission of Miss Viola Garvin. The letter from Stanley Spencer is used by kind permission of Arthur Tooth & Sons Ltd.

THANK GOD THAT I'M AN ENGLISHMAN is from *Nine Sharp and Earlier* by Herbert Farjeon, published by Messrs Dent, and VICTORIA is from *Kings and Queens* by Eleanor and Herbert Farjeon, published by Victor Gollancz Ltd.

The passage quoted from WHY I AM A JEW by Edmond Fleg (translated by Victor Gollancz) is used by permission of Editions Gallimard, Paris. The passage quoted from THE DONKEY OF GOD by Louis Untermeyer, copyright, 1932, is used by permission of Messrs Harcourt, Brace and World Inc.; copyright renewed, 1960, by Louis Untermeyer. The recipe for *gigot d'agneau en croûte* is given by courtesy of Monsieur R. Thuilier, Restaurant Baumanière, Les-Baux-en-Provence.

The self-portrait by David Low is reproduced by permission of the National Portrait Gallery, London; the two Low Cartoons by permission of the *Evening Standard*; the photograph taken in Frankfurt by courtesy of Miss Ursula Assmus. The frontispiece, Moses, the Wilberforce Tondo and the pieces of Staffordshire pottery are reproduced from photographs taken by Mr Edward Schwarz, London. The drawing of *opus reticulatum* was made by Miss Vita Gollancz.

The passage from Pliny the Elder's *Natural History* quoted in Chapter II is taken from a translation made in 1601 by Philemon Holland.

INDEX